# The Serial Killer
# Next Door

## The Double Lives of
## Notorious Murderers

### Richard Estep

# About the Author

**Richard Estep** is the author of numerous books, ranging from paranormal non-fiction and UFOlogy to history and current affairs. These books include *Serial Killers: The Minds, Methods, and Mayhem of History's Most Notorious Murderers,* and *The Handy Armed Forces Answer Book.* He is a regular columnist for *Haunted Magazine* and has written for the *Journal of Emergency Medical Services.* Richard appears regularly on the TV shows *Haunted Files, Haunted Hospitals, Paranormal 911,* and *Paranormal Night Shift,* and has guested on *Destination Fear* and *A Haunting.* He makes his home in Colorado, with his wife and a menagerie of adopted animals.

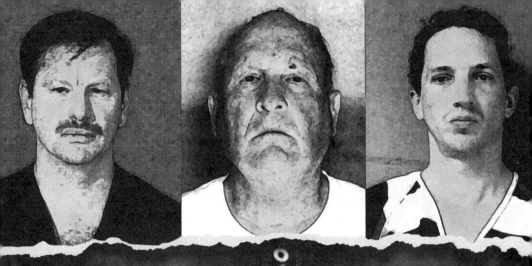

# The Serial Killer Next Door

## The Double Lives of Notorious Murderers

Richard Estep

**The Serial Killer Next Door:**
**The Double Lives of Notorious Murderers**

Visible Ink Press®
43311 Joy Rd., #414
Canton, MI 48187-2075

Visible Ink Press is a registered trademark of Visible Ink Press LLC.

Most Visible Ink Press books are available at special quantity discounts when purchased in bulk by corporations, organizations, or groups. Customized printings, special imprints, messages, and excerpts can be produced to meet your needs. For more information, contact Special Markets Director, Visible Ink Press, www.visibleink press.com

[how did this revert to visibleink.com? argh], or 734-667-3211.

Managing Editor: Kevin S. Hile
Cover Design: Graphikitchen
Page Design: Cinelli Design
Typesetting: Marco Divita
Photo Research: Gregory Hayes
Proofreaders: Larry Baker and Christa Gainor
Indexer: Shoshana Hurwitz
Cover images: Shutterstock.

paperback: 978-1-57859-768-0
ebook: 978-1-57859-817-5
hardbound: 978-1-57859-816-8
Cataloging-in-Publication data is on file at the Library of Congress.

Printed in the United States of America.

# Also from Visible Ink Press

Please visit us at www.visibleinkpress.com.

# Dedication

In loving memory of Richard Hitchcock. Your body may have been confined to a wheelchair, but your heart and mind wander the stars.

# Table of Contents

## Table of Contents

# Photo Sources

Airliners.net: p. 64.

Associated Press: pp. 11 (Alex Brandon), 15 (Ronald Zak), 20 (Julia Pykhalova, *Komsomolskaya Pravda*), 42 (London Metropolitan Police), 71 (The Canadian Press, Nathan Denette), 78 (Bruce Kellman), 85 (*Wichita Falls Times Record News*, Gary Lawson), 101 (Ed Betz), 112 (Texas Department of Criminal Justice), 124 (Dave Chidley/The Canadian Press), 135 (Alexandra Newbould/The Canadian Press), 144 (The Canadian Press/Jane Wolsak), 190 (Frank Gunn/The Canadian Press), 202 (John Byrum/*The Spartanburg Herald-Journal*), 210 (Elizabeth Cook/PA Wire), 248 (Elizabeth Cook/PA Wire).

Dwight Burdette: p. 234.

CMGlee (Wikicommons): p. 38.

Federal Bureau of Investigation: pp. 56, 157.

GoldenStateKiller.com: pp. 51, 58.

James Heilman, MD: p. 109.

Jorobeg (Wikicommons): p. 14.

King County Sherriff's Office: p. 173.

Kingston Penitentiary: p. 192.

Library of Congress: p. 247.

NotFromUtrecht (Wikicommons): p. 245.

Sydney Oats: p. 276.

Pwojdacz (Wikicommons): p. 232.

Rama (Wikicommons): p. 240.

Santa Barbara County Sheriff's Office: p. 46.

Sdgjake (Wikicommons): p. 94.

Shutterstock: pp. 2, 4, 8, 18, 19, 24, 27, 29, 34, 35, 40, 48, 53, 67, 69, 74, 76, 82, 83, 88, 89, 91, 96, 99, 104, 106, 114, 116, 119, 121, 128, 132, 138, 140, 143, 148, 150, 153, 155, 162, 164, 167, 171, 175, 177, 180, 184, 186, 188, 194, 196, 199, 200, 206, 207, 212, 217, 219, 220, 223, 224, 226, 229, 236, 237, 245, 250, 253, 255, 258, 263, 266, 268, 270, 272, 279, 281, 282, 286, 288, 290.

The Chemistds (Wikicommons): p. 182.

Toronto Homeless Memorial: p. 130.

**Photo Sources**

Martin Zeise: p. 261.
Zheng Zhou: p. 11.
Public domain: p. 242.

# Acknowledgments

The author would like to thank the following people: India, for suggesting many of the serial killers covered in this book; the publishing team at Visible Ink Press, particularly Roger and Kevin, for working to make the book better than I left it; patreons for their unflinching support; and Laura, for tolerating a grouchy writer who was researching some terrible things.

# Introduction

They walk among us, living alongside us in the same apartments and neighborhoods as we do. Some farm the food that we eat. Others take care of us when we are sick, diagnosing our ailments and helping nurse us back to health. Still others sell us the homes in which we live or wear the uniforms of the armed forces men and women who protect our national liberty.

They socialize in the same bars as we do or serve us drinks with a knowing smile. Some feel lonely and use online dating apps to meet people like us.

They even look like normal, everyday human beings who seem to have the same hopes, fears, and dreams as the rest of humanity.

Yet they are not us.

They are serial killers.

Growing up, we are taught that monsters are easy to identify. Fairy tales and movies depict them as ugly, grotesque creatures with telltale signs of their evil nature such as a physical deformity or perpetual scowl. The truth is very different. The serial murderer does not like to stand out. He or she wants to survive, if for no other reason than to continue killing and abusing their fellow human beings.

Their number one rule: don't get caught.

There is an art to blending in with the rest of humanity that the serial killer must master if they are to have any sort of longevity once they begin to murder. The trick is to not stand out from the crowd, or—if one simply cannot help it—to not stand out for the wrong reasons.

As a means to an end, creating a second life is a strategy employed by many serial killers. In this way, they can completely divorce themselves from the brutality and evil of their primary interest. More often than not, it is a smokescreen, a part of the mask that is utilised to help them fly under the radar. Some are loners, but others cultivate a family life, marrying and raising children. They settle down, possibly in suburbia, mowing their yards and exchanging small talk with the neighbors.

There is a significant degree of compartmentalization involved with this process, the construction of an entirely separate persona that is walled off from its murderous counterpart. The serial killer is able to switch between the two, flipping the equivalent of a mental switch that invokes the transformation from apparently loving family man or woman into a sadistic, homicidal beast.

As time passes, however, the line between the two lives is increasingly prone to blurring. Elements of the murderous persona bleed across into the life of the mundane. Cracks develop. Red flags appear, sometimes subtle, sometimes gross, but increasingly frequent until they can no longer be missed. Then comes discovery, capture, and, ultimately, if we are fortunate … justice.

It is this duality of identity, the disparity between public and private lives, that many of us find so fascinating. In my first book for Visible Ink, *Serial Killers: The Minds, Methods, and Mayhem of History's Notorious Murderers,* I explored this theme as it relates to many different offenders. Most were well-known criminals such as John Wayne Gacy, Richard Ramirez, and Ted Bundy. These names are iconic; their faces and list of atrocities infamous throughout modern popular culture. For this second volume, my intent was to put some lesser-known serial killers under the microscope. The names that comprise the chapter list for this book tend toward the obscure, but they are no less fascinating … and, unfortunately, every bit as appalling.

The serial killers on whom this book focuses are grouped together in a loose sequence based upon the nature of their public lives. Within its pages, we will meet paramedics, physicians, and nurses; painters, gardeners, and handymen; chefs, accountants, and real estate brokers. There are even entertainers and media personalities such as the author and TV presenter Jack Unterweger. Many were veterans, having served in their country's military—some, such as Colonel Russell Williams, were even on active duty at the same time they were committing murder.

A career is not necessary for a serial killer to maintain a separate life. Steady employment is helpful, true, but hardly essential. Neither is being a lone wolf always the case. We will look at murderers such as Australia's notorious Snowtown Killers, who formed a clique, and couples who killed together, as in the case of Canadians Paul Bernardo and Karla Homolka—the so-called "Ken and Barbie Killers."

Ranging from drifters to high-ranking military officers, it is clear that serial killers can be found in all walks of life. In addition to profiling 30 of them in this book, I have tried to address their motivations for doing what they do. The reader will undoubtedly notice that in many cases there is a sense of deep resentment and anger either at the world and humanity in general or directed at a specific human being—a parent, a spouse, or lover—which is then projected upon innocent victims.

The age-old debate of nature versus nurture arises again and again within these pages, and each individual chapter provides a slightly different answer. Some serial killers seem to be born broken, and whether they were raised in a warm and loving environment or grew up in an abusive, toxic nightmare they would probably have turned out the same way regardless. They are, to put it succinctly, born with bad wiring.

Others seem to be more a product of their environment and might not have grown into killers if they had gotten a better start in life. For every serial killer coming from a broken home, however, there is one whose family loved them and even doted upon them—perhaps even, in some cases, a little too much.

The reader will notice that the sections in this book vary in length. As I immersed myself in legal documents, reports, and other resource materials, it soon became clear that certain individuals were more suited to getting a "deep dive" than others. Shorter chapters are interspersed with longer ones in an attempt to break things up somewhat while still maintaining a structure that groups similar cases together.

Lastly, a word about the level of depth and description in the book seems apropos. The author of any true-crime book walks a fine line between providing an appropriate amount of detail in order to catalog the subject matter and not providing so much that the end result appears both lurid and in bad taste. I have striven to strike a balance to the best of my ability, and if the text errs too far on one side or the other, the responsibility lies entirely with me.

The subject of serial killers is, by turns, both fascinating and abhorrent. It is all but impossible to study them and their behavior without feeling a sense of overwhelming compassion for their victims, most of whom suffer an excruciating ordeal at the hands of these monsters. That sense of sympathy can, in some cases, extend to the family members of the murderers themselves, who oftentimes have no idea whatsoever about their loved one's secret evil side. Our deepest sympathies should certainly extend to the next of kin of the victims whose lives are shattered by the actions of a remorseless predator they will often never meet—sometimes, the emotional damage inflicted upon them is beyond all healing and repair.

Richard Estep
Colorado
16 January 2022

# THE BAYOU STRANGLER
# RONALD J. DOMINIQUE

**M**any of the serial killers covered in this book managed to successfully maintain two separate and distinct lives. One of them was usually a smokescreen: the mask of a career professional such as a soldier, pilot, police officer, farmer, or real estate agent, to name just a handful of trades. Many had families, loved ones who they cared about and who in turn also cared for them.

The other life was the real them, the raw truth of who each of them really was when all pretenses had been dropped. These were lives filled with torture, rape, and murder.

Some found this juggling of two different facets to be relatively smooth and easy. For others, it was more challenging, the source of much stress and anxiety. They would step out of their respectable blue- or white-collar worlds, snatch up a victim, strike, and then go back to their everyday reality as if nothing had ever happened. Not so in the case of Ronald J. Dominique, a serial killer who lived and moved in the same circles as many of his victims did: on the streets and in the homeless shelters of Louisiana.

During the span of just over eight years, he was responsible for the rape and murder of 23 transient men before his capture in 2006. Despite the sheer number of victims, however, he remains relatively unknown to this day.

Ronald Dominique was born and raised in Thibodaux, Louisiana. There was little in his childhood to suggest that he would one day grow up to become a serial killer. He showed no tendency to harm animals or sign of taking joy through causing pain to others. It was a modest upbringing, spent primarily in a trailer park. He had a reputation for being a good kid, for the most part, who liked to run around and play with other children his own age. His social life was unremarkable, and there were no problems at school, so far as we know.

After graduating from Thibodaux High School in 1983, Ronald Dominique had little in the way of career prospects. Interspersed between periods of unemployment were stints as a meter reader and a side gig delivering pizzas. He could never keep a job for very long, having the habit of somehow managing to rub his employers the wrong way. Dominique eventually developed a reputation for having a bad attitude. It became increasingly difficult for him to find work.

Leading a gay lifestyle was less than easy in 1970s–1980s Louisiana. It was not something one tended to advertise, as prejudice was everywhere. Dominique did frequent gay bars on a regular basis, where he liked to dress up as the female singer Patti LaBelle. Singing her hit songs in front of an appreciative audience brought him great joy.

Once he reached adulthood, Dominique's helpful and cheerful personality underwent something of a sea change. He became moodier and more introspective, withdrawing into his shell and interacting less with others. Those who knew him remarked upon the change, but there was no obvious cause that anybody could pinpoint.

Dominique had been a fairly clean-cut kid, not the sort to get into trouble beyond what was normal for young boys. When he got older, all that changed. A series of minor run-ins with the law ensued. Arrests for driving under the influence, speeding, and making harassing phone calls were the first clear signs of problems.

Dominique's meekness and charm helped trick his victims into allowing themselves to be tied up and helped deflect police suspicion even when accusers came forward.

While it is true that none of those offenses should be taken lightly, it is also fair to say that none of them would have landed Dominique in jail for any great length of time. However, there were at least two opportunities to capture Ronald Dominique and imprison him before he went on to murder 23 innocent men.

In 1993, a rape victim came forward and made a report to a police officer about a terrifying interaction that had taken place.

He had accepted a ride from Dominique, the man stated, and the journey had ended in a nightmare: he was tied up, with a gun held to his head, while Dominique sodomized him.

Police officers found the accused rapist and questioned him. Unsurprisingly, his story was very different. Yes, Dominique admitted, the two of them had had sex—but his accuser had consented to it, and it was only when Dominique found things getting "a little scary" that he felt compelled to draw a weapon for his own protection. This caused the man to leave.

The police seem to have taken Dominique's story at face value, because he was never incarcerated for the crime. This was a great shame, because history repeated itself three years later, when a second male victim came forward and told the same story, almost word for word. Once again, the perpetrator tied his victim up while he used a gun to keep him compliant. When the restraints were in place, Dominique traded the gun for a knife and held the blade at the man's neck throughout the ordeal. After he finished, the rapist untied his victim and allowed him to leave with his life. Future victims would meet a very different fate.

This second time, the rape accusation was assigned to the same officer who had dealt with Dominique three years prior. The many similarities between the two sets of victim statements were obvious. Once again, Ronald Dominique found himself being questioned by a cop. He made every effort to weasel his way out of it, claiming that once again, the sex had been consensual, and that both men had requested he tie them up. Why had he pulled weapons on them? the officer wanted to know. Because they had tried to extort him out of some money, Dominique explained. The fact that the likelihood of two different men, some three years apart, both spontaneously deciding to grift him for money was apparently lost on him.

Unsurprisingly, the police did not find his story to be particularly convincing. Charges of rape were filed, and by the summer of 1996, he was jailed and facing years, if not decades in prison. If Dominique had been successfully convicted, then 23 innocent lives would have been saved. Tragically, that's not how things worked out. The case never went to trial, and the charges were dropped. By late fall, Ronald Dominique was released back into society.

The following summer, he took his predilection for violent rape even further. In July 1997, the murders began.

Unable or unwilling to hold down a steady job, Dominique had little money to his name and lived either on the streets or spent the night in homeless shelters, whenever a bed was available.

He hunted for victims in a wide area in the southeast part of Louisiana. With no permanent residence to tie him down, Dominique moved from place to place whenever he felt like it, and he killed when the mood took him.

His first victim was 19-year-old David Lavon Mitchell Jr. He had attended a family gathering during the day and was trying to thumb a ride home when Dominique picked him up. He was assaulted, strangled, and his body abandoned in a ditch near the side of the road. It was discovered on July 14. To make this young man's loss even more tragic, his family, who were already worried by their son's disappearance, learned about his death when it was announced on the TV news. The police officers sent to inform the Mitchell family of David's death had not even made it to their front door yet.

David Mitchell did not fit the profile of Dominique's future victims. He was not homeless; he had a loving family waiting for him at home. He was not an outsider, as many of those Dominique went on to kill would be. What made him vulnerable to the predations of a killer were the fact that he was hitchhiking and was perhaps a little too trusting of the man who pulled over to offer him a ride.

Before beginning his killing spree, Dominique first targeted male hitchhikers as rape victims, a strategy he would carry forward when he added murder to his crimes.

Although nobody caught it at the time, something about the death of David Mitchell didn't quite make sense. His body was found floating in water, and a subsequent autopsy found more of it inside his lungs. This led to the false conclusion that he had died via accidental drowning. Apparently, nobody thought it strange that the dead man's pants and underwear were pulled down around his ankles, something often seen in the setting of sexually motivated murders. A toxicological screen revealed no evidence of drugs or alcohol in Mitchell's bloodstream. How, exactly, does a healthy and unimpaired young man spontaneously drown in a body of water so shallow that he could simply have stood up in it?

Over the span of the next nine years, Ronald Dominique raped and murdered 22 more men, using the exact same technique of entrapment and method of murder. Once he was finished with them, he abandoned the bodies in a variety of out-of-the-way places. As the number of suspicious and unexplained deaths began to rise, the police realized that they might have a serial killer on their hands and established a task force to hunt him down.

As happens with most cases of suspected serial killers, the FBI also assisted with the case, lending its technical expertise to the investigation. Dominique was not yet on the police radar as a potential murder suspect. As he moved from one parish to another, slowly leaving a trail of bodies in his wake, more officers from the various police departments involved joined the search. They were determined to stop him before he killed again.

Finally, in 2006, they caught the break they had been looking for. Forty-two-year-old Dominique had taken a young man named Ricky Wallace back to his trailer, with the intent of raping and murdering him. Wallace refused to allow himself to be tied up, however, and rather than push the issue, Dominique had permitted him to leave. Detectives spoke with Wallace and learned about the incident, quickly realizing that Wallace almost perfectly matched with the pattern of the serial killer's victim type. Based on this information, they went looking for the man who had offered him a ride.

Most importantly, Wallace remembered the location of the trailer and was able to direct detectives there. The occupant was listed as Ronald Dominique. A background check revealed that he had been the subject of two rape accusations back in the 1990s—and both victims had been male.

It was now December 2006, and law enforcement operatives had finally caught up with Dominique. They went to the homeless shelter he was currently staying at to pick him up for questioning. Rather than cause a scene or try to escape, he allowed himself to be handcuffed and went to jail quietly. It was obvious to him that the game was finally up.

For those experiencing homelessness, life is often difficult and challenging at best. During the wintertime, it can be even harder. Perhaps bearing this in mind, Dominique made no attempt to lie his way out of the multiple murder charges he now found himself facing. It may simply have been that a roof over his head and three hot meals a day was a more attractive prospect than spending the rest of his life living rough on the streets.

> Once Dominique started talking, the flood gates opened. Out came victim names, dates, and the exact location of body disposal sites.

This did not track with his stated motive, however. When police asked him why he had murdered his victims in cold blood, Dominique told them matter-of-factly that he needed to keep them quiet because he had already been to jail once (for rape, in 1996) and did not want to end up back there. Murder had therefore seemed like the only viable option.

Quoted in a 2006 interview published in the *Seattle Times*, Sheriff Jerry Larpenter, one of the officers responsible for questioning Dominique, said that he believed Dominique simply developed a taste for murder somewhere along the way. This is not an uncommon development in the life of a serial killer, and it often causes them to increase the frequency of their crimes once the urge to kill takes a greater hold over them.

Whatever his true motivations may have been, Ronald Dominique stayed pleasant and cooperative with detectives as they continued to ask him questions, slowly building up a bigger, more complete picture of his crimes. He even voluntarily consented to giving up a sample of his own DNA, which matched that found on the bodies of some of his victims.

Once Dominique started talking, the flood gates opened. Out came victim names, dates, and the exact location of body disposal sites.

Detectives made exacting notes of everything he said, checked and double-checked. Almost everything matched up. Most tellingly of all, he knew things that only the killer could have known, including precise details about how the victims had died, which were not available publicly via the media.

In court, Ronald Dominique pleaded guilty to eight counts of murder. His rationale for doing so was simple: it was the only way to guarantee that the prosecutors would not push for the death penalty. He got his wish, being sentenced to life imprisonment instead. This also meant that the state was able to skip giving him a trial.

One of the reasons for Dominique's ability to ensnare male victims was his appearance and the vibe he gave off. On a first meeting, he did not appear to be much of a threat. He was overweight, bordering on obese, and short in stature. His health was generally poor. This was not a man who could have physically overpowered his victims under normal circumstances. Neither was he particularly charming, in the traditional sense, unable to flatter his way into the good graces of the men and boys that he targeted.

He was fully aware of his limitations, and instead, put on a meek and mild performance to lull them into a false sense of security. For their part, Dominique's victims found that he raised few if any red flags, and when he offered something they wanted, they felt safe enough to take him up on it. He approached men who were hiking, usually catching them on stretches of road with little or no traffic to minimize the likelihood of being seen. What Dominique offered varied. It could be the promise of a ride to wherever the man wanted to go, or a fistful of money—anywhere up to $300 tended to be enough. He was willing to promise drugs to those with an addiction, if that's what it took to get them to go with him.

Not all his victims were gay men. Some were straight. In the latter cases, Dominique concocted a story about his having a wife or girlfriend who needed the attention of a man. The story went that she had been molested when she was a young girl, and the only way she could have sexual intercourse now was if her male partner permitted himself to be tied up in restraints. He kept a photograph of an attractive woman in the glove box of his pickup truck to help sell the story. She was even willing to pay the man for the inconvenience of allowing himself to be tied up, Dominique would add. Free money and sex with a beautiful woman—an irresistible combination. More often than not, the ploy worked.

After each crime, Dominique would move the victim's body to a remote place, where time and the elements would degrade evidence before the body could be found—in at least one case, leaving little more than a skeleton.

Once they reached Dominique's trailer and consented to being tied up, things would turn nasty. Suddenly, the amiable and low-key man who picked up the hitchhiker up was gone. In his place was a sadistic maniac, one who would not let them out of the restraints alive.

What if the potential victim got back to Dominique's place, didn't like the look of things, and changed his mind at the last minute? Dominique was a relatively cautious man in such cases. Knowing that if he attacked an unrestrained man, the odds were good that he would get a beating in return, he allowed them to leave. This is one reason why he lived to kill another day—no unnecessary chances were taken.

Looking back, it is possible to see the foreshadowing of Ronald Dominique's future serial murders. By 1996, he had not yet taken a human life, but his propensity for violence was beginning to rear its head repeatedly with two violent and sadistic rapes. Although he had not pulled the pistol's trigger or stabbed either of his victims with the knife, Dominique brandished both weapons and relished the sense of power and control that they gave him over his victims. It is likely that the gratification he felt during the rapes was heightened by the presence of the weapons, and when he committed his first murder the following year, it represented the logical next step in Dominique's quest for sexual fulfillment.

Taking a closer look at the 23 victims reveals a number of commonalities between them. All were males, which fits Dominique's status as a homosexual, sexually motivated predator. He was partial to African American men, who ranged in age from the teens through to the mid-forties. Dominique killed eighteen black men and five Caucasians. Of that number, some, but not all, were gay. He liked to target the homeless and indigent, though not exclusively. This partly was because those were the circles in which he moved. These were Ronald Dominique's peers, men who lived on the streets and scrabbled to make a living, just like he did.

In addition, he was fully aware of the fact that when a homeless person disappears, fewer questions tend to be asked. There is a tacit assumption that the missing person may simply have moved on elsewhere, heading to another town or city in search of new pastures. Rarely is it assumed that something bad may have happened to them. There are also few, if any, family members around to ask questions or to file a missing person's report. This goes a long way toward explaining why sex

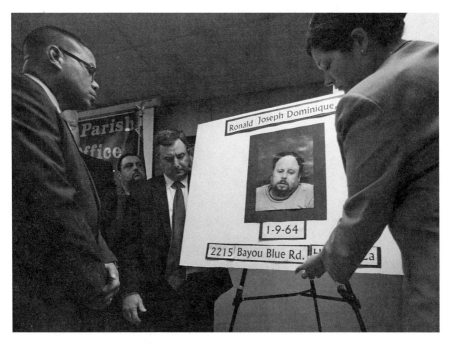

Ronald Dominique's capture is announced at a press conference in Houma, Louisiana.

workers, drug users, and those experiencing homelessness have long been preyed upon by serial killers.

Police noted that a number of the dead men had been involved either directly or peripherally with the illegal drugs market, leading to some initial speculation that their deaths could have been due to feuding between rival dealers. However, drug dealers do not tend to suffocate or strangle their targets when lashing out at them. Shooting and stabbing are far more likely to be the cause of death in such instances.

One of the reasons it took so long to finally catch Ronald Dominique was the sheer randomness of his murders. After killing his victim, the serial killer drove around with the body in the back of his vehicle until he found a dumping site that appealed to him. There was no rhyme or reason to it; he simply chose a place that was isolated and dark. He left few clues behind as to his possible identity. The bodies sometimes took days or weeks to be discovered. In that time, they were exposed to the elements. By the time police crime scene technicians were alerted, they had little to work with in terms of identifying them.

Yet catch him, they ultimately did. As is the case with so many serial killers, it was Ronald Dominique's sloppiness that finally helped bring him to justice—in conjunction with solid detective work on the part of the task force created to identify and bring him to justice. That, coupled with his own willingness to confess to his crimes, meant that the serial killer nicknamed "the Bayou Strangler" will never be free to kill again.

# THE AUSTRIAN RIPPER
# JOHANN "JACK" UNTERWEGER

**C**an a leopard ever truly change its spots? There are those who believe so. Yet there are also those who are convinced that "once a murderer, always a murderer." Such people might point to the example of Johann "Jack" Unterweger.

When he stepped off the plane at Los Angeles International Airport in the summer of 1991, the Austrian-born Unterweger was living the dream. To all outside appearances, the 40-year-old writer and poet was a poster child for the promise of criminal rehabilitation. A convicted murderer, Unterweger had served his time in prison, been released, and gone on to great professional success—so much so, in fact, that he had traveled to the United States to write about its criminal underworld. What better place to accomplish that than one of the country's poorest, most crime-ridden neighborhoods: the infamous Skid Row?

Unterweger chose the Hotel Cecil as his temporary residence. The hotel would later become infamous for the death of Canadian tourist Elisa Lam, who disappeared under mysterious circumstances in 2013. Her dead body was found floating in a rooftop water tank. The cause of death remains unproven to this day, with the coroner's finding of accidental death being disputed by those who suspect foul play.

Once an opulent destination, Hotel Cecil had long been in decline (along with neighboring Skid Row), already well known for transience and vice by the time Unterweger chose it for his base of operations.

Nor was Jack Unterweger the only killer to take a room at the Cecil. During his 1984–1985 reign of terror, the so-called Night Stalker, Richard Ramirez, rented a room on the top floor. It has been suggested that Unterweger may have chosen to stay at the Cecil as a sick homage to Ramirez, though there's no evidence proving it to be true.

A far more likely reason for the Austrian to have picked the Cecil was its proximity to the Los Angeles sex trade. Prostitutes were a common sight in the vicinity of the hotel, and Unterweger used his charm to finagle a ride-along with a Los Angeles Police Department patrol unit. His stated purpose was to observe the seamier side of the city for himself in order to write about it, but in reality, the seemingly earnest writer had far more sinister intentions.

He wasn't in L.A. to observe crimes. He was there to commit them. Because Jack Unterweger was a serial killer.

Much of Unterweger's early life is shrouded in mystery, not least because as an adult, Jack liked to tell stories about his upbringing—stories that would, he hoped, generate sympathy. He claimed to be the son of a U.S. Army soldier, a man who physically abused his son before abandoning him. Unterweger then spent time in and out of orphanages.

As a young man, Jack Unterweger developed a sadistic taste for brutality. His preferred outlet for the rage he felt was women, and more specifically, sex workers. He took to beating them savagely, telling police later that he was symbolically beating his own mother, who had been a prostitute herself and the true target of his ire.

Violence turned to murder in 1974, when he beat 18-year-old Margaret Schäfer unconscious, then strangled her with the straps of her own bra—which would become Unterweger's modus operandi in future murders. He was convicted of the murder in 1976 and sentenced to a minimum of 15 years in prison.

Unterweger made good use of his time behind bars by reading and writing. He wrote poetry and short stories, some of which were intended for children. He also penned an autobiography, which painted him in a sympathetic light. In the manuscript, Unterweger cast himself as an abused child who had grown up to inflict abuse in return. The book, titled *Purgatory; or, The Trip to Prison—Report of a Guilty Man*, went on to earn critical acclaim and reap financial success. It was more fiction than fact, an attempt to misdirect the reader into thinking of its author as something other than the monster he truly was.

Remarkably, there was no shortage of people who bought the book and bought into its message. A grassroots campaign arose, one aimed at getting him out of prison early.

Upon his release from prison on May 23, 1990, Jack Unterweger seemed to be a reformed man. In reality, he was nothing more than an actor playing a part. He knew exactly what to say and do to make people believe that he had turned over a new leaf. After all, his supporters pointed out, hadn't he served his time, successfully completing his mandated 15-year sentence? Wasn't everybody entitled to a second chance?

Unfortunately for seven innocent women, Jack Unterweger succeeded in fooling pretty much everybody. He had been out of prison for less than five months when he started to kill again. The "reformed" murderer began to lead a secret life based on a carefully constructed persona: that of the artist, mistreated and abused as a child, who had done wrong himself because of the wrongs that had been done to him, and had now turned firmly away from the path of crime. In reality, Unterweger returned to killing with almost reckless abandon.

On a trip to Czechoslovakia, he murdered a sex worker named Blanka Bočková by strangling her. The murder weapon was the victim's own bra, which had also been the case when Unterweger murdered Margaret Schäfer. At the time, nobody connected the two killings with the fact that the killer was now out on parole.

There is something intriguing and inherently salable about the murderer-turned-media star, and he was soon living high on the hog. Jack Unterweger was now a man who had everything: women found him attractive and gravitated into his orbit. He had money, the finest clothes, cars, and celebrity aplenty. His truly was a rags-to-riches story. Yet the urge to kill, the anger he felt toward females, had never left him. As he laughed and joked with women, he was secretly seething.

More murders followed. All the victims were female and were engaged in prostitution. As 1990 gave way to 1991, the number of fatal strangulations began to mount. Inevitably, suspicion began to fall upon the recently released and supposedly rehabilitated Unterweger, the darling of the literary world. The police began to take a closer look at his activities, but they did not have the evidence to charge him with any of the murders.

Later that summer, the Austrian journalist was offered a dream come true: the opportunity to fly to the United States and observe the

In the heart of downtown Los Angeles's commercial districts, Skid Row has long been the city's epicenter of homelessness, illicit drugs, and prostitution.

vice-ridden underbelly of Los Angeles in person, then write about it. He jumped at the chance and reached out to the Los Angeles Police Department to see if it would cooperate with an article about crime in the city.

The LAPD consented to show the Austrian writer around the city. Unterweger was a snappy, if somewhat eccentric dresser, wearing tailored suits and completing the ensemble with a cowboy hat. He spoke with an air of confidence and sincerity that tended to win the listener over. Having an accent didn't hurt either; it gave the man an exotic air, something befitting a writer and poet.

Nobody in the United States knew about Unterweger's murderous past. Those he met were easily taken in by his charm and charisma. Shortly after his arrival, he began strangling sex workers that he picked up on Skid Row. Three died before the LAPD's homicide detectives, in conjunction with their European counterparts, made the connection between Unterweger's arrival and the recent spate of stranglings in Austria.

Now wanted for the murders of seven sex workers in his homeland, the 41-year-old Unterweger went on the run. He fled across France,

Italy, and Switzerland with his 18-year-old girlfriend, Bianca, in tow. Finally, the couple made it back to the United States. As he made his way across the country, Unterweger managed to stay one step ahead of the police. They finally caught up with him on February 27, 1992, when he was arrested in Miami Beach. He had been lying low while Bianca worked as an exotic dancer in the city's strip clubs to support them both.

The authorities in Los Angeles wanted Unterweger tried there, but instead he was extradited back to his native Austria. Although there were still those among his supporters who believed him to be innocent, the evidence that detectives working on both sides of the ocean had gathered would ultimately prove otherwise. Forensic DNA testing helped strengthen the case against him.

A photo released by the Austrian police, as authorities began the manhunt anew, shows Jack Unterweger after release from his first prison term.

Unterweger maintained his innocence right up to the end, but it did him no good. He was found guilty on multiple counts of murder, and he would never leave jail alive. Even today, he has advocates who maintain his innocence.

Jack Unterweger might have been convicted of multiple murders and sentenced to spend the rest of his life behind bars, but he ultimately contrived to evade justice. On the night of his sentencing, Unterweger was returned to his cell. He removed the cord from his jogging pants—surprisingly, nobody seemed to have thought to place him on suicide watch—fastened it in a loop around his neck, and then tied it to the curtain rod above his head. He was found, fatally strangled, when the guards came to check on him. He was 44 years old.

Why did he kill? Perhaps the answer lies in his memoir, which, although liberally strewn with outright falsehoods and half-truths, is in places quite plausible. He saw prostitutes as his enemies "and conquered them through my inner hatred."

Unterweger's reputation has had a bizarre afterlife. Many people are unaware of his existence, and if they know of him it all, it is usually because of his connection with the Hotel Cecil, which has seen a resurgence of public interest lately due to a number of television shows. The actor John Malkovich portrayed Unterweger on the stage, in a play titled *The Infernal Comedy*.

For years, it seemed as if the plans for a movie biopic would never quite come to fruition, but 2015 saw the release of the motion picture *Jack*, directed by Elisabeth Scharang and starring actor Johannes Krisch in the titular role. The film was, appropriately, an Austrian production and failed to garner widespread distribution, which makes is likely that Johann Unterweger will remain a resident of the strange no-man's land between infamy and obscurity forever.

# THE WRONG ARM OF THE LAW
# MIKHAIL POPKOV

As I write these words, it is the summer of 2021. Mistrust of law enforcement in the United States is at an all-time high. Other nations are also beginning to experience the same lack of confidence in the police. Yet this has not always been the case. Since the founding of the first centralized modern police forces in the early 1800s, generation after generation was taught to respect and trust the men and women who wore the uniform of a police officer.

While there were countless hard-working and honest officers walking the beat, inevitably there were some who abused the position of trust and responsibility bestowed upon them by society. Few of them did so in a more heinous way than Siberian Mikhail Popkov—also known as "the Werewolf" due to the sheer savagery of his attacks.

Details on Popkov's childhood and upbringing are murky at best, with a number of different (and sometimes contradictory) stories in circulation. Some maintain that the police officer found out that his wife was having a sexual relationship with another man and that his murders were all attempts to take out his anger on many different women. Others claim that Popkov's homicidal behavior was a result of an abusive mother, one who beat him while in drunken fits of rage. A third alternative is that Popkov began killing women simply because he liked the way it made him feel and because his position of authority allowed him to keep getting away with it. At least, this is the story he told detectives once he was finally caught.

Working in the east Siberian city of Angarsk, Popkov prowled the streets in his patrol car, looking for vulnerable women to pick up. He presented himself in a friendly, approachable, and yet also official way, which

The savage nature of Popkov's attacks earned him the nickname "the Werewolf."

caused the women to whom he offered a ride to accept it, more often than not.

Popkov was muscular and athletic, training regularly and engaging in sports in his free time. Overpowering unsuspecting victims was not difficult for him, especially with the majority of his victims being intoxicated.

The true number of murder victims that Mikhail Popkov is responsible for will almost certainly never be known. Police estimates rose from 60, then 80, past 100, to somewhere around 200, based on the number of women who went missing during the 18-year span in which Popkov was actively abducting and killing. His first murder is believed to have taken place in 1992, and the evidence suggests that his last victim was murdered in 2007—although this is by no means certain.

He selected his targets carefully, making sure that each one was walking alone and was away from other people when he approached them. If they staggered and shuffled a little, betraying signs of having had a little too much to drink, then so much the better in his eyes. After getting a woman to sit inside the police car with him, Popkov would drive her to an isolated area and make sexual advances. After intercourse, some were allowed to live. Others, the ones who displeased him in some way, were murdered.

Almost all of Popkov's victims were younger than 40 years of age, with the youngest being 16. He avoided murdering those he thought of as children.

When it came to picking a murder weapon, Popkov had plenty of options to choose from. He was brazen enough to steal them from the evidence room at the police station, using tools impounded from former crimes to commit new ones of his own. He sliced the heart out of one victim's chest and decapitated another with what authorities believed was an axe.

Popkov's nickname—the Werewolf—stemmed from the savage mutilation that he inflicted on his victims. It was not uncommon for him to stab his victims more than 100 times. The sheer savagery of these attacks implies a hatred for those he killed, which he tried to expunge by inflicting severe physical trauma upon their bodies long after they were dead. Popkov subjected the women to severe beating, often using solid objects to break bones and cause blunt force trauma. These weapons ranged from rocks and stones to shovels, screwdrivers, and other tools. Many of Popkov's killings took place out in the woods, which he knew would be effectively deserted late at night, and he developed a habit of slamming his victim's head against the trunk of a tree until she had been battered unconscious.

The fact that Popkov escaped detection for so long was partly because he had a number of advantages that most murderers do not. As a police officer, he had an insider's perspective on the crimes he committed; indeed, on more than one occasion, Popkov had cause to visit the crime scenes that he himself was responsible for. He mixed with detectives and senior officers and was therefore privy to their thought processes and musings on the case. None of them ever suspected that the guilty man was standing right there with them, hiding in plain sight—a member of their own law enforcement community.

DNA testing and forensic evidence led to his arrest in 2012. Police officers investigating the case focused their attention on the drivers of a very specific type of car, one whose tire tread marks were found in the snow near several of the body dumping sites. One such car had been driven by Mikhail Popkov.

In 2015, Popkov was convicted of 22 murders and imprisoned. Perhaps believing that he had nothing else to lose, he would later confess to another 59. He was given multiple life sentences by the judge. It is impossible to say exactly how many women he killed, with estimates ranging anywhere from 80 to 200, and possibly even more.

What were Popkov's motives? If his confession is to be believed, he wanted to "teach and punish" the women he murdered. Something that they did or said, or perhaps simply something about them, triggered a homicidal rage in Popkov. He admitted to wanting to spread fear among the "immoral women" of the city. Yet other women who also accompanied Popkov in his police car escaped unharmed, never realizing how narrow an escape they had just had.

The distinctive tire tread left at crime scenes by Popkov's car helped investigators start with a narrow pool of potential suspects.

The uniformed beast who terrorized the streets of Angarsk gets to experience life on the other side of bars.

During interviews, Popkov tried to paint himself as some sort of moral crusader, killing only those women who he felt deserved it because he disapproved of their sexual proclivities. The fact that he had raped many of his victims seemed to have been lost on him, however, when he made claims of superior morality.

Mikhail Popkov developed a pathological desire to make women do whatever he wanted them to do, to control them as much as possible. Police officers are used to being obeyed, particularly those in the Soviet Union, who are seen as an extension of the state. It is likely that the women Popkov chose to kill were the ones who showed a streak of independence or what he perceived to be disrespect. This was the kind of behavior he deemed worthy of punishment. Despite his easygoing exterior, Popkov never wanted to be liked. He wanted to be feared, and he spoke of a desire to cleanse the streets of the type of woman he so despised.

Although he had an extremely dark side, none of Mikhail Popkov's friends, colleagues, or family members ever suspected he might be a murderer. Indeed, when her husband was arrested and charged with multiple murders, his wife, Elena, and his 27-year-old daughter, Ekaterina, refused to believe that he was guilty—even though he confessed to many of his crimes in court.

Interviewed by the *Siberian Times* in 2015, Elena said, "If I suspected something wrong, of course, I would divorce with him. I support him. I believe him."

Not only did Elena Popkov choose to stay married, but she also regularly visited her husband in prison. So great was the influence he cast over his family that Ekaterina began to study the psychology and behavior of serial killers herself, determined to find what she believed was the "real" murderer for whose crimes her father was convicted. Popkov's mother also flatly refused to believe her son might be guilty.

Russia has had no death penalty since the mid-1990s, and so there is no death row for Mikhail Popkov to sit upon, languishing and awaiting an appeal or stay of execution. Instead, he will simply live out the rest of his life behind bars, occasionally confessing to another murder or two whenever it suits his purpose. This he last did in the summer of 2020, admitting to two more deaths at his hands.

The police officer's rank and uniform, coupled with the misperception of Mikhail Popkov as a warm and loving family man, led people to trust him; for years, none of the detectives investigating his bloody string of murders considered the possibility that their friend and colleague could have been responsible. Even when one of his victims, who miraculously survived the violent ordeal to which Popkov subjected her, identified him, nobody in authority took the accusation seriously.

He truly was a master of hiding in plain sight, and we should be thankful that in the end, this monster's luck finally ran out.

# KILLER ON PATROL
# GERARD SCHAEFER JR.

It is a long fall from grace whenever a police officer winds up behind bars. The list of causes for a cop being imprisoned can be long and varied. Bribery is one of the most common reasons. Quite rightly, we take a dim view of any authority figure who abuses that position for their own personal financial gain.

Busting drug dealers is a common duty for law enforcement, and when a stash of illegal drugs is seized and impounded for evidence, it is not unheard of for a corrupt officer to skim some off the top and sell it themselves. Cops have the connections through which it is possible to distribute drugs and fence stolen property.

There is another category of law enforcement offender, one in which the crimes are far more severe than theft or narcotic sales. Some police officers have turned out to be serial killers.

Such was the case with Gerard Schaefer Jr.

Gerard John Schaefer Jr. was born in Wisconsin on March 25, 1946. His family relocated to Florida. As a boy, he had a propensity for killing animals, an obvious warning sign for what was to come later in his life.

His upbringing was deeply rooted in the Catholic faith, which was reinforced daily by the religious school that he attended. He was a regular churchgoer. Just how sincere his beliefs were is impossible to say, although at one stage, he did give serious consideration to joining the priesthood. What we *can* say for certain is that the adult Gerard Schaefer's treatment of women was about as far from the Christian virtues as it is possible to get.

Schaefer claimed that his father was a violent man, both physically and emotionally abusive. Schaefer's mother bore the brunt of this abuse, some of which undoubtedly occurred in front of her son. There is a strong causal link between children (usually boys) witnessing violent abuse at home and growing up to inflict abuse of their own upon their partner. It is very likely that the seeds of Gerard Schaefer's desire to humiliate, degrade, and physically hurt women were planted in his childhood.

To the casual observer, Schaefer was an ordinary young man. He appeared to show few of the deviant tendencies that were lurking beneath the surface of his apparently normal persona. Yet there *were* red flags, if one knew where to look. He sometimes displayed a puritanical hatred of women who showed what he believed to be an "immodest" amount of their body in public.

Schaefer's former girlfriend, Sondra London, would ultimately go on to publish some of his "creative" writing. She had a unique level of personal insight to the *real* Gerard Schaefer. In her introduction to the book *Killer Fiction*, she recalls trying to restrain Schaefer from attacking his father after the latter called Schaefer's mother a whore. An outraged Schaefer had taken a golf club to his father's head, proving himself more than willing to commit violence when the mood took him. It should also be added that the slur *whore* was something that Schaefer would frequently employ himself when referring to females. He was also not above using other terms of sexually based degradation, such as *slut*, which gives an insight into the way he viewed women.

Gerard wrote out fantasies of future murders in detail. In at least one case, he planned to feed a victim's body to alligators.

It was with London that Schaefer first shared his secret fantasies of murdering other women. By 1965, these fantasies had coalesced from the more general to having a specific focus, a woman that Schaefer spied on. He felt a visceral loathing of the unsuspecting target of his anger, perhaps because of the lustful feelings she aroused in him. Those feelings of lust came not necessarily from a desire to have sex with her but rather the excitement of wanting to murder her. He began to plan the killing down to the last detail, intending to beat his victim into submission, restrain her, and then take her out to the swamp and feed her to the alligators.

Unlike some serial killers, Gerard Schaefer was both intelligent and educated. This showed in his demeanor and manner of speaking. He was more than capable of holding his own in polite conversation and reasoned discourse, but on the other hand, he liked to use slurs in relation to those he considered to be beneath him. The brother of one of his victims later told a reporter that Schaefer "was *too* polite" and "could really pour it on too strong." As charming as the future serial killer tried to be, some people saw through the facade he would put on.

Privately, Schaefer was an elitist, though he could hide it well when it suited his purpose to do so. He was also a racist, sneering at minorities and those who were different from him. A judgmental man by nature, this may have contributed to his choice of law enforcement as a career. The compulsion to judge and control others was a strong motivator for him.

After school, Schaefer went on to college, studied the law, and had the discipline to graduate successfully with a bachelor's degree in the field of criminal justice. After attending the police academy in 1971, Schaefer became a beat

**Only a confession made to a cellmate during his incarceration connects Schaefer to the disappearance and murder of the two women.**

cop with the Wilton Manors (FL) Police Department. He was 25 years old at the time. From the beginning, he did not have a solid reputation among his peers. It didn't escape notice that Schaefer loved to issue speeding tickets, and that he pulled over and ticketed a disproportionate number of females. His colleagues thought that he was weird. They had no idea just how right they were.

Wilton Manors P.D. fired Schaefer shortly after taking him on, but he managed to get hired by the Martin County Sheriff Department as a deputy in the summer of 1972.

It is impossible to say for sure when, exactly, Gerard Schaefer killed his first victims. There are simply too many unknowns to the case. A solid bet, however, would be the afternoon of October 2, 1966. Nancy Leichner, 21, and her friend, Pamela Nater, 20, disappeared during an excursion to the Ocala National Forest. At the time of writing, their remains have yet to be found. Only a confession made to a cellmate during his incarceration connects Schaefer to the disappearance and murder of the two women. While much of what he says must be taken with a huge grain of salt, his claim of having kidnapped them at gunpoint and then killed them does ring true when considered in light of his standard modus operandi, or MO.

On September 8, 1969, Schaefer abducted and murdered 25-year-old Leigh Hainline Bonadies, in Boca Raton. She had known him personally when they were both growing up. Their homes were two houses apart from one another, and the two had become friends—or so it appeared. She had been married for just two weeks when she disappeared. Following Schaefer's arrest, articles of jewelry belonging to her were discovered in his belongings.

Carmen Marie Hallock, or "Candy" to her friends, lived near Schaefer in Fort Lauderdale. The 22-year-old cocktail waitress and student disappeared on December 18, 1969. She had been wearing a black dress and heels when she went to meet an unidentified male. This is significant because Schaefer authored a short story about the murder of a woman who wore the very same outfit. No trace of her was found for four years, until two of her teeth, which had gold fillings, turned up in a search of the home Schaefer's mother lived in. Officers also found the belongings of several other young women who had gone missing in the vicinity.

Before their disappearances, both women had talked about having been offered a job that involved "undercover drug investigative work for the government." While the mysterious man offering the gig was nebulous about the details, the job was sold to them as being both exciting and high-paying, and it seems obvious with hindsight that this was a hook being used by Schaefer to lure them into a meeting with him on terms of his choosing. It may also have been an ill-conceived attempt to concoct a flimsy explanation for the women's disappearances. The truth is: civilians without any sort of law enforcement background are not simply offered dangerous and sensitive work like this.

On December 29, 1969, two girls disappeared from Pompano Beach. Peggy Rahn, 9, and her classmate, Wendy Stevenson, 8, were last seen playing together. Investigators consider Schaefer a potential suspect, although his involvement has never been proven.

It is believed that Schaefer killed numerous other women during the late 1960s and early 1970s, torturing them, raping them, and then disposing of their bodies in places that are still unknown today. By 1972, he was beginning to take risky chances, ones that increased his likelihood of being caught. On a hot day in July of that same year, that's exactly what happened. Schaefer encountered a pair of hitchhikers that he thought were vulnerable. The two women, 17-year-old Pamela Wells and 18-year-old Nancy Trotter, were subjected to a terrifying ordeal at the hands of the sheriff's deputy. He drove them out to an isolated stretch of woodland on Hutchinson Island, handcuffed them, tied them up, and placed nooses around their necks. The island is in Martin County, where the serial killer worked as a deputy. He knew the area well, particularly the parts in which he was unlikely to be disturbed with his victims.

Schaefer lured at least two of his victims (and likely more) with the fiction that they would be working undercover, entering a new life filled with excitement and intrigue.

Stranded in the middle of nowhere, bound, and about to be hanged, the two young women were understandably afraid for their lives. What saved them from meeting the fate of Schaefer's other victims was a radio call. He was still on the clock and had no choice but to leave. While he was gone, the hitchhikers managed to work themselves free and escape. They went straight to the police and reported the fact that they had been captured, subdued, and threatened with death or being sold into slavery. A flailing Schaefer concocted a tall story, claiming that he had been trying to teach Wells and Trotter a lesson regarding the perils of hitchhiking, which was illegal. The sheriff wasn't buying it.

Kidnapping and abusing hitchhikers is frowned upon in police circles. Gerard Schaefer's law enforcement career was effectively over, and his personal troubles were just beginning. Two months later, while he was out on bail and awaiting trial for kidnapping, Schaefer wormed his way into the confidences of two more female victims and did the exact same thing—except this time, he followed through on his threat to kill them both.

Georgia Jessup was 16 and her companion, Susan Place, was 17, when they both ran afoul of Schaefer in September of 1972. They were going out for a day at the beach and accepted the offer of a ride from Schaefer. The two young women were tortured, assaulted, hanged, and their remains were buried in hastily dug shallow graves on Hutchinson Island. The skull of each woman had been bashed in with a blunt object, and their heads were cut off. Schaefer was out on parole and under law enforcement scrutiny, but he simply couldn't stop himself from killing.

On January 16, 1973, Schaefer was finally taken off the streets. He was sent to the Martin County jail for six months on a charge of aggravated assault for his attack on Wells and Trotter, with two years of probation set to follow. As a deputy, Schaefer had booked in prisoners at the jail himself. The experience of being an inmate must have been a sobering one.

Three months later, on April 1, the mutilated bodies of Jessup and Place were discovered. The coroner could not pinpoint a precise date of death but estimated that the two girls had been dead for around five months based on the advanced state of decomposition.

**Strangulation with a noose had almost been the fate of the hitchhikers, and it was certainly the case here. Gerard Schaefer, still sitting in a jail cell, was the obvious suspect.**

Detectives noticed that there were clear parallels between the layout of the crime scene and the abduction of Pamela Wells and Nancy Trotter. Strangulation with a noose had almost been the fate of the hitchhikers, and it was certainly the case here. Gerard Schaefer, still sitting in a jail cell, was the obvious suspect.

Schaefer maintained his innocence, but there was no shortage of evidence linking him with the two murders, along with a string of disappearances which had taken place over the past several years—all of them females. Susan Place's mother told the court that the last person she saw her daughter with before her disappearance was Schaefer. At the time of her meeting with him, he was going by the alias of Jerry Shepherd, claiming to be a student at the University of Colorado. Mrs. Place had made a point of writing down the license plate number of the car Susan had gotten into. The vehicle was owned by Schaefer.

The search of Schaefer's mother's house, where the killer had been living with his wife, Teresa, at the time of the murders, turned up a jewelry box that belonged to Georgia Jessup. Teresa Schaefer also had a purse that was positively identified as Georgia's. She told police that her husband had given it to her. Some of the most damning evidence discovered in the house were a series of written stories and journals detailing the rape and murder of multiple women. The level of detail Schaefer had gone into was borderline nauseating, and the documents were used in court as an attempt to demonstrate the psychopathic nature of his mind.

Speaking in his client's defense, Schaefer's attorney pointed out that if his client could be convicted based on what he insisted were works of fiction, then why wasn't a filmmaker like Alfred Hitchcock (director of *Psycho*) behind bars? Neither the judge nor the jury were convinced, and Schaefer was sentenced to imprisonment. Had the death penalty been an option at that time, it is almost certain that the judge would have imposed it.

Schaefer's journals detailed numerous accounts of gruesome assaults, some of which matched the details of his known crimes. The defense tried to argue they were works of fiction, akin to the movies of classic horror film director Alfred Hitchcock.

Whenever a potential serial killer is identified, detectives revisit missing persons cases and homicide cold cases to determine whether the killer might be responsible for other crimes. One such instance that points squarely at Schaefer is the January 1973 disappearance of two backpackers from Iowa, 18-year-old Collette Goodenough and 19-year-old Barbara Ann Wilcox. The two women vanished just six days before Schaefer was sent to jail. They had been hitchhiking their way east across the United States, making it as far as Florida. Goodenough's diary, passport, and driver's license were all found in cartons during the search of Schaefer's mother's home. Their remains were found four years later, hidden in a thicket close to a canal. Each had been decapitated.

Also found during the property search was jewelry belonging to two missing girls from Fort Lauderdale, who had run away from home on October 23, 1972. Mary Briscolina and Elsie Farmer were both 14 years old. Their skeletal remains were found months later, abandoned in a field amongst the grass and weeds.

On January 4, 1972, 22-year-old waitress Belinda Hutchins went missing. On the day she disappeared, eyewitnesses recalled seeing her climbing into a car like that driven by Gerard Schaefer. Her personal address book showed up in Schaefer's cache of trophies, and the name Belinda appeared repeatedly in the murder/sex "fantasies" that he wrote.

Following his conviction, Schaefer was incarcerated at Florida State Prison, serving two first-degree-murder life sentences. They were cut short on December 3, 1995, when the 49-year-old Schaefer escaped from paying his debt to society. He was brutally murdered in his jail cell. Guards found blood splattered all around the cell. Schaefer had been repeatedly stabbed, including wounds inflicted upon both eyes, and had his throat slit. His killer had targeted Schaefer's face and head for a frenzied knife attack.

> **He told Sondra London that his real tally of victims was somewhere between 80 and 110. Just how accurate that figure may be is open to debate.**

His cellmate was blamed for the crime, although he protested his innocence. Schaefer was hated by his fellow prisoners, not just for his personality, but because of the two big strikes he had against him: he was a former police officer and a convicted sex offender. Convicts will tolerate murderers among their number but cannot abide cops or perverts. In prison, Schaefer was a marked man and had previously been attacked more than once.

Although he had been convicted of two murders, Schaefer slyly alluded to the possibility that he may have been responsible for many more. He told Sondra London that his real tally of victims was somewhere between 80 and 110. Just how accurate that figure may be is open to debate. As with so many serial killers, Schaefer was extremely narcissistic and liked nothing more than to indulge in a spot of grandstanding. It is extremely likely, however, that Gerard Schaefer killed more than two victims—perhaps many more. Detectives considered him to be the prime suspect in several more murders, perhaps as many as thirty. The disappearances span multiple states, including his adopted home state of Florida.

Quoted in the *South Florida Sun Sentinel* in 1995, shortly after the serial killer's death, former FBI profiler Bill Hagerty said that he would rank Schaefer among the top five sickest serial killers he had ever interviewed. That puts him at the head of a large number of very sick and twisted individuals to have crossed the FBI agent's path over the years.

Had he lived, it's possible that Gerard Schaefer would have been released on parole in 2018, assuming he was not convicted of other murders before that happened. There is reason to believe that further murder charges would have been brought against him.

There is nothing wrong with enjoying crime or horror fiction. For millions of readers, the works of authors such as Stephen King and Thomas Harris provide a chilling, but ultimately safe, means of escapist entertainment. The tradition of macabre literature goes back for centuries. No matter how graphic and disturbing some of this fiction can be, however, it is rarely, if ever, written by those who have perpetrated similar crimes in real life.

An exception to this is his book *Killer Fiction*, a collection of writing and drawings by Gerard Schaefer and Sondra London. It first saw print in 1989. As a college student, Schaefer had taken several courses in creative writing and took to writing murder fiction while he was behind bars. The results were extremely graphic and disturbing, with much of his writing involving the torture and degradation of women. A common theme was the female victims defecating themselves, something that Schaefer the writer returned to again and again.

In print, as in real life, Schaefer characterizes women as "whores" and describes in nauseating detail various ways in which they should meet a violent demise. Some detectives and profilers came to believe that the horrific prose depictions Schaefer wrote were, in fact, most likely recollections of things he had actually done, rather than simply warped imaginings. His accounts of raping and murdering women, then raping them again after they were dead, could be accurate accounts of the disappearances of numerous female victims.

# THE BUS STOP KILLER
# LEVI BELLFIELD

Any homicide detective will tell you that there are as many potential motives for murder as there are different human emotions. Some killers are motivated by lust: they crave sex, money, or power over their fellow human beings. Others, by jealously, revenge, or spite.

In the case of Londoner Levi Bellfield, the driving force behind a series of murders and sexual attacks was hatred. Bellfield hated females—more specifically, young, fair-haired women and girls—with such deep-rooted intensity and disgust that he felt compelled to destroy them.

Levi Bellfield was born in London in May of 1968. Living in low-income council housing, it wasn't long before he was running with a bad crowd. Bellfield was drawn to the world of petty crime, and by the time he was 13 years old, he had been caught and convicted of burglary. While a history of theft and relatively low-grade crimes committed during childhood do not necessarily mean that a child will grow up to become a serial killer, it does suggest a disdain and disregard for authority, which may lead to more serious offenses further down the line.

He was the father of eleven children, by several different mothers. Bellfield was consistently abusive toward the girls and women in his life. One of his daughters recalled him raping her mother and then beating her severely. He did the same to many of his girlfriends, showing his intimate partners depths of psychological cruelty that he kept hidden from the world at large. Being in a relationship with Levi Bellfield brought with it the strong likelihood of being sexually assaulted and physically battered.

Bellfield lacked a university education but was by no means unintelligent. He possessed a degree of "street smarts" and instinctive cun-

Wheel clamping is a technique of punishing drivers of improperly parked vehicles. Preventing the car from being driven, a wheel clamp is typically left on until some fine has been paid.

ning that served him well for a time, allowing him to elude the police investigation into the murders for which he was responsible. Physically sturdy, with much of his muscle having been replaced by fat, Bellfield had a love of posing for photos with his shirt off, trying to portray himself as the hard man. He had worked as a nightclub bouncer, relishing the opportunity to exercise power over other people. Bellfield also ran a company that wheel-clamped improperly parked vehicles, no doubt providing some degree of satisfaction at having motorists at his mercy.

Levi Bellfield exclusively targeted young females, preferring blondes where possible. After approaching them and striking up a conversation, he would begin making comments of a sexual nature. This soon segued into a sexual advance, which often was rejected. Bellfield was not a man who took rejection well, seeing it as a direct slight upon his enormous yet equally frail ego. The result was a vicious surprise attack upon his intended victim and usually involved a blunt weapon, such as a hammer or some other striking tool.

Some murderers, such as the American serial killer Israel Keyes, prefer to commit their crimes as far away from home as possible, traveling long distances to put as much space between them and suspicion as possible. Not so with Levi Bellfield, who stuck to the streets he had grown up on. All his attacks took place in west London, his comfort zone. Bellfield lived and worked nearby, running his private business under one of more than 40 aliases.

Nobody can say for sure when his penchant for petty crime turned deadly serious, but one of the first recorded incidents took place in 2001, when Bellfield offered a ride to a woman named Anna-Maria Rennie. Rennie was waiting for a bus when Bellfield approached her. She politely declined his offer, expecting that to be the end of the matter. Instead, Bellfield responded by getting out of the driver's seat and grabbing her, trying to stuff the astonished woman into the vehicle. She fought him off, and Bellfield fled the scene, screaming a string of sexually degrading epithets at her as he left.

On March 21, 2002, 13-year-old schoolgirl Amanda "Milly" Dowler got off the train at Walton-on-Thames and disappeared. She was not seen again until September 18 of that same year, when her remains were found in some woods 25 miles away from the spot where she was last seen. Milly's body was in a state of severe decomposition, and while the cause of her death was impossible to determine, 13-year-olds do not simply die spontaneously. The death was deemed to be suspicious, and the perpetrator needed to be found.

> **On March 21, 2002, 13-year-old schoolgirl Amanda "Milly" Dowler got off the train at Walton-on-Thames and disappeared.**

As soon as Milly's body was located, detectives worked painstakingly to reproduce her final steps. Milly had been out with friends until a little after four o'clock in the afternoon, when she began to walk home unaccompanied. To make sure that her parents didn't worry, she called home and let them know that she was on her way. She never arrived. Growing increasingly concerned, her parents waited three hours and then called police to report their daughter missing. A massive search was launched in the area of her disappearance. Police divers dredged the nearby Hogsmill River. Milly's disappearance made national news, but it was all to no avail. She had been kidnapped by Levi Bellfield.

According to claims he would make years later, Bellfield took his abducted victim to a flat that he owned close to the site of her abduction and sexually assaulted her. He did the same thing the following day, but this time, in the driveway of the home in which Milly lived with her parents, raping her against his car. The rape took place in daylight, but they were never seen. It is nauseating to think what effects this brazen display of depravity would have had on Milly, so close to home, and later, upon her parents, when they heard the specifics of the attack on their daughter. Considering the additional risk of discovery this placed on Bellfield, we can only conclude that he planned the location of this attack in an effort to inflict as much emotional pain and anguish as possible on Milly and her family.

Milly Dowler was assaulted, abused, and tortured for 14 hours, before her abductor strangled her to death. It was an act

Bellfield targeted more than one victim as they exited public transportation.

of extreme sadism and brutality, one that would shock the hardened detectives who investigated it and even the journalists who covered the case, who thought that they were inured to practically every kind of criminal behavior.

Almost one year later, in February of 2003, Levi Bellfield committed his second murder. Marsha McDonnell was 19 years old and lived in Hampton, London. A university student with an aptitude for music, she was taking a year away from her studies. McDonnell was young, light-haired, and was spotted getting off a bus by Bellfield, who had been hanging around, waiting for somebody like her to come along.

McDonnell had been to the movies and could never have suspected that she would be the target of a psychopath. It is not known whether Bellfield attempted to strike up a conversation, propositioning her as he liked to do with other young women; what is known is that he used a heavy, solid object as a club, striking her repeatedly about the head. The nighttime attack took place in the street, in plain sight, but if it was witnessed by anybody, they never came forward.

She was not killed instantly. Bellfield made a clean getaway, leaving McDonnell unresponsive and bleeding on the ground. Despite the best efforts of medical personnel at the hospital, she died there two days later, having sustained significant brain damage during the assault.

By 2003, Bellfield's attacks were growing increasingly brazen. He no longer cared about keeping them secret. Hair stylist Irma Dragoshi, 34, had immigrated to the United Kingdom from Albania. On December 16, Bellfield was driving around West London with two companions in his car when he spotted her waiting for a bus. Parking the car, he got out and ran to the bus stop.

Bellfield approached his unsuspecting target from behind and delivered a heavy blow to her head. It is not known whether he used a weapon, though it is likely that he did—probably a blunt, hefty object that he kept in his vehicle for just that purpose. Dragoshi crumpled to the pavement, hitting her head in the process, and a cackling Bellfield ran back to his vehicle and drove away. If he thought that his companions would keep quiet about his crime, however, he was wrong. Despite Bellfield's denial of responsibility for the assault, one of the men who watched him attack Dragoshi would later testify against him in court.

On May 28, 2004, Levi Bellfield came close to killing again. Kate Sheedy, 18, had just stepped off a bus and was crossing the street, minding her own business, when she was run down by a speeding vehicle. As with Bellfield's other victims, she was young and had blonde hair. The 28th was her last day of school, and Sheedy had spent the evening in the pub, celebrating the special occasion with a few friends.

What should have been the capstone to a wonderful day became memorable for another reason entirely: she was left broken and bleeding in the road after a brutal, completely unprovoked vehicular hit-and-run attack. Accidents do happen, of course, but this was no accident: it was a vicious, premeditated attack. The white van was lying in wait, parked at the side of the road with its engine running but headlights switched off. This gave Bellfield a better chance of taking his victim by surprise.

Kate Sheedy had no chance to get out of the way in time. The van gunned its engine, ran into her, and knocked her down into the road. Its driver slammed on the brakes and threw it into reverse, running over her prostrate body. Then it sped away into the night.

**Kate Sheedy had no chance to get out of the way in time. The van gunned its engine, ran into her, and knocked her down into the road.**

An ambulance arrived and rushed Sheedy to the hospital. Medical imaging revealed an array of internal injuries, many of them serious enough that she was lucky not to have died in the street. Kate Sheedy is a remarkably courageous woman. She fought through the process of healing and rehabilitation, spending months in excruciating pain. Due to a combination of sheer force of will and excellent medical care, she thankfully pulled through. Yet the attack left her scarred, both physically and psychologically.

The police had no idea why she had been targeted. Sheedy had no enemies to speak of, and certainly nobody disliked her enough to try to kill her. Unbeknownst to them at the time, she fit Levi Bellfield's "type": young, light-haired, and attractive. In a marked departure from his other crimes, Bellfield made no attempt to charm Sheedy into going along with him. In fact, the two never exchanged a single word. The serial killer sat, waiting patiently, until he saw a prospective victim that he liked the look of, and then he tried to murder her, in plain sight of the public.

On the night of August 19, 2004, Levi Bellfield attacked student Amélie Delagrange in Twickenham. She was a visitor to the United

Southwest of the city center along the River Thames, London's suburban Twickenham district is home to the largest rugby stadium in the world.

Kingdom from her native France, and she had spent the evening socializing with friends before walking home alone. The specifics of what happened to her remain unknown, but, in all likelihood, she was spotted and approached by Bellfield, who was lurking in the shadows, waiting for just such an opportunity to come his way.

If he followed his standard MO, Bellfield would have spoken to Delagrange and tried to charm her. After she rebuffed his advances, Bellfield attacked her, striking her in the head with a solid object, before making his escape.

Delagrange did not die instantly. She was found in a near-comatose state by a passerby, who immediately called 999, summoning the police and emergency medical services to the scene. Paramedics did the best that they could, rendering urgent care and transporting her to the hospital, but her head trauma was too severe. She died in the intensive care unit later that same night.

The similarity between the murder of Amélie Delagrange and that of Marsha McDonnell in 2003 immediately caught the attention of investigating officers. Both were young women who had died in a very similar manner, being bludgeoned to death with a heavy, blunt implement of some sort. In both cases, the fatal injuries were inflicted upon the head. The two murders had also taken place relatively close to one another.

After his attack on Delagrange, Bellfield stole her cell phone. Although he didn't particularly need it, it may have been a feeble attempt on his part to pass her murder off as a robbery gone bad, rather than the work of a serial killer. Whatever the reason may be, he was foolish enough to use the phone in the town of Walton-on-Thames. This was the same town from which Milly Dowler had been abducted.

Now that a link had been established between the Dowler and Delagrange murders, detectives started looking for a common denominator between the two. They reasoned that the killer had not been on foot when he abducted Dowler and may well have driven to Twickenham in order to kill Delagrange. If they could identify a vehicle that was in both Twickenham and Walton-on-Thames on the days that both crimes were committed, they would have their man.

The work of a homicide detective may appear glamorous on TV, but in reality, it requires countless hours of monotonous, repetitive, and painstaking work. Officers pulled footage from every known video camera in the vicinity of each crime scene, then sat down to trawl through every single second of it, looking for the killer's car.

Finally, after watching hour after hour of traffic driving by, they found it: a white Ford Courier van was caught on camera in both places. A search of the country's vehicle registration records showed that there were around 25,000 similar Ford Couriers on British roads. Each and every owner was a potential suspect. Although it would take time, detectives would ultimately learn that one of those owners was Levi Bellfield. Both Bellfield's current

A pattern soon emerged. He had a habit of approaching young women at bus stops and trying to engage them in conversation.

spouse and at least one of his exes told detectives that he was a likely candidate for the murders of Milly Dowler and Amélie Delagrange.

With Bellfield in their sights, the police placed him under constant surveillance. A pattern soon emerged. He had a habit of approaching young women at bus stops and trying to engage them in conversation. Although this did not lead to an attack, detectives found the behavior suspicious and felt that they finally had enough evidence to obtain a warrant for his arrest.

Officers launched a dawn raid on Bellfield's house on November 22, 2004. Going from room to room, they were surprised to find that he was nowhere to be seen. Then they searched the attic and discovered their man hiding in the darkness—undoubtedly not the action of an innocent man. He was placed in handcuffs and escorted to the police station for what would be the first of many interviews.

In the courtroom, Bellfield tried to play mind games with Kate Sheedy, leering and pulling faces at her and her boyfriend. Yet if her ordeal had proven anything, it was that Sheedy did not lack for courage or resolve. She stood up and testified against the man who had tried to kill her, helping secure the conviction that would send him to prison. If Bellfield had expected to intimidate her, he was to be disappointed. In addition to the charge of attempted murder with regard to Sheedy, he was convicted on murder charges for the killing of Amélie Delagrange and Marsha McDonnell.

On February 25, 2008, the judge imposed a sentence of life imprisonment, guaranteeing that Bellfield would never walk free again, but justice had not entirely been served—for the time being, at least. There was still one more victim to be taken into account.

Despite the evidence, and the fact that he was the police's prime suspect in the murder of Milly Dowler, Levi Bellfield continued to deny any involvement in her death. Undeterred, detectives continued to build a strong case against him.

CCTV camera footage retrieved from the street in which Milly Dowler disappeared picked up a red car that belonged to Bellfield's partner. She later told police that she had not been driving the car on March 21, 2002; Bellfield had decided to borrow it, so he was behind the wheel. In all likelihood, he was out trawling for a victim, saw Milly walking home alone, and decided that she fit the bill.

In an interview with UK TV's Sky News, Detective Chief Inspector Colin Sutton—who had been on Bellfield's trail for years—recalled

the serial killer's strange behavior during his interviews at the police station. Bellfield affected an air of complete disinterest toward the murder inquiry of which he was the center, even going so far as to turn his chair away from the interviewing police officers and facing the wall instead.

If Bellfield was trying to convey the impression that he wasn't involved in the murders of several young women, he went about it in completely the wrong way. Lounging back in his chair with his legs extended, the accused killer's behavior was better suited for a comfortable couch at home than for a criminal investigation. In fact, this behavior was so odd, it was positively jarring, and even Bellfield's own lawyer pointedly told him to show some

Police manually sifted through CCTV footage from cameras near Bellfield's crime scenes to discover common elements, which turned up vehicles traceable to Bellfield.

respect for the proceedings. This was not the behavior of an innocent man; on the contrary, it was the posture of somebody with a great deal to hide.

On June 23, 2011, Levi Bellfield was convicted of murdering Milly Dowler. She was Bellfield's first victim (that we know of), but hers was the last killing for which he was prosecuted. He steadfastly maintained his innocence for five more years, until finally, in 2016, he confessed to having abducted, raped, and killed Milly.

In the wake of the revelations about their father, Bellfield's children understandably disowned him. Speaking to BBC news, his eldest daughter, Bobbie-Louise, said that he could "rot in hell," a sentiment with which most of us can heartily agree. Bobbie-Louise Bellfield wrote a letter of condolence to the parents of Milly Dowler, apologizing for the atrocities that her father had inflicted on their daughter. Being the spouse or child of a serial rapist and murderer usually has a serious impact, and many experience problems with depression and substance abuse. Some attempt suicide, unable to live with their relationship to a bona fide monster.

> **At the time of writing, Levi Bellfield remains the only serial murderer incarcerated in the British criminal justice system to be the subject of multiple complete life sentences.**

In 2016, Bellfield underwent what he claims to be a sincere conversion to the Islamic faith. As part of this process, he changed his name to Yusuf Rahim.

At the time of writing, Levi Bellfield remains the only serial murderer incarcerated in the British criminal justice system to be the subject of multiple complete life sentences. There is no possibility of parole; he will die in prison. Yet there has been public outrage at Bellfield's claim that he now suffers from posttraumatic stress disorder (PTSD) and has been offered counseling to treat not only those symptoms but also anxiety and clinical depression. The British taxpayer is footing the bill for Bellfield's course of treatment, which many find to be unacceptable.

In 2019, Bellfield attempted to take his own life in his prison cell. The suicide attempt was unsuccessful, and at the time of writing, he remains in prison.

In a pattern that is seen over and over again with male serial killers, particularly those who combine sexual assault with the act of murder, Levi Bellfield had an inherent lack of respect for the female gender. He saw girls and women as being far inferior to himself, perceiving them as objects to be used rather than peers and fellow human beings. For some reason, he found blondes particularly objectionable. A former girlfriend recalled finding photographs of blonde female models that Bellfield had taken out of magazines. Their faces had been cut up and disfigured, a tangible externalization of the anger he felt toward such women.

On first contact with a potential victim, Bellfield could be extremely charming. He would flatter, cajole, and use humor to get his way. If his advances were rebuffed, however, a very different side to his personality would emerge. Bellfield became domineering and controlling. He often flew into a rage, the anger fueled by a sense of unfairness. "How DARE you reject me?" Bellfield would think, as his outrage quickly turned into aggression.

In the eyes of Levi Bellfield, the biggest mistake a female could make was to reject him. He was completely self-centered, caring for nothing whatsoever beyond his own needs and desires. This came along with a colossal sense of entitlement, the kind of pathologic personality that believes that, in the event of a female denying him her attention or failing to give him whatever it was that he wanted, he was totally justified in simply taking it from her—by force, if necessary.

Levi Bellfield, the scourge of west London.

According to the police officers who grilled Bellfield on his role in the murders, he was extremely arrogant and showed signs of narcissistic behavior. His murders were not acts of impulsive rage. On the contrary, they were coldly premeditated and thought out in advance. Levi Bellfield had sufficient organizational skills to abduct and hide his victims, sometimes in broad daylight, and got away with it for several years. He devised a plan to fly under the radar of law enforcement, and the strategy served him well, right up to the point where it no longer did.

Detective Chief Inspector Colin Sutton, one of the few people who undeniably knows the mind of Levi Bellfield best, voiced the opinion that the murders for which he was convicted and imprisoned are almost certainly just a small sample.

In 2019, the hunt for Levi Bellfield was fictionalized in the three-part TV drama series *Manhunt*, starring Martin Clunes as DCI Sutton and Welsh actor Celyn Jones as Bellfield.

The true scope of Bellfield's crimes remains uncertain, and even though he will never walk out of prison a free man, he has little motivation to come clean regarding the others. The British public and the loved ones of those he brutalized can only take cold comfort in the knowledge that Levi Bellfield will never again have the opportunity to take another innocent life.

# THE GOLDEN STATE KILLER
# JOSEPH JAMES DEANGELO

The state of California has seen more than its fair share of serial killers through the years. The Zodiac Killer, who remains unidentified to this day, shot his victims dead and then taunted both the authorities and the media with a series of cryptic cyphers purporting to contain clues that would aid in his capture.

During the era of peace and love, the infamous Manson Family murdered actress Sharon Tate and her companions at the bidding of their unhinged patriarch, Charles Manson.

Perhaps the best known was Richard Ramirez, the infamous Night Stalker, who terrorized the citizens of Los Angeles and its surroundings during a 16-month reign of terror spanning 1984 and 1985. His nickname was based upon Ramirez's MO, which involved breaking into the homes of unsuspecting women and couples after dark, subduing any male that might be present, and then repeatedly assaulting the female occupants. Once he was finished, Ramirez usually (though not always) killed them.

Before Ramirez haunted the streets of L.A., however, there was another so-called Night Stalker: Joseph James DeAngelo. Despite a long list of rapes and murders, he managed to evade detection for decades, until justice finally caught up with him in 2018. When the identity of the serial murderer nicknamed both the Original Night Stalker and the Golden State Killer was finally discovered, it came as a major shock to the public—because the perpetrator had once worn the uniform of a California police officer.

Joseph James DeAngelo Jr. was born on November 8, 1945, to U.S. Air Force sergeant Joseph James DeAngelo Sr. and his wife Kath-

In 1973, Joseph James DeAngelo joined the police force of Exeter, California, a small city on the eastern edge of the agriculture-heavy San Joaquin Valley.

leen. He was a result of the post–World War II baby boom.

One of the most disturbing incidents of his childhood took place when he was nine years old. DeAngelo is said to have witnessed two airmen rape his sister, Constance, who was just seven years old. The incident was related to Buzzfeed news reporter Stephanie K. Baer in 2018 by Constance's son, Jesse, who said that his mother had told him the story herself. The DeAngelo family was stationed on a U.S. air base in Germany at the time. The experience would almost certainly have traumatized young Joseph for life, and more alarmingly, planted the first mental seeds that rape was an acceptable, even desirable thing to do.

DeAngelo Sr. was a domestic abuser and beat Kathleen so often that it finally came to the attention of the Air Force. He was told that if the beatings continued, he would be drummed out of the service. It is not uncommon for spousal abusers to also beat their children. In the 1940s and 1950s, an adult delivering a beating to a child was often excused under the guise of it being discipline. We can reasonably assume that all four of the DeAngelo children—Joseph Jr. and his three siblings—were beaten by their father on more than one occasion. There are also reports from within the family that Kathleen was not beyond hitting the children herself, when the mood took her. During his murder trial in 2020, DeAngelo's sister would submit a corroborating statement to the court that said that their father was abusive to his children, both physically and mentally.

Joseph Sr. and Kathleen divorced, and both remarried. As is often the case, the children remained with their mother, returning to the United States, while their father settled in Korea and started another family. According to prosecutors at his trial, Joseph Jr. showed a propensity for hurting animals and breaking and entering.

After leaving high school in 1964, he enlisted in the U.S. Navy as a damage controlman the following year. DeAngelo served in the Vietnam War for 22 months. On leaving the service, he went to college, graduating with a degree in criminal justice. This prepared him for a career in law enforcement. He was hired on by the Exeter Police Department in May 1963.

By the early 1970s, the future looked bright for him. DeAngelo married in 1973, and the couple had three children. He worked as a police officer in Exeter between 1973 and 1979. His assignment was to the burglary unit, visiting the homes of those who had just suffered a break-in, taking a report, and trying to catch the burglars. After nightfall, when he was off the clock, DeAngelo was breaking into homes himself, rummaging through the residents' property and taking anything he thought might have value. This truly was a case of the fox guarding the chicken coop.

His fellow police officers recalled Officer DeAngelo as being an outsider in the department. He had little in the way of a sense of humor, or so it seemed to them, preferring to remain aloof while everybody else blew off steam with jokes. He was also something of a know-it-all, which, coupled with his always serious personality, only served to further distance him from his colleagues.

"I liked him," one former colleague told the *Los Angeles Times*, "but he's not the type of guy that I'd have over for a barbecue."

Theft was something that had always appealed to him; the reason DeAngelo was drummed out of the field of law enforcement was because he was caught shoplifting, stealing items that he could have bought legally for just a few dollars—such as a can of dog repellant and a hammer. When he was caught, DeAngelo put on a highly dramatic performance,

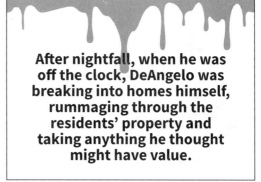

After nightfall, when he was off the clock, DeAngelo was breaking into homes himself, rummaging through the residents' property and taking anything he thought might have value.

crying out loudly and attempting to fake a heart attack, in hopes that the store security guard would let him off. He was not successful. Police arrested him, and he admitted to the officer taking the report that he had put on a show in an attempt to avoid trouble.

This was another sign of DeAngelo's pathologic personality. He could be incredibly calm and calculating one minute and utterly impulsive the next. The thrill of stealing from a store outweighed the limited monetary gain, which was by no means nearly enough to offset the risks. One botched theft cost him an entire career.

With his prospects of a law enforcement career now dashed, DeAngelo took work wherever he could find it. During the 1980s, he found work as a mechanic with Save Mart grocery stores. By all accounts, he was a solid enough employee. Nothing he did at work hinted at the dark side of his personality, the dual life that he was leading after night had fallen.

There was also a real thrill to be had by invading a stranger's personal space, intruding upon their most private places. DeAngelo got off on the sense of power this gave him, but after a while, the act of intrusion wasn't enough. That's when he turned to rape—and ultimately, murder.

It took on the form of a twisted game. The Golden State Killer did not strike randomly. He preplanned his attacks, watching his victims far in advance of carrying out the actual crime. He enjoyed seeing them come and go, noting such things as what time they went to bed, how frequently visitors came and went, and how many people lived at home with them. He also cased the residences, applying the experience he had learned working (and committing) burglary to figure out the best way of gaining access. Sometimes he even broke in, walked around the property, analyzing the layout, the entrances, and the exits. He did not steal on these reconnaissance excursions, for fear of tipping off his intended victim.

DeAngelo started out by making crank calls to his targeted addresses, breathing heavily into the phone receiver until the other person hung up. He liked to instill a sense of fear, or at the very least nervousness, into his intended victims, who were always either women or couples. Sometimes, he would call back after a rape had taken place, and then threaten to come back to kill the victim.

Both before and after his crimes, DeAngelo would use the phone to harass or psychologically torture intended victims, surviving family, and the authorities.

These phone calls weren't restricted to those DeAngelo targeted. He loved to call the police anonymously and taunt them, telling the operator that he was going to rape a new victim very soon, and there was not a thing the cops could do about it.

His break-ins happened at night. DeAngelo used a gun to control his victims and keep them from trying to escape or fight back. Any male present was forced to strip naked and lie face down, while the intruder stacked dinner plates on his back. If the terrified man tried to move, the clattering of the falling plates would alert DeAngelo.

Once the male, who was seen to be the greater threat, was rendered compliant, DeAngelo took his time assaulting the female. It was not unusual for him to spend hours committing these appalling sexual assaults, even taking a break to fetch food and drink from the couple's own fridge.

Why not simply kill the male immediately? Two reasons suggest themselves. Firstly, had DeAngelo murdered the man straight away, his female victim would never have believed she had a chance of surviving the encounter and would have been far more likely to scream, resist, or try to flee. Leaving the male alive gave her something to hope for—and, indeed, there were times when DeAngelo satisfied himself

**Waking up to find a masked intruder pointing a gun in your face would be enough to discombobulate anybody.**

with rape and did not kill either of his victims, choosing instead to sneak out of the residence and disappear into the night, taking whatever valuables he could find along with him. It was for these crimes that he was known as the East Area Rapist prior to becoming the Golden State Killer—a nickname that would be applied later. Police investigators believe that DeAngelo's sexual assaults outnumbered his murders by about four to one.

Secondly, it is likely that he became aroused at the thought of making the male lie there, powerless to stop it, while DeAngelo assaulted his partner within earshot. Before this, he would typically cover the female with his gun while forcing her to tie up the male.

DeAngelo's method of entry usually involved prying open an unlocked window or door. Wearing a full-face ski mask, he waited until his victims were asleep before entering their bedroom and shining a bright flashlight in their eyes. The victims were usually groggy, disoriented, and temporarily blinded by the flashlight beam. Waking up to find a masked intruder pointing a gun in your face would be enough to discombobulate anybody.

Joseph DeAngelo's criminal career started out with petty shoplifting and then graduated to full-fledged breaking and entering. By the mid-1970s, he was committing burglary after burglary in the city of Visalia, which resulted in his being given the nickname of "the Visalia Ransacker." Cash, jewelry, or guns—anything with a price tag was fair game. In the summer of 1975, DeAngelo stole a .38-caliber revolver during one of his break-ins. He started to carry it on future burglaries.

A couple of weeks later, on the night of September 11, DeAngelo broke into the home of a professor named Claude Snelling. He pulled that same gun on Snelling's 16-year-old daughter, who had been fast asleep in her bed, and tried to kidnap her. DeAngelo had been snooping around the house for the past few weeks and had now decided to make his move. Things did not go according to plan. Professor Snelling woke up and challenged the intruder, who shot him dead before making his escape.

At the time of his early home invasions, DeAngelo was motivated primarily by the urge to rape and steal. If he had been able to kidnap Claude Snelling's daughter without disturbing anybody else in the house, let alone killing her father, it is likely that he would have done so. That would change in due course.

DeAngelo was almost captured in December of that same year, when he was caught red-handed scoping out a potential victim's residence. A police officer got the drop on him and even fired a warning shot. DeAngelo panicked and threw up his hands, but then tried to turn the tables on the cop, drawing his pistol and shooting back. Fortunately, the bullet hit the officer's flashlight, which shattered, causing several wounds but not killing him. DeAngelo ran off into the darkness.

The East Area Rapist loved the notoriety he was receiving because of his crimes. Throughout his reign of terror, entire communities lived in fear. Residents became more diligent about locking their doors and windows, adding better locks to increase home security. Guard dogs became more common, and sales of firearms rose significantly. According to police sources, the number of burglaries being committed actually went down, due to the increased level of public vigilance that the rapes and murders had elicited.

On February 2, 1978, he committed what seemed at first to be an unrelated double murder. A married couple, Brian and Katie Maggiore,

As the killer's infamy grew, his methods grew more cautious. Fear of revealing his identity ultimately led him to stop leaving any of his victims alive.

were out for a stroll with their dog. The Maggiores were minding their own business when suddenly they found themselves running for their lives from an armed assailant, who shot them both dead. There was no obvious motive, and this was not a mugging.

After canvassing the neighborhood for eyewitnesses, the police spoke with a local resident who watched the Maggiores being pursued by a masked man who was armed with a handgun. He was seen to gun them both down and then flee on foot. Homicide detectives theorized that the Maggiores had spotted DeAngelo on the prowl, perhaps lurking around a house that he was preparing to break into, and that he had killed them for it to protect his identity. For some years, there was some debate as to whether the Maggiores were murdered by the Golden State Killer or not. The issue was finally settled during his trial, when Joseph DeAngelo confessed to their murder.

It was a close call for the East Area Rapist. By 1979, DeAngelo was becoming increasingly concerned about being discovered and caught. He wore a mask in order to prevent his victims from seeing his face, and he tied them up to ensure they would not escape. On the night of October 1, something happened that caused his MO to change—a home invasion and attempted rape went disastrously wrong. Having broken into the home of a young couple who lived in Goleta, DeAngelo managed to subdue his victims but unexpectedly lost control of the scene when the couple were able to escape and scream for help, forcing DeAngelo to flee the scene himself.

> Once he was through, ... DeAngelo shot both victims dead in cold blood. On his way out, he went through the fridge and took a few bites of turkey that had been left over from Christmas dinner.

He must have decided that this incident was a little too close for comfort, because after the events of that night, the East Area Rapist no longer even considered allowing his victims to live. Though he would still assault women, he had now fully committed to murder.

It is entirely possible that, with the transition from a primarily rape-based focus to one with murder at the forefront, DeAngelo found that he found the latter more fulfilling. Between 1976 and 1978, the sexual assaults had been taking place just weeks or sometimes even days apart. In the first half of 1979, they reduced to being, on average, a monthly occurrence. After the flubbed home invasion in Goleta, the interval between attacks widened to a matter of months. The Golden State Killer was slowing down.

Almost three months after the bungled assault in Goleta, DeAngelo broke into a residence occupied by 44-year-old Robert Offerman and 35-year-old Debra Manning, in the same town. This time, he was determined not to get caught. It is unlikely that he deviated from his standard MO during the assault, holding both at gunpoint and forcing Manning to tie up her male partner. Once he was through, however, DeAngelo shot both victims dead in cold blood. On his way out, he went through the fridge and took a few bites of turkey that had been left over from Christmas dinner.

A man and a woman lay dead at his own hand, and Joseph DeAngelo still had the stomach to take food from their fridge and eat it.

Detectives interviewed the neighbors, who recalled having heard either gunshots or firecrackers late on the night of the murder. The property belonged to Offerman, and it was his primary residence. Both he and Manning were divorcing their spouses and were now spending the night at his place. DeAngelo most likely spotted Manning and tailed her to the property, then waited until late at night before breaking in. Their bodies were discovered by a friend of Offerman's. Both had died in the bedroom. Manning was found naked on the bed, her limbs bound, and Offerman was on the floor beside her, his body leaning against the bed.

DeAngelo struck again on March 13, 1980, in Ventura County. He broke into the home of Lyman and Charlene Smith and, after molesting Charlene, beat them both to death with a log intended for their wood-burning fireplace.

The 43-year-old Lyman was a respected attorney and was due to become a judge. Charlene was ten years younger than her husband. The Smiths' bodies, trussed up and left on a blood-soaked bed, were discovered the following day by their 12-year-old son.

The Golden State Killer went quiet for the next five months. When he surfaced again in August, the attack mimicked that of his last two home invasion murders, targeting a newlywed couple who made their home together in Laguna Niguel. The Harringtons were both medical professionals: Keith was enrolled in medical school, and Patti worked as a nurse.

The last time anybody (other than their murderer) had contact with the Harringtons was on Sunday, August 17, when Patti spoke with her father-in-law, Roger. He owned the home they lived in, and she invited him over to dinner on the evening of the 21st.

A planned community in coastal Orange County, California, Laguna Niguel is a sleepy, upscale residential neighborhood near the Pacific coast.

When Thursday came around, Roger arrived at the home and found nobody answering the door. He let himself in with a set of keys and found the bodies of his son and daughter-in-law in the bedroom. The bed linens and comforter had been pulled up to the pillows, covering both victims' heads. They had been dead for approximately four days.

No murder weapon was found, but the Harringtons had been killed with blunt force trauma. Both were wearing night attire, consistent with their having been disturbed by an intruder while they were sleeping or still in bed.

There were no more assaults for the remainder of 1980. The holidays came and went. The next attack came on the night of February 6, 1981. DeAngelo deviated from his newly established routine by targeting a woman who was home alone, rather than a couple: 28-year-old Manuela Witthuhn, who lived in Irvine. Witthuhn was married and lived with her husband David, but he was in the hospital at the time of the attack.

After forcing his way into the house and sexually assaulting Manuela, the killer used an unidentified blunt object to inflict fatal head trauma upon her.

David not only had to deal with the sickening knowledge of what had happened to his wife, coupled with the fact that he had not been home to protect her, but he also bore the burden of being a potential suspect. To an extent, this is understandable. When a husband or wife dies, the investigation almost always begins with their spouse. In selecting a victim who was home alone, the murder did not fit the pattern of DeAngelo's previous couples' murders. It was only after his 2008 death that the rape/murder was proved to have been committed by the Golden State Killer. By that point, the emotional problems caused by the crime had destroyed the life of David Witthuhn too.

As if the attack itself wasn't cruelty enough, the serial killer repeatedly phoned David Witthuhn after the killing, breathing heavily on the line and threatening to come back and kill him too. According to Witthuhn's second wife, Rhonda, she and David were the recipients of these threatening calls for years, demonstrating that Joseph DeAngelo took as much perverse delight in abusing the families of his victims as he did in committing the crimes themselves. They could never relax, living in a state of constant fear that Manuela Witthuhn's murderer would one day come back and make good on his threats.

Now came a five-month pause between attacks. His need to kill sated for the time being, DeAngelo was presumably focused upon his personal life during that time. He reverted to his familiar pattern in July, selecting another unsuspecting Goleta couple on the night of the 27th.

Cheri Domingo, 35, and her partner, Greg Sanchez, 28, were at home in bed when DeAngelo broke in. Neither of them went quietly; their neighbors heard them screaming at approximately three o'clock in the morning, along with what was almost certainly gunfire. Unfortunately, they wrote it off as somebody celebrating, rather than a double murder taking place.

**Neither of them went quietly; their neighbors heard them screaming at approximately three o'clock in the morning, along with what was almost certainly gunfire.**

Neither Domingo nor Sanchez owned the house. Domingo was house-sitting while the property was up on the market, awaiting a new tenant.

Later that same morning, a visitor came to the residence and found the couple dead in the bedroom. Both had sustained significant head injuries, delivered by a blunt object. Sanchez had also been shot in the face. Detectives instantly connected the murders with those of Robert Offerman and Debra Manning, who had lived just a few blocks away from the crime scene. Eighteen months after their murder, Joseph DeAngelo had returned to one of his old stomping grounds in order to kill again.

Despite the recognized commonalities between the two sets of murders, the homicide investigation ultimately went nowhere. Following the July murders, not only were there no further Golden State killings in 1981, but the serial killer also went dormant for the next five years.

Joseph DeAngelo committed what is believed to have been his final murder on May 4, 1986, when he broke into an Orange County home occupied by an 18-year-old named Janelle Cruz. She lived with her family, but they were out of town on vacation at the time of the attack. After being sexually assaulted, she was beaten to death with a blunt object, her body left in a blood-soaked bed to be discovered the following day.

After murdering Janelle, DeAngelo did something unusual for a serial killer—he stopped killing. There has been much speculation as to why. One commonly floated theory is that he was simply getting too old to handle the physicality that was required. He was 41 at the time of the murder, which can hardly be considered old, but it may have been the case that subduing and assaulting victims half his age was getting increasingly difficult for him. He may just have decided to "quit while he was ahead."

Whatever the reason, the Golden State killer simply dropped off the grid. He stayed in the vicinity of Sacramento, whose citizens he had terrorized and murdered for years, and settled down to a life of mostly quiet domesticity. He raised his children, who in turn made him a grandfather.

Undoubtedly, Joseph DeAngelo thought that he had gotten away with it.

He was wrong.

One of the aspects of the Golden State Killer investigation that frustrated investigators the most was the fact that they had viable DNA samples of the killer in their possession and had ever since 1980. The problem was that the samples did not match anything on file in police records or databases. The perpetrator, it appeared, had managed to stay off the law enforcement radar for decades.

Indeed, even at the time of his capture, Joseph DeAngelo had not been arrested or spent time in jail. To most people, he was just an ordinary, everyday grandfather, enjoying his sunset years of retirement in California. It would take the advancement of DNA-matching technology, coupled with the invention of a new social craze, to reignite one of the United States' biggest cold cases and finally bring it to a successful conclusion.

Ultimately, the key factor in Joseph James DeAngelo's identification and capture was the rise of the genealogy website.

Over the last few years, more and more people have become fascinated with exploring their own family tree. Thanks to the ubiquity of the Internet and the rise of websites and services that help explore one's personal genealogy back through many generations, it is now simple for somebody to figure out their ancestry or to connect with relatives they never knew existed. This process is made significantly easier with the submission of a DNA sample,

Despite leaving behind plenty of evidence, DeAngelo's biometrics had never been recorded to enable a match until, decades later, investigators reopened the case using modern DNA matching techniques.

usually a simple swab of the inner cheek. Analysis of that sample can be extremely revealing—sometimes more so than anybody would ever have suspected.

Investigators hit upon the idea of comparing the Golden State Killer's stored DNA samples, which had been gathering dust for years, with those submitted by the public to a genealogy website. What might have seemed like a long shot actually paid off handsomely. There wasn't an exact match on the killer—that would have been too easy, and DeAngelo wasn't stupid enough to put his DNA out there like that. One of his relatives, however, had done so with their own sample, and that was the next best thing. Thanks to months of painstaking work, analysts finally made a breakthrough.

They couldn't identify the murderer, but they were able to identify his specific branch of the family tree—which was huge. From there, old-fashioned detective work led them to their prime suspect: 72-year-old Joseph James DeAngelo. His DNA sample came from a tissue that he had discarded in a trash can and a swab of the handle on his car door while he was shopping. It was also noted that the East Area Rapist had said "I hate you, Bonnie," to a victim during one of his attacks. A search of DeAngelo's background re-vealed that he had once been

There wasn't an exact match on the killer—that would have been too easy, and DeAngelo wasn't stupid enough to put his DNA out there like that.

engaged to a woman named Bonnie Colwell and that the relationship had been broken off with some acrimony on his part.

It all added up. Just like that, the Golden State Killer's cover was blown.

Thanks to a triumph of technology, ingenuity, and sheer dogged-ness, the detectives now knew that they had their man. All that remained was for them to go and pick him up from his home in Citrus Heights, near Sacramento.

After the initial shock of finding himself unmasked and taken into custody by the police had worn off, DeAngelo clammed up. He refused to help detectives or cooperate with the investigation in any way, pre-ferring instead to simply sit there quietly, staring off into space. It is likely that, during this period, he was frantically reviewing his options—which were few.

When he finally did start talking, it became apparent that he was attempting to lay the groundwork for an insanity defense. Yes, DeAngelo admitted, he had been responsible for dozens of rapes and multiple murders, but it wasn't his fault. A voice inside his head had told him to do it—a voice that he named Jerry.

If he thought that would somehow get him off the hook, he was wrong. The detectives saw straight through his feeble attempt to blame another personality for his crimes. Now that his identity was revealed, the amount of evidence stacked up against him was monumental.

For somebody as dangerous as Joseph DeAngelo, there could only ever be one appropriate sentence: life imprisonment without the possibility of parole. Even though he was frail and aged at the time of his trial, the only way justice could still be served in some way was to deprive the Golden State Killer of his freedom for what remained of his life. Prosecutors waived the death penalty in exchange for a confession of guilt, something intended to provide closure for his victims' next of kin, though some of them were infuriated that he was going to dodge Death Row. He confessed to 13 murders and 13 rape charges, only a percentage of the sexual assaults he had actually committed.

At the conclusion of his trial and the imposition of sentencing, which took place in August 2021, the families of several of DeAngelo's victims had the chance to speak about the harm that he had done and the pain he had caused. It was pointed out that he had gotten the opportunity to marry and start a family, raising children and grandchildren—which his 13 murder victims had all been denied. He listened dispassionately and then, in what was most likely a feigned show of remorse, told them "I'm truly sorry to everyone I've hurt."

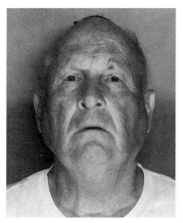

By the time of his capture, DeAngelo had assimilated entirely into normal life. His neighbors never would have suspected the retired grandfather of his infamous streak of crimes.

DeAngelo's former wife, Sharon, revealed that her husband used a laundry list of excuses to explain his nocturnal disappearances. He would claim to be hunting pheasants or making a long-distance drive to visit his parents. She filed for divorce following his arrest in 2018.

As noted previously, prior to marrying Sharon, DeAngelo was engaged to a woman named Bonnie Colwell. To her great credit, Colwell would come forward at DeAngelo's trial to show support and solidarity for his victims. Although she was not permitted to testify, as she was not a witness, Colwell wrote in a letter to the judge that she broke it off with DeAngelo because he was both abusive and manipulative.

The last straw came on the night he appeared outside a window at Colwell's parents' home, insisting that the two of them were going to go and get married. To emphasize the point, he was brandishing a pistol, which he pointed at her. Fortunately, Colwell did not acquiesce. Instead, she fetched her father, who saw DeAngelo off. The engagement was ended that same night.

DeAngelo's marriage to Sharon Huddle may not have been a happy one, according to his neighbors, who recalled hearing pitched screaming matches through the walls of their home. Undoubtedly, DeAngelo harbored a lot of resentment toward females in general—it is probably that this resentment grew to outright hatred, which was then taken out on strangers.

Some neighbors described him as being paranoid and told of the time DeAngelo left an enraged voicemail, threatening to murder them and their dog, because he found its barking annoying. Interviewed by ABC News, one neighbor, Grant Gorman, said that DeAngelo said that he would "deliver a load of death." The thing that stood out most about him to other neighbors was his foul mouth and loud voice, which everybody in the street heard at one time or another.

Did Joseph DeAngelo first engage in rape because, as a young boy in Germany, he witnessed his sister suffering the same ordeal? Partially, perhaps. Coupled with an aggressive temper and a violent mindset, this precipitating incident may have been the first step on the road to his becoming a serial rapist and murderer. The question of whether an otherwise normal young boy was irretrievably warped because he was part of such an awful experience, or whether he was simply "born bad," is one that psychologists still struggle to answer with any degree of certainty.

Although many of those who knew him personally recalled DeAngelo as being a nice guy, vindictiveness was a defining trait of his personality. The obvious delight he derived from tormenting not only the police and the authorities but also his victims and their families paints a picture of a man who liked to induce as much fear and pain as he possibly could. Making the survivors of his sex attacks believe that he might one day return to murder them was the very height of cruelty. For some reason, Joseph DeAngelo was mad at the world and liked to take that anger out on innocent strangers whenever the opportunity presented itself.

Another valid question is: can he be properly characterized as insane? At first glance, his horrific crimes seem like the work of a criminally insane offender. Yet careful analysis reveals that DeAngelo knew exactly what he was doing. For one thing, he modified his methods and techniques to stay one step ahead of the police. During the early murders, he left his victims tied up. The bindings he used to do so were evidence and could have helped detectives link the murders. In the later killings, he took the ligatures with him and left the bodies of his victims unbound.

> For some reason, Joseph DeAngelo was mad at the world and liked to take that anger out on innocent strangers whenever the opportunity presented itself.

On those occasions when there was a threat that he might be caught or identified, DeAngelo showed no hesitation whatsoever in taking a life. Whether it was a loving father protecting his daughter or an innocent couple walking their dog who were simply in the wrong place at the wrong time made no difference to him. Once they registered as a threat, it was over. He pulled the trigger and made his escape. There is a cold, calculating nature to these events that suggests that DeAngelo was willing to go as far as necessary to secure his own best interests. As reprehensible as his actions were in those instances, it cannot be denied that they were also rational—they obeyed a sense of internal logic.

This finding was borne out by the fact that a psychological evaluation found him competent to stand trial. The bottom line is that Joseph DeAngelo knew exactly what he wanted and was willing to inflict any amount of pain and suffering in order to get it, consequences be damned.

No discussion of the Golden State Killer would be complete without making a tip of the hat to crime writer and researcher Michelle McNamara. Self-admittedly obsessed with the case, McNamara (who had no background in law enforcement) spent countless hours poring over case reports, reviewing eyewitness testimony, and talking with other "web sleuths" in an attempt to unmask him. She was convinced that the key to the case would be found in a DNA match of some sort, and she was absolutely right.

Tragically, McNamara died in 2016, before Joseph James DeAngelo was finally brought to justice. She had done arguably more than anybody else to not only keep the memory of the victims alive but also to push for active investigation into the case to continue. Her book *I'll Be Gone in the Dark: One Woman's Obsessive Search for the Golden State Killer* stands as a fine testament to this remarkable woman and her unique contribution to bringing a murderer to justice.

It seems fitting that the final word on the Golden State Killer be given by one of the women he raped, Jane Carson-Sandler. In a remarkable display of bravery, she faced her attacker down in the courtroom and told him: "DeAngelo, I want you to look at me—and I want you to remember what I say. You didn't destroy my life in your cowardly, cruel, and sick behavior. One quarter of me, being a Christian, I want to say to you: 'May God have mercy on your soul.' Then there is another three-quarters of me that want to say to you, 'Buddy, just rot in hell.'"

Bravo, Jane. Bravo.

# THE KILLER COLONEL RUSSELL WILLIAMS

O ver the course of their lives, some killers manage to master the art of hiding in plain sight. A number of them—usually, those who are successful professionals—contrive to leverage their chosen profession for cover. Their elevated and respectable position in society is used as a smokescreen. The murderer cultivates the perception that they are beyond reproach. More often than not, it works ... for a time, at least.

The military has produced its share of murderers. Charles Whitman, the University of Texas–Austin tower sniper, was a former Marine. Jeffrey Dahmer, the so-called Milwaukee Cannibal, served in the U.S. Army. Gary Ridgway, the Green River Killer, was a sailor in the U.S. Navy. Dennis Rader, known as B.T.K. (Bind, Torture, Kill), served in the Air Force.

Most of these men joined the enlisted ranks, and few of them climbed the military career ladder very far. All were socially awkward to some degree and lacked either the requisite intelligence or education to gain an officer's commission.

A prime exception to this rule is Russell Williams.

Williams was born in the United Kingdom in 1963 but emigrated to Canada with his parents when he was a child. His father was a metallurgist whose work took him to several different countries. From a relatively young age, Russell Williams was on the path to some kind of greatness. He was enrolled in a prestigious private boarding school, Upper Canada College in Toronto, where he did well academically, leading the way to attaining a degree in economics at the University of Toronto. His fellow students would recall him as a withdrawn, though not

A twin-engine business jet, the Challenger was often used by the Royal Canadian Air Force to transport VIPs.

quite reclusive, young man, albeit one who liked to play the occasional practical joke. They paint a picture of a fastidious and detail-oriented personality, who was a disciplined and motivated student.

These character traits are important for anybody who wishes to become a pilot, and Russell Williams undertook flight training while still a university student during the mid-1980s. Always an ambitious young man, he had his eye on a military career. The Royal Canadian Air Force seemed like a natural fit, given his passion for aviation, and his undergraduate degree meant that he could be commissioned as an officer. Williams did well in the Air Force. Not only was he a skilled pilot, but he was also a natural teacher, and before long he was serving in the role of flight instructor. By 1991, he had attained the rank of captain and had also gotten married.

The position of fighter pilot is one of the most coveted assignments in the military. Many are attracted to the glamour, excitement, and prestige that accompany such a role. These are the pilots who Hollywood makes movies about. Yet the truth is that the backbone of any modern air force is its transport fleet, which takes care of the mundane, unglamorous, but absolutely essential work that keeps a military running daily.

Russell Williams became a transport pilot, flying the CC-144 Challenger jet through much of the 1990s. Some of the high-profile passengers he flew around included Queen Elizabeth II and Prince Philip of Great Britain, and the Canadian prime minister, giving him one of the most trusted positions in the Air Force at that time. In order to enjoy a successful career as a military officer, however, it is also necessary to punch some staff and administrative tickets along the way. The newly promoted Major Williams assumed a role in the Air Force department for military careers and also applied himself to earning an advanced degree.

The main objective for most career officers is to obtain a command of their own. In the case of now Lieutenant-Colonel Williams, this came in the summer of 2004, when he was given command of a transport squadron. His career continued to advance over the next few years, and by 2009, he had achieved the rank of colonel. This promotion made him eligible for the position of commanding officer at Canadian Forces Base Trenton, a key hub for military transport aviation and one of the world's busiest air bases. It was an awesome responsibility and one that perfectly suited Colonel Williams. Yet when his superiors awarded him this prestigious assignment, they could never have foreseen that the whole house of cards upon which this man had built his life was about to come crashing down.

Because Colonel Russell Williams was a serial rapist and a murderer.

It began with a theft, or more accurately, a series of thefts, along with some breaking and entering. The stolen items were articles of women's underwear. Russell Williams had gotten into the habit of breaking into the homes of women when they were out and stealing their bras, panties, and other intimate items. He would then put them on himself and pose for pictures, presumably for the purpose of sexual gratification. Sometimes, he photographed himself masturbating on beds. Williams did this more than 80 times, collecting a hoard of stolen trophies along the way. Many of the victims of these thefts were underage girls, some as young as 11 years old.

One of the more alarming aspects of these break-ins was that Williams would often turn his attention to items that belonged to children, photographing himself naked with teddy bears and articles of young girls' clothing covering his crotch. Although there is no evidence to suggest that he ever molested a child, the potential was most certainly there.

For a while, Williams was content with this illicit side of his life, entering the homes of strangers and gratifying himself sexually in their bedrooms, but it would not satisfy his lusts forever. He took to shedding his clothing outside the victims' house and entering the property while naked. Before long, he took the next step and began physically assaulting women. He chose his targets carefully, looking for females who lived alone.

His first physical attack took place in September 2009, when he entered the home of an unsuspecting woman while she was sleeping. Williams tied her up and blindfolded her. Then he took a string of humiliating photos of his bound victim, running his hands over her naked body. Less than two weeks later, he assaulted another female in her home. This time, he hit her repeatedly in the head. Williams's propensity for violence was now ever present, though bizarrely, he did allow her to take some aspirin after the sexual assault when she told him that she had a headache. Again, he took a series of photographs throughout the attack.

> **Williams would often turn his attention to items that belonged to children, photographing himself naked with teddy bears and articles of young girls' clothing covering his crotch.**

On November 16, the 47-year-old colonel broke into the home of 37-year-old Air Force Corporal Marie-France Comeau for the first time. This was to be a reconnaissance outing: Williams had met the corporal before and wanted to be certain that she lived alone. Comeau was out at the time, and Williams made entry via a window that led down into her basement. After searching the place and satisfying himself that his intended victim had no roommate or live-in partner, he went through her personal possessions, trying on some of her underwear and playing with her sex toys. Not content with this, he also took photographs of himself wearing the items before slipping out into the night.

Breaking into an innocent woman's home, riffling through her intimate clothing, trying it on, modeling it, and posing for pictures with sex aids are all significant red flags that pointed to Williams being a very dangerous man. Had he been caught entering or leaving the house, forced to answer some very difficult questions by the police, and embarrassed to the point where his career was put in jeopardy, then things might have been different. Perhaps that would have provided him with such a shock that he would have been scared away from taking his crimes to the next level.

Perhaps. We will never know for sure.

Instead, Russell Williams got away with his illicit scouting expedition, and that only served to embolden him. He returned to Comeau's home on the night of November 25, 2009. This time, the corporal was home. Williams used the same window to slither down into the basement, then found himself a hiding place in the shadowy recesses. His plan was to wait for her to fall asleep and then come out of hiding to attack her.

The plan was stymied by Corporal Comeau's cat, who had come down to the basement and quickly scoped out the presence of an intruder. When Comeau went down to find her pet, she found it sitting motionless, its gaze fixed on the intruder's hiding place. Williams knew that his hand had just been forced. He lunged at Comeau, using a heavy flashlight to batter her repeatedly across the head. Taken completely by surprise, the corporal was unable to defend herself effectively, although she did put up what resistance she could.

Once his victim was on the floor, Williams tied her to a steel post and partially covered her face with duct tape. Comeau pleaded with her attacker for her life, telling him repeatedly that she did not want to die and did not deserve it. The colonel was indifferent to her heartfelt pleas. He continued to sexually assault and physically abuse the helpless woman until she finally died of asphyxiation after Williams taped her nose and mouth shut.

One aspect of Williams's MO that stands out is his compulsion to visually document everything. He took photographs of Comeau's body in different parts of the house, both before and after her death. He videotaped his brutal and hours-long sexual assault on her inside the master bedroom, and he even photographed the cleanup process he went through before fleeing the scene. In addition to the videos and photographs, which would later be used as evidence against him in court, Williams stole several pieces of his victim's underwear.

The best laid plans of mice and men are no match for the investigative skills of the common house cat.

The body of Marie-France Comeau was found the next day by her boyfriend when he came to visit. It had been placed in her bed.

Corporal Comeau was under the command of Colonel Russell Williams. Indeed, he even had the gall to write a letter of condolence to her bereaved, grieving parents after her body was discovered. It was a brazen attempt to maintain his smokescreen of innocence.

The killing of Marie-France Comeau only served to embolden Williams, who had taken the step from committing sexual assault to carrying out an actual murder. When it became apparent that he had gotten away with it, he began looking for his next victim.

He found that victim on January 27, 2010. Williams would later tell police that while he was driving through a Belleville neighborhood, he spied 27-year-old Jessica Lloyd running on a treadmill through the window of her home. Once again, he broke into his intended target's home while she was out and made sure that nobody else lived there.

> **The killing of Marie-France Comeau only served to embolden Williams, who had taken the step from committing sexual assault to carrying out an actual murder.**

Late the following night, Williams was lurking in her backyard, patiently waiting for her to turn out the light and go to sleep. Then he broke into the house, subdued Lloyd, and tied her up before subjecting her to a brutal and sustained sexual attack, making the terrified woman change into several different sets of underwear in the process. He also recorded the assault on video.

By all accounts, Lloyd was a warm, caring woman who was popular and community oriented. She was also smart enough to know that her only chance of surviving was to remain calm and endure everything her attacker put her through. Williams lied to her, claiming that he was going to release her once the ordeal was over.

Rather than kill the blindfolded and restrained Lloyd in her own home, Williams forced her into the passenger seat of his car and drove her to his residence. There, he made her take a shower. According to testimony Williams gave later, Lloyd suffered several seizures, perhaps brought on by having been struck in the head. She asked her captor to make sure her mother knew she loved her, in the event of her death.

Williams kept up the pretense that he was going to let Lloyd go, but in reality, he would use a rope to strangle her to death. Before that, he bludgeoned her with a flashlight until she was unresponsive. Three days later, after keeping Lloyd's body hidden at home, Williams took it out and abandoned it. It went undiscovered for several more days, and a search was put on for the missing woman.

Time was running out for the killer colonel, however. Suspecting that the assaults on Marie-France Comeau and Jessica Lloyd may have been carried out by the same perpetrator, police set up a checkpoint in the area of Lloyd's house. On February 4, 2010, an eagle-eyed officer stopped Williams and noticed that the tread pattern they were looking for looked a lot like that on the colonel's vehicle. The police had themselves a credible suspect and started watching Williams's movements. They soon found out that boot prints taken from Jessica Lloyd's home also belonged to him.

Three days later, Williams was arrested. Detectives oversaw a search of his home and turned up his cache of souvenirs. Once he saw the evidence the police already had and were continuing to acquire, the dam broke. Williams confessed to it all. He asked for a map and pointed out the spot where Jessica Lloyd's body could be found.

One has to wonder whether his capture provided relief for the man whose secret life was becoming increasingly violent and was on its way to fully taking him over.

When police officers obtained a warrant to search Williams's home, they found hundreds of sets of women's underwear. These included bras, panties, swimsuits, and lingerie. On computer hard drives, they also discovered thousands of pictures of the colonel wearing many of them and posing for the camera. Sometimes, he combined his Air Force uniform with the women's clothing and took pictures of

Among his other mistakes, Williams kept evidence of his crimes. Investigators discovered souvenirs from his many victims, a well-organized scrapbook, and hard drives filled with thousands of photos that together proved his guilt.

himself masturbating for these shots. Williams also kept pictures of his victims' drivers licenses and other documents, all of it stored at his residence. There were also newspaper clippings and police reports concerning his crimes. This collection was meticulously stored and cataloged in a neat and organized manner.

This compulsion to collect, to document, and to catalog, and doubtless to revisit these trophies, constituted a huge blind spot for a man who had built his career upon mitigating risk. Pilots, particularly military pilots, are trained in the art of risk assessment and management. They do not take unacceptable risks, things that represent an unacceptable hazard to their aircraft. The field of aviation has developed a pervasive culture of safety. Williams's stash of clothing and pictures from his crime scenes represented a huge risk to him if it was ever discovered—as, indeed, it ultimately was. Yet he was compelled to keep it anyway. This urge was strong enough to override the knowledge that hanging on to these things was very much not in his best interests.

If his own testimony is to be believed—and any statement made by a serial predator should be taken with a grain of salt—then Russell Williams began to act on his sexual urges sometime around 2007. There is a clearly linear progression from his desire to dress in women's clothing and take pictures of himself, to breaking into the homes of strangers (he preferred to target single women under the age of 30) and stealing their clothes, to assaulting, and ultimately killing them.

While there is no such thing as the perfect military officer, Colonel Russell Williams certainly came close—for all appearances, at least. His superiors at the Royal Canadian Air Force were absolutely blindsided at the arrest of one of their senior officers on such serious charges. Had his dark and seamy side not been discovered, it is highly likely that he would have achieved the rank of general, or even higher. The colonel was just one promotional step away from joining the upper echelons of the Canadian military command structure.

Williams was a golden boy, on his way to the very top. For years, he was able to maintain a convincing facade of being an officer and a gentleman, moving effortlessly in the professional and social circles that are required for senior officers.

When Williams was arrested, the high command rushed to find a qualified replacement to take over the top spot at CFB Trenton. There was also fallout in the media, and the Air Force found itself attracting lots of unwanted attention in the national and international press. The concept of a serial killer was nothing new, but never before had one of them been a high-ranking military officer.

Inevitably, one question was asked more often than any other: just how was it that Williams had gotten away with what he did? Weren't there warning signs that underneath the carefully cultivated facade of a doting husband and professional career lurked a violent, sadistic maniac? As with so many people of this type, Williams was a skilled performer, adept at fooling his friends, neighbors, colleagues, and perhaps even his wife. The answer seems to be no, there really weren't.

According to a February 9, 2010, article in the *Toronto Star*, Williams's neighbors described him as someone who loved animals, particularly his pet cat, and made a point of carefully checking the lawn for frogs before breaking out the lawnmower. It's hard to reconcile this image of a man who was so kind to animals with that of the cold-blooded torturer, rapist, and murderer that Williams ultimately turned out to be. Which one was the true Russell Williams?

"He was the last person I would have thought of," the article quotes Bill Page, one of Williams's neighbors. As human beings, we all have a blind spot when it comes to our judgment of other people. We tend to assume that if somebody seems polite, well-spoken, educated, and holds a position of authority or high status in society, that person is most likely to be trustworthy. Williams was able to parlay this innate bias to his personal advantage for a while, hiding in plain sight and even living just a few doors down from one of his victims.

Unlike most serial predators, when captured, Russell Williams made almost no attempt to defend himself. In fact, he admitted to his crimes, pleading guilty to 88 separate charges of murder, rape, and breaking and entering. He showed a little remorse for his crimes, offering written apologies to the next of kin of his murder victims, but how much of that was genuine is impossible to say. Showing his coldly and calculating side, Williams claimed that one of his main reasons for pleading guilty was to avoid racking up a large legal bill that his wife would have to pay.

Relieved of freedom, it would not be long before Russell Williams would be relieved of his military rank and awards.

The judge handed out two life sentences for the murders, with no parole permissible for the first 25 years, and further sentences for the sexual assaults and the break-ins. If Russell Williams ever gets out of prison, he will be in his 70s. The Royal Canadian Air Force moved swiftly to strip the disgraced former colonel's military rank, revoke his decorations and awards, and even have his uniform burned in an attempt to completely expunge him from their ranks. He is rightly seen as a stain on the reputation of the service, albeit one for which the Air Force bears no fault, in this writer's opinion.

Could the military have spotted Williams's pathologic tendencies during its officer selection process? That's doubtful. Although the RCAF had a fairly rigorous screening process for its officer candidates, Russell Williams was an accomplished actor when it came to covering up his desires and peccadilloes. Scrutiny of his personal history turns up few of the traditional red flags for a serial rapist and murderer. He was a motivated, educated, highly functioning young man, without any hint of scandal or wrongdoing.

Thankfully, the homicidal military officer was caught before he was able to claim more victims. The case of former colonel Russell Williams should serve as a cautionary tale for society at large and force us to ask: How many others like him are out there, hiding behind the respectability of a military uniform?

# KILLER PILOT
# ROBERT LEE YATES

**R**obert Lee Yates served with distinction in the U.S. Army, a helicopter pilot and flight instructor whose career included several overseas deployments. (Indeed, once the nature of his grisly crimes came to light, investigators began looking at missing person cases in Europe, North America, and Africa.) He stayed out of trouble and even attained a number of medals during his stint in the military, which spanned two decades—although much of that time was spent dormant, with the majority of Yates's known killings taking place during a two-year murder spree in the late 1990s. Considering the fact that Yates served at numerous military installations during his career, scattered throughout the continental United States and abroad, some law enforcement officials suspected that the actual death toll may have been significantly higher.

His known victims were all female, with one exception: 21-year-old Patrick Oliver, who was murdered along with 22-year-old Susan Savage in the summer of 1975. The two were enjoying a creek side picnic in Walla Walla, Washington, when corrections officer Robert Yates, who was 23 at the time, committed what is believed to be the first two of his many murders. Investigators suspect that Yates happened upon the pair by chance and took them by surprise, though his motives for committing the murders in the first place remain opaque even to this day.

Yates shot both victims multiple times, inflicting defensive gunshot wounds to their arms while they tried desperately to shield themselves, before killing each with a fatal shot to the head. He then moved the bodies across the creek and concealed them as best he could. When detectives finally arrived at the scene, they were baffled. There was no apparent motive for somebody to have killed Oliver and Savage in this way. They had no known enemies, nor were they carrying much in the way of money or valuables. Nor did sexual assault appear to be the reason. After chasing down a few promising leads, detectives finally grew frustrated when the trail went cold.

It would remain that way for the next 25 years.

His next murder took place in 1988, when Yates picked up a young woman named Stacy Hawn, aged 23. She, too, died of a gunshot wound to the head. He was on leave from the Army at the time of her murder.

In 1996, some 21 years after the Oliver-Savage murders, Yates began killing again. This time, his victims were no longer the result of random encounters. Instead, he prowled the red-light districts and poorest areas of Spokane, Washington, picking up female sex workers or runaways. He sometimes drove a van, which doubled as a mobile and convenient place for him to have intercourse. Yates also owned a white Corvette, a flashy car that left its mark on the memory of some witnesses, who recalled at least one of his victims getting into it and never being seen again.

His MO was to pick up a vulnerable female, usually one he believed to be engaged in prostitution, solicit sexual favors from her at an out-of-the-way location, and then shoot her multiple times until she was dead. To ensure the latter, Yates always preferred to finish the victim off with at least one head shot from a small-caliber pistol. He also wrapped and bound each woman's head with plastic bags, either to help asphyxiate them or to contain some of the blood. The bodies were often left in fields, ditches, and garbage dumps, usually in a seminaked condition.

Yates haunted Spokane's seedier areas, often choosing victims from among the city's sex workers.

As the Spokane murders continued through 1997 and into 1998, the police realized they had a serial killer on their hands. The method of killing, plus the fact that each victim's body was found in an isolated spot that was still close to a road, made this very clear. By the time he was done, Robert Yates had murdered ten women in Spokane, all in the same way, and all with connections to prostitution.

One of Yates's would-be victims managed to escape from his clutches. Christine Smith, 32, was a sex worker whom Yates talked into his car and paid for oral sex on August 1, 1998. As she was performing the act, Yates shot her in the back of the head. Although the wound bled heavily, as head injuries tend to do, Ms. Smith clawed her way out of Yates's vehicle and escaped. The fact that she had been shot in the head at point blank range and somehow managed to survive was truly remarkable. The only thing that had saved her life was the relatively small caliber of her assailant's pistol.

Two years later, after his arrest, Christine Smith saw an arrest photograph of Robert Yates in the newspaper and immediately recognized the man who had picked her up and then tried to kill her. Only then did she realize that she had narrowly escaped death at the hands of a serial killer.

When a serial killer is captured, sloppiness or an excess of confidence usually plays a role in their downfall. In the case of Yates, he not only had driven a distinctive car when picking up some of his victims—a white 1977 Corvette—but he also had been less than diligent about cleaning it thoroughly afterward. Yates had been seen driving through Spokane's red-light area on more than one occasion and had even been stopped by police for speeding. By the time he became a murder suspect, Yates had sold the Corvette to a friend, but there was still a paper trail connecting him with ownership of the car. This would prove to be crucial in his downfall.

On August 26, 1997, 16-year-old Jennifer Joseph's body was found in a field outside of Spokane. She had been arrested for prostitution prior to her murder, making her a good fit for Yates's target demographic. The cause of death was multiple gunshot wounds, which had come from a small-caliber handgun—the same handgun used in the murders of other women, who had also been found with plastic bags over their heads.

The police were looking for the owner of a white Corvette and began working their way methodically through the state's database of Corvette owners, investigating each one and crossing them off the list before moving on to the next.

Finally, it was Yates's turn to be questioned. He seemed like a promising suspect. For one thing, records showed that he had gotten a speeding ticket in the same area where some of the victims had been found. Detectives noted that during the in-person interview, Yates seemed restless, displaying a higher-than-normal level of anxiety.

Blood stains were picked up by forensic teams, who carefully analyzed the Corvette. Yates could offer no convincing explanation as to

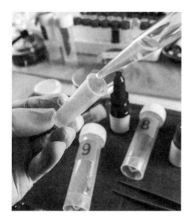

Police quickly discovered evidence connecting Yates to the crimes, including blood found in his white Corvette and semen found at the scenes.

why blood stains from Jennifer Joseph were found inside his car, along with a missing shirt button.

Police had taken semen samples from many of the murder victims, and DNA testing proved a positive match with that of Robert Yates. His fingerprint was lifted from the plastic bag that had been used to asphyxiate one of the dead women, and natural fibers further tied him to the case. There could be no doubt that this former military helicopter pilot was responsible for the murder of multiple women.

Yates's wife, Linda, hadn't the slightest inkling that her husband, the father of her five children, was a serial killer. The revelation made to her by detectives came as a huge shock, but what happened when officers searched the family home somehow managed to make things even worse.

Excavation of the back yard revealed that Yates had buried the body of one of his victims there, just a short distance from the house. Every day that she had gone outside or stood at the window gazing out, Linda Yates had been looking at the unmarked grave of Melody Ann Murfin, a 43-year-old mother of two. Her remains were so decomposed that the coroner would have to rely upon Murfin's jewelry to identify her. Linda was sickened when she learned of this. She had even unknowingly planted flowers at the site to brighten up the view of her yard.

In a 2000 interview with reporter Nicholas Geranios of the Associated Press, Linda Yates said that she confronted her husband and demanded to know how he could have brutalized his victims in such a way and then gone back to living a seemingly ordinary married life. He chose not to answer her.

However, she admitted that with the benefit of hindsight, there were some definite red flags that she had missed. Claiming that he was going on a hunting trip, Robert Yates dressed smartly and applied cologne—hardly the sort of thing one does when going out to stalk wildlife in the woods. He would also burn credit card statements before she could see them, but Linda managed to catch a glimpse of charges for a motel that was frequented by sex workers and their johns.

Robert Yates eventually developed impotence, or so he claimed. There were also indications that he was a Peeping Tom, drilling a hole in the wall so he could spy on his neighbors having sex. On discovering this, Linda quite understandably left her husband, but the separation was brief. The couple reconciled after 18 months, on the rationale that it was for the good of the children to have a father in their life.

It is easy to see why Linda Yates believed her husband to be having extramarital affairs, but no spouse can be expected to realize that her husband is a rapist and serial killer based on that information alone. Robert Yates did at least provide for his family financially, and his children loved him, despite his frequent mood swings, even if his wife no longer did. It is noteworthy that one of Yates's daughters reported him to the police for striking her, but things went no further because he was arrested on murder charges before an investigation could be completed.

The Yates's eldest daughter, Sasha, expressed horror and disbelief at her father's actions when she confronted him in the courtroom during his murder trial, demanding to know how he could have done such heinous things while simultaneously raising them to have decency and traditional family values.

**He would ... burn credit card statements before she could see them, but Linda managed to catch a glimpse of charges for a motel that was frequented by sex workers and their johns.**

When asked about his son's upbringing, Robert Lee Yates Sr. described him as a young man who did well at sports and in the classroom, having none of the red flags that serial killers and other violent criminals often display. Few parents ever suspect that their child would turn out to be a serial killer, and to his credit, Yates Sr. sat through his son's trial. One can only imagine his shock as the prosecution recounted the appalling crimes his son had committed.

Examining what little is known about his childhood and upbringing, there are few clues as to why Robert Lee Yates became a monster in later life. He was brought up as a Seventh Day Adventist, attending church on a regular basis. Those who went to school with him remembered nothing particularly remarkable about Yates. He was neither memorably good or bad, although those who went to school with him and talked to the media came down more on the side of him being a "decent guy."

During the trial, Yates professed remorse and claimed that he had turned to God. The victims' next of kin who were present in the courtroom that day certainly weren't buying it. Whether this represented genuine contrition on the killer's part or was simply a cynical ploy to try and garner sympathy from the judge, jury, and public will never be known, but it did not move the judge to leniency.

At the conclusion of his murder trial in 2000, Robert Yates was sentenced to 408 years in prison. As part of a plea deal, Yates had confessed to many of his murders in an attempt to stave off the death penalty. Unsurprisingly, however, he had been less than honest about the extent of his crimes, and when more victims were discovered, the prosecution team pushed for the death penalty.

In December 1997, 24-year-old Melinda Mercer died after being shot in the head three times. Yates dumped her body on a refuse site in Tacoma. The following October, he murdered 35-year-old Connie La-Fontaine Ellis, leaving her body in a ditch, again in Tacoma. Her corpse was found with his signature plastic bags taped over the head, covering a single gunshot wound. The coroner estimated that she had been dead for at least a month.

Robert Lee Yates (right), with his defense attorney, looks at the jury as his sentence is read.

Both women had been heroin users who had turned to sex work to fund their addiction. In each case, the bullets had come from a .25 caliber pistol. Although there are 16 known victims of Robert Lee Yates, it's likely that there are several others. Serial killers are creatures of habit, for the most part, and it's entirely possible that Yates murdered women while he was stationed at various military postings throughout his career.

In 2002, Robert Yates was sentenced to death. This means that he would die strapped to the execution table and given a lethal cocktail of medications into a vein. Instead, fate intervened in the form of an appeal process, made on the basis of multiple appeals and hearings.

In most states, a death sentence takes a long time to carry out—as well it should. This complicated the case of Robert Yates because in 2018, Washington removed the death penalty as an option from its legal system, stating that there was no evidence to prove it was an effective deterrent. Unless there is a significant change in the law, Robert Yates may have escaped death by lethal injection and will now spend the rest of his life in prison.

# ANGEL OF DEATH
# VICKIE DAWN JACKSON

There are few members of society more trusted than a nurse. We quite rightly see them as the angels of healthcare, working long hours to care for the sick and injured. Sometimes, a skilled nurse is all that stands between a patient and death.

Smetimes, though, on thankfully rare occasions, it is a nurse who deliberately pushes the patient through death's door themselves. Such was the case with Vickie Dawn Jackson.

Little information is on record about her childhood and upbringing. What little we do know comes mainly from two sources: her ex-husband and her daughter, both of whom spoke to the media when Jackson's crimes were brought to light.

After gaining her credential as a licensed vocational nurse at night school, Jackson found employment at several local healthcare facilities before finally getting hired in the small town of Nocona, Texas, just south of the Oklahoma border, where she had lived since she was a child. The town was served by a single hospital, Nocona General. One facility, with 38 in-patient beds, was perfectly adequate to meet the needs of a population of a little over three thousand people.

Vickie Dawn Jackson accepted a job there in 2000. Her husband was a nurse aide at the same hospital. Hospital administration saw no obvious red flags. Good nurses could be hard to come by, especially in rural areas like Nocona.

Unfortunately, Vickie Dawn Jackson was the farthest thing imaginable from a good nurse.

Every drug is potentially a double-edged sword. On the one hand, when dosed properly and used ethically, they can help heal or alleviate pain. On the other hand, if given to excess, they can kill. Mivacurium chloride is no exception. It works at the junctions between the nerves and the muscles, blocking the electrical signals that the human nervous system uses to send commands. This makes it a potent skeletal muscle relaxant.

Mivacurium chloride is often used by physicians who are about to intubate a patient, passing a plastic breathing tube into the windpipe. It temporarily paralyzes the patient's muscles, including those muscles that are used to breathe. This commonly happens during surgery prep, just as the anesthesiologist is sedating the patient and rendering them unconscious. The medication is very safe when used by a skilled and diligent clinician, one who has a well-thought-out treatment plan in place, and who is carefully monitoring the patient's condition.

In the wrong hands, however, mivacurium chloride can be a very effective murder weapon. Given inappropriately, the drug will stop the

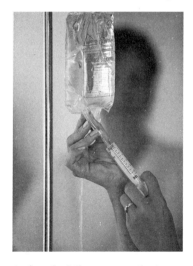

Jackson's victims were patients who were otherwise in generally good health. Each received a fatal dose of mivacurium chloride, which the nurse would sneakily inject into the patient's IV bag.

patient from breathing, sending them into respiratory arrest, followed very soon after by cardiac arrest and death. Vickie Dawn Jackson injected a large bolus of the drug into the IV bag of her patients. Shortly afterward, they died. Jackson's colleagues were usually unable to resuscitate them.

Jackson had a reputation around town as a nice, friendly lady—a real sweetheart. Few outsiders had anything bad to say about her. The same could not be said of her own family, however. Her former husband and her daughter both said that she was volatile, prone to blowing up at the slightest provocation. She also was not averse to physical violence, her husband revealed, though it was directed primarily at their children rather than at him.

Jackson's daughter, Jennifer Carson, told the Associated Press that her mother was "a baby face on the outside but was hell on the inside." She also stated that she had thought her mother was capable of harboring murderous intent but questioned whether she would go through with the deed. Time and circumstance proved her right on the first count but wrong on the second.

By 2001, the number of deaths occurring at Nocona General Hospital was beginning to raise eyebrows. That number was double what it ought to have been. It wasn't just that there were a lot of deaths, however; several of them were completely unexpected. Patients who should not have died, based on the severity of their illness, were nonetheless going into cardiac arrest. All of them were seniors, ranging in age from the 60s to the 90s. One was 100 years old.

In February 2001, hospital authorities were concerned enough to involve the police department, who in turn brought in the Texas Rangers and the FBI. Medical records were scrutinized for each death that had taken place at the hospital between late 2000 and early 2001. Investigators looked at the names of the staff who were present when a patient went into cardiac arrest and died. In each case, one name repeatedly came up: Vickie Dawn Jackson.

The patients had died overnight. Nurse Jackson worked the night shift.

An audit of the hospital's drug inventory examined each medication that had been given over the preceding few months, accounting for every injection and pill received by patients. The final stock count was tallied. A large quantity of mivacurium chloride turned up missing. This wasn't the sort of medication that somebody might steal to abuse or sell, such as morphine, fentanyl, or Valium. Nobody goes home and takes a paralytic drug to make themselves feel good.

There had to be another explanation.

Now that foul play was suspected, law enforcement personnel took the distasteful but necessary step of exhuming some of the recently deceased patients. FBI analysts scrutinized the blood of several patients to

Prosecutors had enough evidence to put Jackson away, including posthumous tests confirming the presence of mivacurium chloride in past patients who had died mysteriously.

whom Jackson had had access. The tox screen came back positive for mivacurium chloride. The only problem was that none of those patients had been prescribed the drug by a physician. There was no clinical reason for it to have been present in their bloodstream. The only logical explanation was that somebody had administered it with the intent to cause harm. That somebody was, of course, Vickie Dawn Jackson.

Investigators, who had previously searched her home, sat down with her and asked her questions. Over the course of several interviews, her story changed. First, she admitted to having used mivacurium chloride, but only once. Then, she reversed course and claimed that she had never given it. Who had thrown a used container of the drug into her trash can at home then? Not her, Jackson insisted. Her husband had done it. He was to blame for all the murders because he had carried them out himself. That theory was quickly discarded in light of all the evidence against Jackson herself. It was clear that nobody else had been in a position to kill every single one of those patients.

As detectives and FBI agents slowly built a case against her, Jackson was bonded out of jail and enjoyed a measure of freedom. She was not considered a flight risk, and she proved this evaluation correct by staying in Nocona. Unable to work as a nurse for obvious reasons, she picked up a job working in a food store instead.

In the summer of 2002, she was arrested and sent to jail. There were complications along the way, resulting in her first trial being declared a mistrial. It took more than four years, but by the fall of 2006, preparations were almost complete to bring the case back to trial a second time. Jackson was facing multiple counts of murder, and the court case was expected to be long and hard-fought. On October 3, however, the defendant surprised everyone by entering a plea of "no contest" to the ten murder charges.

This unexpected plea obviated the need for a trial. Somewhat unusually for the state of Texas, despite the fact that Jackson had taken the lives of ten people, prosecutors did not push for capital punishment. Instead, the judge sentenced her to life imprisonment.

It is somewhat unusual for a serial killer not to want to defend themselves in court. No matter how overwhelming the evidence stacked up against them may be, there is often the almost pathological need for them to grandstand in front of the courtroom. Many recognize that this could be their last major opportunity to hog the spotlight before being removed from the public eye and thrown into prison. Vickie Dawn Jackson was a rare exception. She sought neither fame nor infamy and had no desire to take part in any sort of media spectacle. Instead, her plea of no contest allowed her to achieve two objectives, both of which were extremely important to her.

First, no guilty plea would go on her record. Although a judge could (and almost certainly would) find her guilty, she would not be admitting to any of the murders she had committed. It was a way of refusing to accept responsibility for her crimes, avoiding the issue entirely rather than acknowledging it and facing it head on. Throughout the multitude of police interviews, she steadfastly insisted that she had not killed anybody.

Second, on a more practical level, it would spare Jackson's daughter from being forced to take the witness stand and testify against her mother. It is not difficult to appreciate why a parent would want to spare their child an experience like that. Interviewed in 2006 by the Associated Press, Jackson added that she also wanted to spare the families of the deceased patients from having to hear the specific details surrounding their deaths while listening to evidence in the courtroom.

Shown on her way into a pretrial hearing, Vickie Dawn Jackson would plead no contest to the ten murder charges she faced.

What was Vickie Dawn Jackson's motive for ending the lives of ten human beings? Certainly not a desire for fame. Did she simply revel in having the power of life and death over others? This is not an uncommon motive among serial murderers in the medical profession, such as the United Kingdom's infamous "Dr. Death," Harold Shipman. Sometimes, the individual finds themselves in a position to kill and takes that opportunity to satisfy some base inner urge.

In Jackson's case, however, one of the FBI agents who had been assigned to the investigation offered a simpler, more prosaic theory: the patients made her mad by being (in her estimation) overly needy. Most of the patients who died were relatively stable. No life-or-death illnesses were present to explain their deaths. Yet Jackson viewed them as irritants, and as she grew increasingly angry with them, she took drastic steps to prevent that irritation from ever bothering her again.

Unfortunately for her, she was as bad a liar as she was a nurse. It never seemed to cross her mind that the drastic increase in patient deaths would raise a red flag, especially when they were all taking place across the same shift. The missing mivacurium vials were the proverbial smoking gun. There was no way for her to fudge the hospital inventory list. Once questions began to be asked, it was the beginning of the end for her.

Although it is cold comfort to the families of her dead victims, Vickie Dawn Jackson's death toll could have been far worse than the ten people she killed. Her colleagues confirmed that she had been present at a number of other near-fatalities, situations in which patients had stopped breathing but had been saved by the efforts of the resuscitation team. These patients tended to be younger and healthier than those who had died, but their fate could have been just as bad.

At the time of writing, Jackson is still in prison, serving out her life sentence. Assuming that there are no further complications between now and then, she will be eligible for release and parole during the 2040s.

# PARAMEDIC, PHYSICIAN, AND POISONER MICHAEL SWANGO

I t is a sad yet inescapable truth of the medical profession that patients die. Every doctor who practices medicine for any length of time understands and accepts it. Throughout the span of a physician's career, he or she might see hundreds of patients die—sometimes, that number may run into the thousands.

With that said, there are limits. In certain cases, however, there comes along a medical provider who experiences a little *too much* death and dying. The reason for this is both simple and horrifying: they are directly responsible for killing their patients. Rarely, this can be put down to incompetence. This doesn't happen often, because most medical schools have a rigorous and challenging curriculum. The training and education that goes into the making of a physician means that only the dedicated and qualified are granted the privilege of practicing medicine—usually.

All doctors make mistakes. In the United States, medical errors are the third leading causes of in-hospital fatalities, accounting for more than 170,000 deaths each year. Each instance is tragic, and every hospital has its own systems designed to minimize and mitigate such problems when they occur—or preferably, prevent them from happening in the first place. There is, however, one thing that no safety system can reliably prevent: a murderer.

On the face of it, Michael Swango had an ordinary, unremarkable upbringing. Born in Tacoma, Washington, in October 1954, he was raised in Illinois. a hard-working kid who did well at school. A strong student with solid grades and several extracurricular activities under his belt, he followed his father's example by joining the military. Unlike his

The death of a patient from medical error can weigh heavily on hospital staff. A series of mysterious deaths can destroy morale entirely.

father, who had served in the Army, Swango chose the Marine Corps.

The Marines have a richly deserved reputation for instilling discipline in their new recruits. Swango was already a motivated young man when he enlisted, and his time as a marine served him in good stead when he left the Corps after completing his term of service in 1980 and then enrolled in college. His new goal in life was to become a physician. He continued to be a strong and dedicated student, and his grades were more than good enough to gain him admission into medical school at Southern Illinois University.

It was here that Swango's troubles began. He soon developed a reputation for flakiness. Whether his sense of self-discipline had deserted him or the demands of medical school were simply too much, Swango slowly but surely fell behind his classmates. He took a side job working as a paramedic on a 911 ambulance, which provided him with both extra income and valuable clinical experience but also robbed him of study time and added more stress to an already tense period of his life.

Struggling to keep up, Swango began cutting corners. His classmates and his instructors noticed, and for a time there was a genuine possibility that he would not make it to graduation. More troubling than his nose-diving academic performance were suspicions that he was cheating—Swango was caught falsifying an assessment report on a pregnant patient. His fellow students reacted to this news with disgust. This was a significant integrity failure, and it almost got him expelled from medical school.

After an investigation by the school was concluded, he was allowed to stay on, complete some remediation training, and finally graduate with the status of M.D. in April 1983. He was lucky not to have been thrown out.

More stress was to come when he moved to Ohio to begin his residency. This is a challenging period in any new doctor's career, when the hours are long, the pressure is intense, and the stakes are high. Michael Swango had managed to finagle himself a spot at a major hospital at Ohio State University. In the summer of 1983, they unwittingly took on the neurosurgery resident from hell.

Swango spent a year there before being thrown out in June 1984. In between, he committed at least one murder. Cynthia (Cindy) Ann McGee was 19 years old and had a passion for gymnastics. Cindy had been hit by a car and sustained injuries that were serious enough to hospitalize her. Swango was one of the doctors assigned to her care.

On January 14, 1984, he walked into Cindy's room at the hospital. He carried a syringe filled with potassium. We all have quantities of this naturally occurring metal in our bodies; without it, the body would be unable to function. In significant quantities, potassium is an extremely painful drug when injected into the bloodstream. It causes an intense burning sensation as it works its way through the body.

Like every other substance, too much of it can be toxic—sometimes, fatally so. There is a good reason why potassium constitutes part of the lethal injection cocktail that is administered to condemned prisoners during the process of legal execution. Concentrated boluses of potassium chloride will stop the heart from beating, causing a sudden, catastrophic drop in blood pressure, which kills the person receiving it.

Nineteen-year-olds, even those who have been involved in car accidents, generally do not go into cardiac arrest and die. Years after her death, Swango would finally confess to having murdered Cindy McGee and would be convicted for the crime. However, there had been multiple complaints about his behavior from the nursing staff at the hospital. Patients seemed to have the habit of dying when he was around, in numbers that were great enough to arouse suspicion.

Nurses are trained to notice things. They are skilled observers. It wasn't long after Swango first arrived at Ohio State University that they noticed him going into patient rooms shortly before the patient became seriously ill. Some of those patients died. The more fortunate ones almost did but recovered at the last minute.

Nobody could prove anything, but it was clear that the recently arrived Dr. Michael Swango was the common denominator. This, in conjunction with his spotty track record from medical school, should have been a red flag. An investigation was

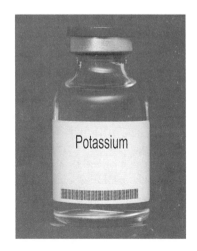

Potassium, an essential mineral in small amounts, will, in large quantities, kill a person—painfully.

conducted during Swango's time at OSU, and at its conclusion, the concerns of the clinical staff were set aside, though he was let go from his residency, which constituted a black mark on his record. Being dumped from his residency after the first year would have served as a warning to other clinical sites that Dr. Swango could bring serious problems to their door if they allowed him to practice there. Swango himself knew this and hit upon an obvious solution: he lied about his past, and he moved on.

After being quietly shuffled out of the OSU residency program in the summer of 1984, Swango saw few options available to him. He needed some source of income to put food on the table, so he went to Quincy, Illinois, and gained employment as a paramedic. Although he had a reputation from medical school as a poor doctor, several of his fellow paramedics and EMTs remembered him being a solid field medic. He also struck people as being a nice guy, someone fun to be around—at first.

> **These stories all had a similar theme: they involved the death or serious injury of other human beings, usually people who had required the life-saving services of the medical profession.**

He could also be quirky, to say the least. Swango had a habit of cutting out and keeping clippings from the local newspapers. These stories all had a similar theme: they involved the death or serious injury of other human beings, usually people who had required the life-saving services of the medical profession. Speaking as a paramedic myself, while this "hobby" of Swango's seems a little macabre, many emergency medical services providers are interested in studying significant illness and trauma. Usually, this is because each medical emergency holds its own lesson, and each has the potential to teach us something that will make us better at our chosen profession.

Was this the case with Swango? It seems unlikely. His fascination with death went back to medical school, when his interest in cadavers was noticed by his peers and deemed to be rather weird, even in those circles. He gravitated toward accounts of grotesque death and graphic wounding—the stranger, the better. The truth is that Michael Swango wasn't remotely interested in saving lives—instead, his attention was focused on learning how to end them, quietly and on his own terms.

In 2014, Quincy's KHQA TV news reporter Ross Green interviewed some of Swango's former colleagues. Fellow paramedic Brent Unmisig recalled hearing another EMS crew recounting their experience of arriving on the scene of a car wreck, only to find Swango perched on top of the car, taking photographs of the victims inside. Significantly, he was wearing civilian clothes at the time of the incident, rather than an EMS uniform. He was off-duty and must have been listening to a radio scanner when he heard about the wreck taking place. Rushing to the scene of an accident, not to render care but to photograph those who are hurt or possibly even killed in it, is in extremely poor taste, to say the least. Any paramedic doing so today would be fired for this offense. Yes, the 1980s were a different time—but they weren't *that* different.

Perhaps this was just hearsay, medics gossiping among one another. Yet the following day, Unmisig had his own personal encounter with Swango's dark side, and this one was much more harmful than inappropriate photographs. He and Swango were working together, and Unmisig accepted Swango's offer to buy him a soda. That turned out to be a huge mistake, as he soon became extremely ill, and he remained that way for 72 hours. Soda is not generally considered to be a viable source of food poisoning—unless, that is, something is deliberately mixed with it that will cause illness. In light of later events, it became apparent that the cup of soda Paramedic Unmisig was given had almost certainly been poisoned by the man who bought it for him: Michael Swango.

One day Swango had brought in poisoned donuts and deliberately left them in a place to which everybody had access. When a number of EMTs and paramedics became seriously ill, he was instantly the number one suspect. Stories about him had been floating around the EMS agency for a while. As soon as his fellow paramedics had reason to suspect that he had poisoned them with ant killer, they immediately called the police. Swango was duly arrested and charged with multiple counts of aggravated battery. Yet none of his colleagues had actually caught him red-handed in the act; they had found bottles of the poison in his kit bag and put two and two together. This was proof enough for them, but in a court of law, it became a "he said/she said" situation, and the angry paramedics were on potentially shaky legal ground.

In court, however, Michael Swango was not a compelling witness. Paramedics

Swango laced a box of doughnuts with pesticide, then left the poisoned treats where his coworkers could help themselves. The same poison was later found in his bag.

are typically very loyal to one another, but that loyalty falls by the wayside when innocent people have been deliberately harmed. Swango was found guilty on all but one count and sentenced to five years' imprisonment. Surely, an offense serious enough to merit a prison term would prevent him from ever practicing medicine again—wouldn't it?

No, it would not.

Behind bars, Swango was the model of good behavior. He focused on his personal physical fitness, working out every chance he got, and made sure to avoid trouble. That got him out of prison after serving just half the time he was sentenced to. The summer of 1987 saw him once again plotting on a way to gain access to patients. His reputation as a paramedic was pretty much shot; no ambulance service would ever have taken a risk in hiring him.

The next few years were spent working in a series of lower-level medical jobs, such as laboratory technician. To be clear, this is important work—doctors and physician assistants rely on accurate lab values to make sound clinical decisions. But working in a laboratory did not afford Swango the prestige that he felt was due to him, in light of his licensure as an M.D.

How could he possibly complete his training as a physician? Swango gave the matter some thought. He knew that his felonious background would prevent him from ever getting a residency again—no hospital administrator of sound mind would hire a convicted poisoner—but perhaps, he mused, there was some other way. If his criminal background could not be expunged, maybe there was something that Swango could do to soften the blow.

His solution was to forge a document purporting to have come from the State of Illinois Department of Corrections. Dated August 23, 1988, the fake document was typed up on what looked a lot like DOC letterhead and in part read:

*DATE OF ENTRY (DOE) INTO SYSTEM: AUGUST 23, 1985.*

OFFENSE: Battery (felony); to wit, violation of Chapter 38, Ill. Rev. Stat., Sect. 12-4—intentional application of physical force to an individual with resultant bodily injury caused by said force.

SUMMARY: Releasee was involved in altercation which escalated to physical confrontation involving multiple parties. Releasee struck a blow with his fist with resultant bodily injury. Injured individual subsequently fully recovered.

SENTENCE: Six (6) months followed by eighteen (18) months probation.

The entire single-sheet document was nothing more than a tissue of lies. Swango was trying to claim that he had been sentenced to six months in prison, rather than five years, for the crime of basically being part of a fist fight—the kind of thing that might happen in a bar or any other public place. It was much easier to play down the lie of having gotten caught up in a fracas than it was to defend having poisoned his coworkers. His argument basically boiled down to "boys will be boys," and Swango, an accomplished and capable liar, was perfectly willing to look the head of any medical residency program straight in the eye and sell it to them.

He would still have to rely on any potential administrator not digging too deeply into the matter; the whole thing could be exploded with a single phone call, if somebody was willing to put the work in to gather all the facts. Showing an almost unbelievable level of arrogance and effrontery, Swango also forged a letter testifying to his good character, purporting to be written by none other than the governor of the state of Virginia, Gerald L. Baliles.

"Reputable citizens who are familiar with your conduct since your conviction(s) advise me that you are leading an upright, law-abiding life," the fraudulent letter gushed, "and they recommend that your civil rights be restored. Relying on these recommendations, I am removing your political disabilities."

This refers to the fact that felons are not able to run for office, serve on a jury, or most crucially in Swango's case, hold a medical license. He typed up the letter on fake Commonwealth of Virginia Governor's Office letterhead paper and forged the governor's signature with a flourish. Along with the fraudulent letter from the Illinois Department of Corrections, he had drawn up two "get out of jail free" cards that would help him finagle his way back into the medical world once more.

The only question was: would they work?

Running from his criminal history but determined to continue killing, Swango began forging documents and concocting cover stories. These helped him land work at hospitals where his true reputation wasn't yet known.

Regrettably, they did. In 1991 and 1992, Swango began shopping himself around to various residency programs throughout the country, finally landing himself a spot in South Dakota. The truth about his past ultimately came to light, and Swango soon found himself back at square one. His big mistake had been trying to join the prestigious American Medical Association, a highly respected membership group for doctors. It looked into Swango's application with a greater degree of scrutiny than the institution in South Dakota had and toppled his house of cards with a background check.

Relocating once more, this time to New York, he managed to talk his way into yet another residency, this one at a Veteran's Affairs (V.A.) hospital facility. The year was now 1993, and shortly after the new doctor started making rounds, his patients began to die.

One of the people he saw during his tenure was a male patient who had multiple chronic illnesses and ailments. According to Swango's notes, on the afternoon of July 26, he was called to attend the patient again, and arrived to find him dead. He made no attempt to perform a resuscitation but instead simply issued a time of death. It was only seven years later, when the patient's body was exhumed as part of an extensive criminal investigation into Swango's activities, that pathologists discovered that abnormally high levels of epinephrine were present in the cells of his major organs.

We all have epinephrine in our bodies—it is adrenaline, something our adrenal glands produce regularly. In normal amounts, it is a useful part of the human biological process. Yet medical professionals also carry doses of epinephrine in ampoules and vials. It is used primarily to treat severe allergic reactions, dangerously low blood pressure, and cardiac arrest. Epinephrine is a useful and therapeutic drug when given under the correct circumstances, but it is also a double-edged sword. Give a significant dose of the drug to a patient intravenously, and it can cause serious cardiac dysrhythmias and death.

Following the exhumation of Swango's V.A. patient, the coroner's report concluded: "The presence of detectable metanephrine, combined with the absence of undetectable normetanephrine, in these samples from an unembalmed, exhumed decedent, strongly suggest a perimortem exogenous administration of epinephrine."

In other words, Michael Swango had used an injection of epinephrine as a murder weapon.

Trying to keep one step ahead of his shady past, Swango filled out the paperwork to change his name, but he was never able to hide for very long. It didn't help matters that his face still popped up on TV true crime shows, where a coworker would invariably recognize him and report Swango's true identity to management.

Michael Swango began to develop a reputation around the hospital as an odd bird. There were raised eyebrows at his choice of attire—rather than wear scrubs to work, he chose instead a set of military fatigues. This may have been an attempt to gain some credibility with veterans, although his service record as a former marine should have sufficed to do that. Whatever the reason, it was not an appropriate manner of dress for a doctor working in the civilian clinical environment.

**It didn't help matters that his face still popped up on TV true crime shows, where a coworker would invariably recognize him and report Swango's true identity to management.**

He killed again on the night of September 23, 1993. Still at the V.A. hospital, Swango (now using the alias of Dr. Kirk) was called to treat a male patient who was struggling with respiratory issues. The nurse who was taking care of him judged that, although he needed some help with his breathing issues, he was not at imminent risk of dying. The problem was serious, but it should not have been life-threatening.

Two other doctors accompanied Swango to the patient's bedside. They worked to place a central line catheter into the patient's chest, a more effective means of getting drugs and fluid into the bloodstream than through a peripheral I.V. This can make all the difference if the patient's condition should suddenly deteriorate. Once the central line was in place, the two other physicians left, leaving Swango the only doctor taking care of the patient. He was also the last physician to see the patient alive, accompanied by a nurse from the hospital's float pool.

The nurse watched Swango administer a vial of sodium bicarbonate via the central line. Sodium bicarb is a base medication that is used to reverse or offset the effects of acidosis inside the body—in other words, it helps restore the pH balance to somewhere within the normal range. Every seasoned medical provider knows that bicarb does not play well with other drugs inside an IV line; if it's followed up with a medication that has a more acidic pH, the two tend to consolidate within the IV, clogging it up and forming a kind of sludge. To offset that effect, it is common practice for a provider to flush the line with a saline injection immediately after administering sodium bicarb. Saline is basically just low-concentration salt water and helps get rid of any lingering traces of bicarbonate that might cause problems in the tubing.

This is why the nurse was not at all surprised to see "Dr. Kirk" withdraw a syringe from the pocket of his lab coat and chase the sodium bicarb injection up with a bolus of fluid. She assumed, quite understandably, that this was simply a benign saline flush to clear the IV line in preparation for giving future drugs.

She was wrong.

A short while later, the patient went into cardiac arrest. No attempts were made to resuscitate him, which was appropriate; he had a legally valid Do Not Resuscitate order, drawn up in consultation with his own physician—at least, that's what *should* have happened. In reality, many of the DNR orders that were filed with Swango's patients were forgeries, authored by Swango himself.

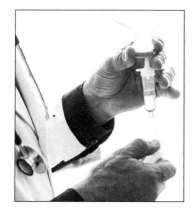

While performing a normally routine procedure, Swango passed a fatal substance off as saline, injecting it into a patient's IV line right under a nurse's nose.

Another unusual aspect of this particular patient's death was that Swango stayed in the dying man's room from the moment he administered the medications until the time of his death.

This struck the attending nurse as being highly unusual. Doctors tend to be busy people, and this is even more true in V.A. hospitals, where the patient-to-physician ratio is often quite high. The care providers who staff such facilities work hard, and it's rare to find them standing still in one place for very long. Dr. Kirk/Swango remaining at the patient's bedside until he suddenly and unexpectedly died was so out of the ordinary that the nurse recounted it to FBI agents during the subsequent investigation. It wasn't a great stretch of the imagination to conclude that something was very fishy about the respiratory patient's death.

Other things did not quite add up either. The sharp-eyed nurse noticed that Swango had falsified the time of death on the patient care report, which is a critically important legal document. There was no obvious reason for him to do so, other than to try and distance the patient's death from the unidentified medication that Swango had injected into his central line.

Despite the peculiarities surrounding this unusual in-patient death, coupled with his status as the resident oddball, Swango was still not on the hospital administration's radar on October 3, when he poisoned his next victim with neuromuscular blocking agents. Much as the name implies, these medications block the control signals being transmitted between the nerves and the muscles which they service. This blockade results in paralysis. Medications such as these are used to paralyze patients who have been sedated, so that a skilled

**The sensation of slowly suffocating while being utterly powerless to do anything about it would be nothing less than terrifying.**

medical provider can insert a breathing tube into their trachea. In the hands of somebody like Michael Swango, however, they are more than capable of killing.

In this instance, his murder weapon of choice was succinylcholine, a potent and fast-acting drug that begins to work in less than a minute after it has been injected into the patient's I.V. line. A normal dose of "sux," as medical providers sometimes call it, will totally relax the patient's body for anywhere from four to six minutes. Larger doses will keep them paralyzed for longer periods of time.

There is a reason that such patients are given sedatives before receiving a succinylcholine injection. Imagine what it must feel like to be unable to breathe, unable to move a muscle in your entire body, and yet also be conscious and aware of everything that is happening to you. The sensation of slowly suffocating while being utterly powerless to do anything about it would be nothing less than terrifying. It is for this reason that patients who are injected with succinylcholine will often be given a medication such as midazolam first; this not only sedates them, significantly reducing their anxiety, but also induces a sense of amnesia, so that they will not be troubled by emotional trauma after the procedure has been performed.

It is safe to assume that Dr. Michael Swango did not bother to sedate his patients before killing them. He is known to have stood over them at their bedside, watching them die. Swango almost certainly enjoyed the sense of power this gave him and would probably not want to have lessened that sensation by making his victim more comfortable first.

The fact that Swango had murdered this patient would only become clear in 2000, during an FBI investigation into the doctor's criminal activities. A toxicological analysis of the dead man's tissue samples showed the presence of succinylcholine, a drug for which the patient had no legitimate medical need and was not listed anywhere on his treatment charts.

Three months after he began his residency at the V.A. facility, and having murdered multiple patients, word of Swango's past misdeeds reached the attention of the hospital administration. Once more outed as a fraud, he was summarily dismissed, and word was put out to every teaching hospital in the United States, warning them to be on the lookout for him.

Michael Swango's medical career was now completely stalled—in the United States, at least. No academic institution would take him on. The alternative seemed obvious: he would travel overseas. After some deliberation, he decided upon Africa as his next destination. He reasoned that an African country would be only too happy to welcome an American doctor into one of its hospitals and would hopefully not look into his background too closely.

He was right. The winter of 1994 found Swango making rounds at Mnene Hospital in rural Zimbabwe. It was yet another clean slate for the man who had burned through several of them already. The question was—how long before Swango's past caught up with him?

At first appearances, this new doctor was a great addition to the medical team at Mnene. The hospital was faith-based, and he cunningly played the devout Christian, attending church services on a regular basis. Behind the scenes, however, it was the same old story. Dr. Swango left a trail of dead patients in his wake.

It wasn't long before the nurses made the same observation that their counterparts back in the United States had. The new doctor wasn't incompetent: he was a cold-blooded killer. Each time, the pattern was the same. A patient who was unwell or injured, but far from critical, suddenly took an unexpected turn for the worse and died. Dr. Swango was either in their presence or had been shortly before their death.

One patient spoke of being woken up one night by a sharp pain in his buttock. He opened his eyes and turned to find Swango, syringe in hand, standing at the foot of his bed. After the doctor left his room, the patient became seriously ill, finding it difficult to breathe. Had nurses not been alerted to his gasps and rushed to his bedside, it is likely that another unexplained death would have been laid at Swango's feet. As it was, the patient went on to suffer serious, debilitating side effects.

Confronted with the patient's testimony, Swango flatly denied it. He had not injected the man with anything, the doctor insisted. The patient stuck to his guns. He had no reason to lie, and it wasn't difficult for him to identify the American doctor, whose features were so distinctive in an African hospital. A search of his room revealed the cap from an intramuscular-gauge needle lying on the floor beneath the patient's bed.

A different nurse, who worked alongside Swango in the operating theater, would later tell an FBI agent about the time they were preparing a pregnant patient for a cesarean section delivery. The patient suddenly developed great pain and broke out in a sweat. The nurse discovered that this had happened directly after Dr. Swango had injected her with an unidentified substance—something he insisted was just "water."

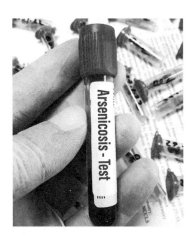

The nurses took their concerns to higher authorities. Swango's response was to play the victim card. His story was that he was being persecuted, and that he bore no responsibility whatsoever for any of the questionable deaths. The hospital fired him. Almost anybody else, put in Swango's position, would have slunk away with their tail between their legs before popping up somewhere else to try the con all over again. Not Michael Swango. He lawyered up and launched a full-on legal assault against the hospital system, alleging unfair treatment at their hands. The sheer effrontery of this move is almost

Swango's career in Zimbabwe left a trail of victims poisoned with injections of arsenic. Even his own wife was not immune to his murderous attempts.

unbelievable, particularly when viewed in light of the fact that Swango's face and criminal history were still appearing on true crime shows back in the States.

Fortunately, Swango's bid to be allowed to return to medical practice in Zimbabwe was unsuccessful, even with the help of an attorney. Although he was never convicted of a single murder while living in Africa, the number of suspicious deaths that took place around him was too great to simply ignore. The question was not whether Swango killed patients in Zimbabwe but rather how *many* he murdered.Estimates range from the single digits all the way up to 50 or 60. There were also a number of nonfatal poisonings, which seriously impacted the health of the victims. One case in point is Swango's African landlady, who he successfully poisoned with arsenic before leaving her residence. Another was Swango's own fiancée, nurse Kristen Kinney, who tragically took her own life in 1993. Before her death, Kinney had experienced a range of unexplained symptoms, all of which were consistent with arsenic poisoning. Upon forensic examination, the toxin was indeed found to be present in her body.

> **Before her death, Kinney had experienced a range of unexplained symptoms, all of which were consistent with arsenic poisoning.**

Finding himself *persona non grata* throughout Zimbabwe's medical system, he now began to cast a wider net, moving from place to place and taking work wherever he could find it. He continued to apply to hospitals for work, most notably one in Saudi Arabia. Swango did obtain work there, but on the flight over to Saudi Arabia on June 27, 1997, his plane stopped to refuel in Chicago. It was there that American authorities arrested him, after his passport was flagged in an immigration database.

Michael Swango's past had finally caught up with him. The V.A. is a federally funded agency, which meant that the lies he had told and the fraud he had committed had some major legal ramifications. The government takes the control, tracking, and administration of narcotic medications very seriously, and rightfully comes down hard on those who abuse these controlled substances. This policy resulted in Swango being sentenced to 42 months in prison, beginning in 1998, but crucially, this sentence did not address any of the murders he had committed. One cannot help but be reminded of the notorious mobster Al Capone being taken off the streets on charges of tax evasion.

The presiding judge recognized that Swango was a known and convicted poisoner, because his court disposition document read: "While the defendant [sic] is serving his sentence he shall not engage in any duties that directly require the preparation or deliver of foods [sic] or dispensation of medication pharmaceuticals."

Now it was a race against time to prove that, in addition to being a fraud and a swindler, Swango was also a killer. The FBI knew, based on his earlier five-year sentence being commuted to two and a half years, that he would almost certainly be the model of good behavior behind bars. Their biggest concern was that he would be out of jail by 2000 and could drop off the radar and be back up to his old tricks before anybody could put a stop to it.

Michael Swango was off the streets, for the time being. Now the priority was to build a watertight murder case against him, to make sure that justice was truly served. This put law enforcement in a race against time, and they pulled out all the stops. FBI agents and detectives flew across the country and overseas to gather evidence and interview witnesses. The bodies of some of Swango's former patients were exhumed and autopsied. Medical records were reviewed in exacting detail, with experts searching for even the slightest discrepancy.

In the end, it was close. He was due to complete his sentence and walk free from jail on June 15, 2000. Federal agents filed an array of serious charges against him just 96 hours before, on June 11.

Although an exact count of his total number of victims remains unknown, after initially proclaiming his innocence yet again, Michael Swango eventually pled guilty to three charges of murder. He had finally reached a point in his life where the lies, denials, and smokescreens meant nothing. Ever a calculating man, he took the deal offered to him by the prosecutor because if he was found guilty, the possibility of being either executed or extradited to Zimbabwe to answer murder charges there lay in his future. The best option for him was to remain in the United States and serve out the rest of his life in relative safety.

Shown in the custody of U.S. marshals, Swango is now serving his life sentence at a higher-than-maximum security penitentiary, the USP Florence ADMAX.

Swango is currently imprisoned at the U.S. Penitentiary, Florence Administrative Maximum Facility (or USP Florence ADMAX), in Colorado. His extremely high-security prison (nicknamed "the Alcatraz of the Rockies") houses some of the most hardened criminals in the United States; men such as Oklahoma City bomber Terry Nichols, Unabomber Ted Kaczynski, and one of the founding members of Al Qaeda, Mamdouh Mahmud Salim. Internees at the ADMAX are kept in isolation for 23 hours a day, with an hour given over to exercise.

Over the years, numerous reporters, authors, and other interested individuals have written to Swango in the hope of securing an interview. Their queries have all been in vain. The murderous former doctor seems resigned to living out the rest of his days in peace, quiet, and isolation. As far as his motive for killing so many patients is concerned, all we can do is speculate, because he himself is likely to take that secret to the grave.

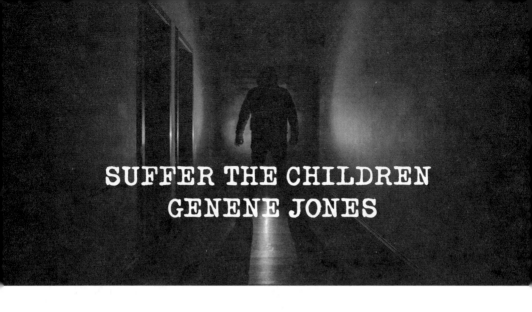

# SUFFER THE CHILDREN
## GENENE JONES

Clad in a dark blue prisoner's uniform, Genene Jones cut a pathetic figure as she sat in San Antonio's Bexar County courtroom on January 16, 2020. To the casual eye, the heavy-set, matronly 69-year-old looked like nothing more than a particularly morose grandmother. In actuality, she was one of the most prolific child killers in the history of the United States, and a black mark on the medical profession to which she belonged.

Peering at reporters and photographers from behind thick-rimmed black spectacles, the stone-faced former nurse was still absorbing the fact that she had just been sentenced to spend, at the very least, the next 20 years of her life in prison.

Although some serial killers derive enjoyment from the fact that their victims put up a fight, others prefer to prey on those who are defenseless and vulnerable. There are few who are less capable of protecting themselves than young children. As a pediatric nurse, Jones had the sacred duty of healing those infant charges who were entrusted into her care. Instead, she deliberately snuffed out dozens of innocent lives during a medical career that would be remembered for all the wrong reasons.

As a child, Genene Jones never quite fit in anywhere. She was born on July 13, 1950, in Texas. She was abandoned by her biological parents and placed in the care of a couple who adopted her. Little is known about her childhood, other than the fact that she had three other adopted siblings, one of whom—a younger brother—died in an explosion at the age of 16. Jones never got over his death.

In 1968, at the age of 17, she married a young man her own age. Four years later, they had a son together. To help support their family,

Jones took a job in the field of beauty and cosmetology. A daughter followed in 1977. This was the same year that Jones decided to pursue a career in medicine, enrolling in nursing school. She and her husband divorced, on the grounds that he abused her physically and emotionally, but Jones did not let that prevent her from finishing up her education.

After completing her schooling, Jones earned the credential of licensed vocational nurse (LVN) in the state of Texas and began looking for work. Although an LVN is not trained to the same level as a registered nurse, they perform skilled and important work, much of it in the form of hands-on patient care. Just as today, there was no shortage of work for licensed nurses.

From the very outset, she earned a reputation among her colleagues as a somewhat unusual character. She was boisterous and loud, never missing the opportunity to tell a crude or smutty joke, preferably one laden with profanity. That's not necessarily unusual in the medical field, where a black and often highly inappropriate sense of humor is sometimes a necessary coping mechanism. Jones liked to relate stories with a sexual bent to them, tales of men she had supposedly slept with, or wanted to, replete with lurid and graphic details. She was nothing if not an attention seeker.

She also had a hot temper and was not the sort of person to take a perceived slight or insult lying down. Nobody pushed Genene Jones around. She could be argumentative and confrontational when provoked, quick to anger, and slow to forgive. Her coworkers were sometimes wary of "poking the bear." More than one doctor or nurse had gotten on the wrong side of her abrasive personality.

Jones's hair-trigger temper quickly taught her colleagues to avoid "poking the bear."

The fall of 1978 saw her start a new job in the PICU (pediatric intensive care unit) at San Antonio's Bexar County Medical Center Hospital (BCMCH). Typically, the sickest and least stable children are admitted to PICUs—those who require round-the-clock treatment and monitoring. The nurse-to-child ratio is usually very low. The latest addition to the nursing staff worked the night shift and made a name for herself as being technically adept, clinically proficient, and confident to the point of arrogance. PICU nursing is some of the most difficult, challenging, and high-stress work in the medical field. It drew Genene Jones toward it like a moth to a flame. For all of her issues, she was regarded as an excellent nurse, knowledgeable and dependable.

Nobody suspected that she might also possess murderous tendencies.

It is only natural to be upset by the death of a child. Almost any healthcare worker will tell you that such losses tend to hit them harder than the death of an adult, and this is doubly true if the caregiver is a parent themselves. One tends to see all the Christmases that the child will never grow up to have and the gaping hole that the loss will carve into the heart of their family. There is no shame whatsoever in a medical provider crying at the loss of such a young patient. I have done this myself on more than one occasion. Yet Genene Jones took this a few steps further than most would consider to be normal, wailing and sobbing in anguish over the bodies of her dead patients—children that she, personally, was responsible for killing.

> Genene Jones took this a few steps further than most would consider to be normal, wailing and sobbing in anguish over the bodies of her dead patients....

At first glance, it is difficult to see such displays of histrionics as being anything other than cold, calculated attempts to not only cover her own malfeasance but also to generate sympathy—while also making herself the center of attention. One possible alternative explanation would be that the outbursts of grief were genuine and reflected the fact that Jones had a pathologically unstable personality. Showing such an exaggerated sense of remorse while literally standing over the body of a child that one has just killed is hardly the action of a sane and balanced individual. It should also be pointed out that Jones seemed equally upset over the death of any child in the ICU, whether it was her own patient or not, and whether she had personal contact with the deceased child or not. Some of them had been in her care for prolonged periods of time—weeks or even months.

One of the patients for whom Jones would one day be convicted of murder was an infant named Joshua Sawyer. Joshua died in 1981 when Jones administered an overdose of phenytoin into his IV line. Phenytoin (more commonly known by the trade name Dilantin) is most often given to control seizure activity. In excessive doses, however, it can also *cause* seizures and can cause total cardiovascular collapse. Joshua went into cardiac arrest shortly after Jones had injected him.

Shortly after Christmas of that same year, an infant named Rolando Santos was admitted to the hospital with pulmonary issues. Respiratory viruses are in full swing throughout the winter months, and emergency departments can be inundated with children suffering from such seasonal ailments as respiratory syncytial virus (RSV). Rolando's pulmonary issues were more serious, however, and at just four weeks of age, he required more advanced and aggressive care.

During the first month of life, the human respiratory system is poorly developed and has little in the way of oxygen reserves. Still, after a thorough assessment by highly skilled pediatricians, it was determined that Rolando Santos was relatively stable—and certainly not at imminent risk of dying. Yet that's exactly what happened three days after his admission. Rolando experienced a number of unexplained seizures and went into cardiac arrest. The medical team was able to resuscitate him successfully, but the root cause of the arrest eluded them. No matter how many sets of labs they ran or images they took, they couldn't figure out why he had experienced the sudden, drastic downturn.

On New Year's Day, 1982, he took another turn for the worse. This time, the cause was found. He was bleeding, both internally and externally, due to excessive levels of heparin in his bloodstream. Physicians were able to stabilize Rolando by administering a drug that counteracted the effects of heparin, and they also transferred him out of the pediatric ICU to a different ward in the hospital. This combination of actions—combating the blood thinner and putting him beyond Nurse Jones's reach—undoubtedly saved young Rolando's life.

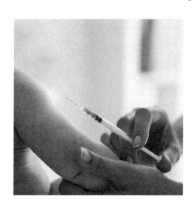

During the course of her career, it took colleagues a while to notice that children left alone with Jones had an increasingly low survival rate.

It would be discovered later that Genene Jones used several different types of drugs to murder. In addition to the anticonvulsant phenytoin, some of the children were killed by blood thinners, the most common of which is heparin. This type of medication prevents the blood from clotting, and their presence in the body means that when a blood vessel begins to bleed, it tends to keep on bleeding—sometimes to the point where the unfortunate patient goes into shock and dies. One telltale sign of their use is when the site of an IV or a needle injection refuses to stop bleeding, even after direct pressure is applied to it for a considerable length of time. Even experienced physicians prescribe blood thinners sparingly, taking the time to weigh the pros and cons of their use, and levels of the drug within the bloodstream are repeatedly checked to ensure that they are within the established safe range.

During Jones's early days at BCMCH, none of her colleagues put two and two together. Children were experiencing seemingly unexplained seizures—which happens more often than most people realize, particularly if the child is running a fever. The strange thing was that the seizures occurred almost exclusively when Nurse Jones was around, rarely when other nurses were providing care. A pattern was forming. At first, it wasn't at all obvious, but over the course of Jones's tenure at the hospital, the number of child deaths began to steadily escalate. The majority of them were infants, who tend to be much more vulnerable than older children because of their inability to speak out and ask for help.

Slowly, Jones's colleagues began to notice—not just the increasing number of pediatric fatalities but also the fact that Genene Jones was the common denominator. Death seemed to visit the hospital when she was on shift. She seemed to have an unnerving attraction to the bodies of dead babies, insisting on taking them to the hospital morgue herself, wrapping each tiny body up and talking or singing to them. More and more often, Genene Jones was raising eyebrows, and her fellow nurses began to keep a closer eye on her. They did not like what they saw, and they weren't shy about speaking out.

By the summer of 1982, relations with her coworkers became increasingly fraught. Management had heard whispers about Jones and ordered a low-profile investigation, which determined that she had been present when at least ten children had died. Although it stopped short of declaring her (or anybody) guilty of murder, or even incompetence, the confidential report did point out what everybody who was aware of the situation already knew: there was no way, statistically speaking, that this was a string of unfortunate accidents or simple bad luck. The odds against that being the case were simply astronomical. The situation cast a dark cloud over the entire PICU and tarnished the reputation of everybody who worked there—particularly those in positions of leadership. There was not enough evidence to lay responsibility for the deaths at the door of any one individual with any degree of certainty, but everybody was convinced they knew who the guilty party was.

Ultimately, Genene Jones resigned rather than accept a position working elsewhere within the hospital. If the internal report had been shared with law enforcement personnel, lives might have been saved. Instead, the primary suspect was permitted to simply move on. No fuss was made, and no scandal blew up to besmirch the hospital's name. Administrators must have realized that the report's assessment had been correct when they reviewed the pediatric death rates inside the facility and found that they had plummeted now that Nurse Genene Jones no longer had access to patients there.

> **The fact that Jones was regarded as being extremely competent and clinically professional actually worked against her.**

The fact that Jones was regarded as being extremely competent and clinically professional actually worked against her. Had she simply been terrible at her job, the deaths would have been no less tragic, but they would have been easier to forgive. The truth is, she knew exactly what she was doing, knew the safe dose of every medication she used, and knew what the harmful effects would be when given to children. There was undeniably malicious intent at work.

Once the term "serial killer" is used in reference to a specific individual, there is a tendency to focus on victim mortality: the number of patients that person has killed. In the case of Genene Jones, however, there were also many "near misses"—children who experienced unanticipated seizures, serious lapses in breathing, vomiting, and other life-threatening side-effects that, fortunately, did not prove to be fatal.

After her resignation from BCMCH, Jones found work at a small, single-physician children's clinic in nearby Kerrville, where she worked for Dr. Kathleen Holland. A pediatrician by specialty, Dr. Holland had worked with Jones in San Antonio and was looking for a nurse with substantial experience dealing with children. She had caught wind of the scuttlebutt circulating about Genene Jones but was willing to give her a chance to escape the cloud of negativity she had accrued at her last job. The well-meaning physician couldn't seem to accept that the newly hired nurse could also be a serial killer, though proof of the matter wasn't long in coming.

Shortly after Jones's arrival, pediatric patients started to have inexplicable seizures and other unexpected medical emergencies—always after having spent time in the care of Nurse Jones. It was only afterward, when more pieces of the puzzle had been assembled, that something else became clear: Jones always tried to have the child's parents leave the examination room, leaving her and the patient alone together. A number of parents did just that, giving Jones the opportunity to inject an overdose of medication into their child.

The death of 15-month-old Chelsea McClellan while visiting the clinic in September of 1982 would raise more red flags. Jones had only been working at the clinic for a month. Little Chelsea's parents took her to the clinic twice, and each time, she suffered a seizure. Each seizure came immediately after she had been touched by Jones. The first time, Jones and Dr. Holland were able to resuscitate Chelsea; during the second, Jones gave the child two injections at the physician's direction.

The shots were supposed to be immunizations, but in reality, Jones had filled the syringes with one of her favorite overdose medications—succinylcholine. This is the same paralytic medication that was used by Dr. Michael Swango (see the earlier chapter for more details) to stop his victims from breathing. As a nurse working in a PICU, she had ready access to this and a number of other drugs that are lethal when given in excessive dosages.

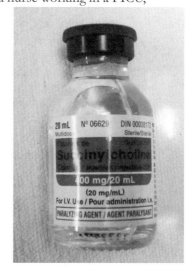

Despite the best efforts of Dr. Holland, an EMS crew, and other medical providers, Chelsea McClellan died in the emergency department of a local hospital a short time after her second visit to Kerrville.

Incredibly, in the early stages after Chelsea's death, no blame was attached to Nurse Jones. She even had the audacity to attend the little girl's funeral, offering her condolences to the McClellan family.

Gossip about Genene Jones was now spreading like wildfire among members of the San Antonio medical community. Like members of any other profession, doctors and nurses hang out together when they are off shift, and many of them like to talk shop. The stink that Jones had brought

Succinylcholine is used in low doses to cause a mild paralysis only for the aid of other procedures, such as intubation. In higher doses, the medication can cause general paralysis and suffocation.

down on Bexar County Hospital, which hadn't made news yet but was well-known to many care providers, had now been transferred to Dr. Holland's clinic. Word was out about the unusually high number of sick and dying children ending up in emergency departments after paying the doctor a visit. By the end of September, that word had reached the ears of the police.

In the wake of Chelsea McClellan's tragic death, Dr. Holland became suspicious. Jones had recently mentioned to her that a vial of succinylcholine had gone missing, and she had ordered a replacement. Now, apropos of nothing, the nurse reported that the original vial had somehow reappeared—but there was no cause for alarm, she explained, because it showed no signs of having been tampered with. Something about the way Jones spun this story didn't sit right with the doctor, who waited for her to leave the clinic before taking a closer look for herself.

Carefully examining the vial, she discovered that there were two separate and distinct puncture marks, where there should have been none. This is a telltale sign of drug diversion (unauthorized use) and usually means that somebody has used a needle to withdraw some or all of the vial's contents, then made a second puncture in order to inject a substitute back inside to replace the stolen medication. Most commonly, such a thing would be found when narcotics were being stolen by an addict—but the doctor knew that there was no such thing as a succinylcholine addiction. The only reason somebody would have to surreptitiously siphon off a supply of the drug was almost too awful to contemplate.

Holland confronted Jones and demanded an explanation. Jones was not forthcoming and told her to get rid of the vial entirely. The doctor knew this would be tantamount to destroying evidence, hardly the act of an innocent and wronged person. Jones was casually suggesting that she commit a crime.

She was left with only one option: this was now a matter for the authorities. It had to be reported. To her credit, now that she was confronted with the truth, Dr. Holland did not hesitate to do the right thing.

Investigators would later confirm exactly what the doctor had suspected. The clear liquid sloshing around inside the vial wasn't succinylcholine at all. It was mostly 0.9% sodium chloride—salt water, also known as "normal saline" in its medical form.

After looking deeper into the issue, the district attorney in Bexar County became gravely concerned about Jones and her activities. There simply should not have been so many deaths in one PICU as Bexar County had seen. Something was plainly not right. In February 1983, an investigation was launched. The medical records of every single pediatric patient who had died at BCMCH between 1978 and early 1982 were put under the microscope. If there had been any conceivable doubt about the culpability of Genene Jones, the string of deaths and severe illnesses connected with the clinic in Kerrville put them to rest.

> There simply should not have been so many deaths in one PICU as Bexar County had seen. Something was plainly not right.

Chelsea McClellan's body was exhumed, and tissue samples were extracted. They tested positive for the presence of succinylcholine, a drug that had never been prescribed to her and one that should not have been found anywhere in her body. It had come from the double-punctured vial that Jones claimed to have lost and subsequently rediscovered—the same vial she had told Dr. Holland to get rid of.

A grand jury was convened to investigate the deaths. Initially, Jones was cooperative and accommodating, but as time passed, she stood behind her Fifth Amendment right to avoid testifying further. In 1984, the case went to trial.

At its conclusion, Genene Jones was sentenced to 99 years of imprisonment for the murder of Chelsea McClellan. Shortly afterward, she was sentenced to an additional 60 years, this time for her unsuccessful attempt to murder Rolando Santos with a heparin overdose. If all had gone according to plan, she would have died in prison. However, in an unusually lenient move for the traditionally uncompromising state of Texas, the law allowed her to get a massive reduction in her sentence if she didn't get into any trouble while in prison. Jones dutifully kept her nose clean, and under the terms of her original sentence, the Texas legal system would have had no choice but to release her from prison in 2018.

There were few, if any, who wanted to see her freed. Particularly vocal (and understandably so) was Petti McClellan, the mother of Chelsea, who refused to countenance the idea of her daughter's murderess

Genene Jones, in an inmate photo from the Texas Department of Criminal Justice taken before being put up for her second trial, stood a 100 percent chance of release in 2018 unless she could be convicted of more of her crimes.

being let out. Another who objected was the young boy she had tried to murder when he was just four weeks old. Rolando Santos told San Antonio–based KSAT reporter Paul Venema that his attempted killer should never be released "because she killed a lot of babies. I think something like that deserves the death penalty."

The death penalty wasn't on the table, and before Jones was due to be released, prosecutors were able to build a second case against her; this time, they indicted her for the murder of Joshua Sawyer, along with four other children, in a plea deal. While Jones pled guilty to the murder of Joshua, she would not publicly accept responsibility for the remainder of the deaths. One can only imagine how frustrating that must have been for the family members of her other victims, which could number anywhere between 40 and 60.

The guilty plea did at least allow the judge to keep Genene Jones in prison, by issuing a life sentence. While some may not see this as being justice, it is the closest that the law allows.

Presenting at her sentencing were the family members of several of Jones's victims. Joshua Sawyer's mother, Connie, had the opportunity to address Jones directly. "I hope for you to live a long and miserable life behind bars," she told the stone-faced woman who had murdered her son.

It is easy to agree with this sentiment.

It is always a difficult thing to try and fathom the motives of those who become part of the healing profession, only to then turn their skills to murdering the very patients they have undertaken to treat. For some, the reason for killing is a sick desire to possess the power of life and death over their fellow human beings. Others are exacting a form of projected revenge on somebody who they believe wronged them earlier in life, often a parent, sibling, spouse, or a rival.

The case of Genene Jones may not be as straightforward as all that. Some of those who were part of the case as it unfolded have taken the view that Jones reveled in being in a position of responsibility, and for her position as a senior PICU nurse to remain stable, she decided to "help things along" by creating an ever-increasing number of critically sick children. In other words, she was killing for job security. Others think that the only way she could derive true emotional fulfillment was by pushing some children all the way to death's door, only to help bring them back again, to great applause and plaudits.

To play devil's advocate, it may be that she never meant to kill; her intent might plausibly have been to render the children gravely unwell, and then nurse them back to health, casting herself in the role of health-care hero along the way. Even if one chooses to entertain this notion, it does nothing to lessen the severity of Jones's actions. As a trained nurse, she was fully aware that the medication overdoses she was giving had the capacity to kill. Whatever her motive, she was willing to accept the risk of her patients dying in order to satisfy her own perverse emotional needs.

Journalist Peter Elkind, the foremost expert on the case and author of the superb book *The Death Shift: Nurse Genene Jones and the Texas Baby Murders*, had the opportunity to sit down and interview Jones prior to the beginning of the murder trial. Jones presented herself with obvious intelligence and a forceful personality, but he also notes that she took pleasure in gossiping about her coworkers and their personal vices. This suggests that, in addition to having a vindictive streak, Jones was also deeply insecure. Putting herself in a position to be seen as a savior of sick or dying children may have been a direct result of that insecurity, a way for her to build up her ego and self-esteem—in the sickest possible manner.

During their interview, Jones flatly denied having killed any of the children who had died while in her care. She went on to retract that statement, claiming variously that she had killed the babies herself and, later, that the voices in her head were responsible. The truth of the matter will never be known, not least because Genene Jones may no longer be certain herself.

In April 1991, a 26-year-old man broke into the Bangor, Maine, home of acclaimed horror novelist Stephen King. The author's wife,

In a scenario eerily reminiscent of a Stephen King plot, Genene Jones's nephew sought to accost the famed horror author at his own home to further his own literary career.

Tabitha, had the terrifying experience of being confronted by a stranger in her own house. The man claimed to have a bomb in the backpack he carried. After confronting Mrs. King, he locked himself in the attic and refused to come out.

Fortunately, the police were able to take the intruder into custody without any further incident. The backpack bomb proved to be nothing more than a hoax.

The reason behind the break-in was bizarre. In 1987, King had published the bestselling novel *Misery*. It tells the story of Annie Wilkes, the self-proclaimed "number one fan" of a writer of historical fiction named Paul Sheldon. By turns charming and psychotically deranged, Annie kidnaps the author and keeps him captive in her home, forcing him to write a sequel to her favorite series of novels. When Sheldon attempts to escape, Annie—a former nurse—hobbles him in a truly uncomfortable scene, which made readers of King's book and viewers of Rob Reiner's movie adaptation wince. As the story progresses, it also transpires that, during her nursing career, Annie was a serial killer. Many of her victims were infants.

Whether written on the page by King or portrayed on screen in a powerhouse performance by Kathy Bates, Annie Wilkes is a truly iconic, larger-than-life character. She has come to define the crazed, obsessive "super fan" that all celebrities fear.

What does this have to do with the break-in at the Kings' home? The intruder was convinced that Stephen King had based the character of Annie Wilkes on the life of his aunt and wanted the writer to help him publish a sequel that he had written himself.

The man was Genene Jones's nephew, Erik Keene, thus proving that sometimes, truth really is stranger than fiction.

# THE RED SURGE
# ELIZABETH WETTLAUFER

**W**ithout insulin, we would be unable to live. This naturally occurring hormone is secreted from the pancreas and allows sugar to enter the cells of our body. (Biology students are taught that insulin is the key that unlocks the cell.)

One troubling facet of the disease diabetes occurs when the body produces too little insulin or becomes resistant to what insulin it does produce. Ever since the early twentieth century, medical science has addressed this problem with injections of external insulin. Just like anything else, however, it is possible to have too much of a good thing. The only organ in the human body that does not require insulin to process sugar is the brain, which takes its supply of glucose directly from the bloodstream. If somebody is injected with an excess amount of insulin, all of the free-floating sugar in the bloodstream rushes into the body's cells, leaving none for the brain.

The end result: seizure, coma, and, ultimately, death.

It is not difficult to understand insulin's potential as a murder weapon. A massive, fatal insulin overdose may not look suspicious, particularly if it occurs in an elderly or greatly sick and unstable patient. Unlike narcotic medications such as morphine or fentanyl, it is not considered a controlled substance. It can be obtained with relative ease, particularly by those working in healthcare.

One such person was Canadian serial killer Elizabeth Wettlaufer.

Elizabeth Parker was born on June 10, 1967. She was raised in Zorra, a township in Ontario, Canada. Her parents, Doug and Hazel, were both extremely devout Christians. They followed the Baptist faith and tried to inculcate in young Elizabeth their religious beliefs. By and large, they were successful. The Parkers were very traditionalist, to the point that they could accurately be described as fundamentalists.

Theirs was a very old-school, black-and-white view of the Bible and the word of God. They lived by the credo that the man was head of the household and that his commands should be obeyed without question. For females such as Elizabeth and her mother, obedience was a major virtue, both to God and to the patriarch of the family. Doug was a preacher in his spare time and was comfortable in the pulpit, sharing his beliefs with a similarly minded congregation of his neighbors. Elizabeth and her brother Robert attended many of these church services, listening intently to their father's sermons.

Under these strictures, any sort of homosexual behavior was a big no-no. This was confusing for young Elizabeth, who developed sexual feelings towards other females when she was growing up. This was impossible to reconcile with her family's belief system, which had no tolerance for girls who showed lesbian or bisexual tendencies. Exhibiting behavior like this—or even simply advocating it—was a fast way to get oneself exiled from the family and thrown out of the church. It was a knife edge that Elizabeth Wettlaufer constantly found herself walking.

Inevitably, her parents found out about their daughter's so-called "perversion." Their solution was to send Elizabeth to conversion therapy, a completely unscientific program whose adherents claimed that it could convert those who underwent it from a homosexual orientation to a heterosexual one. There is no clinical evidence to support the use of such "therapy"; in fact, quite the reverse is true. Conversion therapy has been demonstrated to cause psychological and emotional harm on those

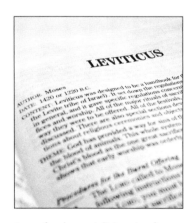

Some fundamentalist sects of Christianity interpret the words of the Bible in ways that allow them to not love their neighbors.

who undertake it, particularly if they are forced to do so. (In fact, on December 8, 2021, Canada made conversion therapy a criminal offense.)

In an attempt to please God and her parents, Elizabeth dutifully agreed to enter the program. Because of her parents' stringent beliefs, she was convinced that she had no other option. When Wettlaufer emerged from "therapy," it seemed at first as if it might actually have been successful. She felt better, she claimed, and was much less confused and conflicted than she had been before. Her desire to be with other women would return, however, and be present throughout her life.

Determined to further her education, Elizabeth enrolled at the Baptist Bible College in London, Ontario. She was a motivated student who performed well academically, and after graduating with a degree, she moved on to attend nursing school.

Her time in the nursing program was far from plain sailing. Wettlaufer was dealing with a series of mental health issues, such as depression. One can only speculate as to how much of her emotional distress was caused by her experiences with conversion therapy and the deep sense of shame and wrongdoing that accompanied her lesbian tendencies. To cope with these and other stressors, she drank heavily and began to abuse prescription painkillers and sedatives—medications with a high risk for addiction. Nevertheless, she overcame these obstacles to the extent that she graduated as a licensed nurse in 1995.

At about the same time she was training as a nurse, Wettlaufer was also undergoing a crisis of faith. Despite her best efforts, she still found herself attracted to other women, and it became next to impossible for her to reconcile those feelings with what she thought God wanted of her. She found temporary solace in alcohol, which would ultimately cause her to lose her job after arriving on shift while significantly impaired. The facility that employed her had no choice. The potential risks associated with an intoxicated or drug-influenced nurse administering medications and caring for vulnerable patients simply could not be ignored.

In some places, practicing medicine while in such a condition would result in the revocation of one's nursing license or certification. This did not happen in Wettlaufer's case. If it had, eight lives would unquestionably have been saved. While the motivations of the nursing administrators who allowed her to keep working as a nurse were laudable, the consequences of their decision would prove to be catastrophic.

Crucially, there was no black mark on her record, which meant that after being fired, Wettlaufer had a good chance of landing a job elsewhere, once a little time had passed.

**To her credit, Wettlaufer did seek professional help for her addiction issues. She returned to church on a regular basis, attempting to mend her relationship with God.**

To her credit, Wettlaufer did seek professional help for her addiction issues. She returned to church on a regular basis, attempting to mend her relationship with God. There was still the thorny issue of her sexuality, however, and she attempted to deal with this by dating and ultimately marrying Donnie Wettlaufer, a man she knew from the Baptist church. For a time, things seemed to be going better, but before long, Elizabeth Wettlaufer's mental health was deteriorating once more.

Then she began to hear voices. They were neither kind nor friendly. The voices were critical of the urges she felt and some of the life choices she had made. To make matters worse, she started to think about killing people she knew. As Wettlaufer grew progressively angrier at life, the universe, and everything, these mental murder scenarios grew increasingly detailed. She thought about killing her husband, her colleagues, and her therapist. More alarming still, while she was working with at-risk elder patients, her thoughts turned toward murdering them.

Before long, Wettlaufer's behavior started to garner complaints from patients, family members, and colleagues. She could be abrasive, difficult, and mentally scattered. She developed a reputation for inaccurately dosing patient medications, a big no-no in the medical field. At the time, it did not appear that she was doing this deliberately, but subsequent events would lead people to wonder.

In June 2007, Elizabeth Wettlaufer, now 40, was offered a job at Caressant Care Nursing Home in Woodstock, Ontario. It is a sad fact of life that long-term care facilities such as this find it extremely challenging to attract and retain nursing and support staff. The work is hard, the emotional toll can be high, and staff is underpaid. There never seem to be sufficient personnel or resources to meet the growing needs of an aging population. This is true everywhere, and Canada is no exception. Wettlaufer's employment record held little in the way of red flags, and in a matter of hours after completing her job interview, she started working directly with residents at the facility.

On paper, she seemed like a great employee. None of her medication errors, attitude problems, or substance abuse issues reached her new employer. Behind the scenes, her marriage was beginning to unravel. Thanks to the Internet, Wettlaufer had made a number of female friends. Her intentions toward them were not always platonic, and when her husband found out, it led to a breakdown in their relationship. When the two separated and began the slow process of getting divorced, she moved in with another woman, one who had already become her lover.

Later that same year, the murders began.

Many of the residents in Wettlaufer's care were vulnerable, and due to conditions such as dementia, could sometimes be difficult. A person suffering from Alzheimer's can be loud and verbally abusive, often to a degree that would frazzle the nerves of even the most stable caregiver. Needless to say, Elizabeth Wettlaufer was not the most stable caregiver.

She had little patience for the vulnerable people in her care. The angrier she got, the more frequent her fantasies of killing them became. Violence was not an option—it would be quickly detected, and Wettlaufer knew that striking one of her charges would land her in a world of trouble. Insulin, on the other hand, was another matter. It was commonly used, easy for her to get hold of, and above all, a quiet means of inflicting harm. She began to experiment with it, giving injections of the hormone in varying dosages to the patients who got on her bad side.

At first, the victims of her insulin poisoning fell sick but survived the experience. Nurses and other care providers are trained to spot the signs and symptoms of low blood sugar, or hypoglycemia: a sudden, unexpected onset of altered mental activity coupled with pale, sweaty skin and a rapid heart rate. The problem can be offset if diagnosed in time and countered with the administration of glucose in one form or another, such as concentrated paste or fruit juice.

Rather than administer the insulin directly into a vein through an IV line, as might be done in a hospital, Wettlaufer used an insulin pen to inject it into the subcutaneous tissue of her victims' bodies. It is easy to hide small puncture wounds such as this by selecting sites that are in rarely visible areas of the body, such as between the folds of skin.

The first round of insulin poisonings was, thankfully, not fatal. For Elizabeth

Retirement should be the most enjoyable time of a person's life, but sometimes seniors experience elder abuse at the hands of so-called health workers.

Wettlaufer, however, there soon came a revelation: the more often she injected her helpless charges, the more satisfying she found it to be.

Two months after her arrival at Caressant, on August 11, 2007, she set her sights on 84-year-old James Silcox. Silcox was a veteran who had served in the Canadian Army during World War II and now, after suffering a major stroke, fully deserved to be given the best care possible in his twilight years. He could sometimes be a challenging patient to handle, primarily because he had diminished cognitive faculties. On the night of his death, he would not stop calling out in a loud voice. This repeated interruption to her nightly routine made Wettlaufer angry, and she responded by injecting him with a fatal dose of insulin. He died in his bed, in the early hours of the morning, after experiencing a precipitous drop in his blood glucose levels.

**Wettlaufer would later describe the sudden, overbearing urge to commit murder her "red surge."**

When Silcox's body was examined by a physician, nothing suspicious was noticed about his death.

Elizabeth Wettlaufer had gotten away with murder for the first time. Four months later, on December 22, with the Christmas holiday season in full swing, she did it again. This time, her victim was another 84-year-old man, Maurice Granat, who went by the name "Moe."

Wettlaufer began to see herself as an instrument of God's will, rationalizing her cold-blooded murders as being her way of "returning people God wanted to be with him." The fact that they were all people who had angered or irritated her in some way did not seem to register.

Wettlaufer would later describe the sudden, overbearing urge to commit murder her "red surge." Anything could trigger the red surge, and those who unwittingly did so would find themselves the recipient of the enraged nurse's insulin pen.

Another resident, 63-year-old Michael Priddle, was afflicted with Huntington's disease, an inherited disorder of the central nervous system in which the nerve cells within the brain slowly begin to die. This makes for an undignified and extremely distressing deterioration in the health of the person who suffers from it. Although the symptoms can be slowed and mitigated somewhat with various treatment options, there is currently no cure for Huntington's.

The disease is an awful thing to suffer, but it is doubtful that Wettlaufer had her patient's best interests at heart when she took it upon herself to once again play God, injecting him with an overdose of insulin. "It's his time to go," she rationalized, before administering the hormone. This time, her murder attempt was unsuccessful, and he lived for another four years. Yet again, there was no suspicion of foul play. One reason was that the employee whose task it was to report a potentially suspicious death was Wettlaufer herself. The fox was guarding the chicken coop.

Having killed two residents and assaulted several more, Wettlaufer confessed to her live-in girlfriend what she had done. Incredibly, rather than report her to the authorities for murder, the girlfriend instead advised her to "not kill anybody else." If the advice stuck, it wasn't for very long. Wettlaufer was drinking again and felt her life spinning out of control once more. She needed something that would help restore that sense of control, and that something was exercising the power of life and death over another human being.

She did try to right the ship. Three years passed with no further killings. Then, in 2011, the red surge came back. This time, her victims were three elderly ladies: 87-year-old Gladys Millard, 95-year-old Helen Matheson, and 96-year-old Mary Zurawinski. Back at home, Wettlaufer's personal life was still a mess.

She was unable to sustain a healthy relationship, and she continued to abuse a variety of prescription medications, particularly strong pain killers such as Dilaudid. Wettlaufer had access to such controlled drugs at work and rarely wasted an opportunity to pilfer some. The easiest drug hauls came when she raided the supply of a patient shortly after their death, when few if any questions would be asked about where the medications had gone.

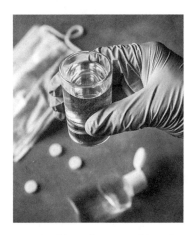

Her reputation at work suffered as she began to display increasingly erratic behavior at the care facility. She would disappear for long breaks, possibly to take drugs or to sleep off their effects. It was inevitable that her struggles did not go unnoticed forever, especially as she began to make more medication errors and was cautioned about them by her supervisors. Warnings were also issued in relation to her hitting on her female colleagues.

Many health workers try to blunt the effects of their difficult work with substance use, both legal and not.

Wettlaufer murdered 90-year-old Helen Young and proceeded to confess it to her pastor. Rather than turn her in for murder, the pastor granted her forgiveness and absolved her of the sin, albeit with the admonition that he would be forced to take action if she ever killed again. Thus was another chance to end her murder spree wasted.

Matters finally came to a head in the spring of 2014, when Wettlaufer murdered her final victim at Caressant: 79-year-old Maureen Pickering. Her personnel file, which included multiple medication errors and other issues, had now gotten too large to be ignored. She was fired. Citing the medication errors, facility management categorized her as being too great a risk to have around patients.

That should have ended her career. Instead, she very quickly picked up a nursing job at another long-term care facility, Meadow Park. The nurses' union to which she belonged backed up Wettlaufer's appeal against her termination. In addition to demanding a $10,542 cash settlement, the nurses' association attempted to get her personnel record (and its multitude of medication error complaints) sealed up so future employers would not be made aware of her past behavior.

The hiring was by no means a foregone conclusion. The references that Wettlaufer had listed on her job application had all worked with her at Caressant and raised the issues of her medication errors and negative interactions with other employees. Meadow Park hired her anyway. This is partially explained by the fact that she had gotten a letter of reference from Caressant as a condition of the settlement negotiated by the union.

Nobody, it seemed, was willing to openly state that Elizabeth Wettlaufer was a liability working with at-risk patients.

Wettlaufer could have used the new job at Meadow Park as a chance to turn over a new leaf. Instead, she was soon giving full reign to the red surge once more, and she murdered 77-year-old Arpad (Art) Horvath with another insulin overdose. Wettlaufer's colleagues found Horvath unresponsive in bed during their early morning rounds, and he died shortly afterward.

In September 2014, just a few weeks after Horvath's death, a significant quantity of controlled medications—narcotics—disappeared from Meadow Park's supply without a trace. The day before, Elizabeth Wettlaufer had turned in her letter of resignation—and she left the same day that the drugs went missing.

Perhaps recognizing that she needed help, Wettlaufer checked herself in at rehab. When she checked out again, she went right back to work—not at Meadow Park but rather picking up temporary nursing jobs wherever she could find them. Predictably enough, more intentional insulin overdoses followed. Fortunately, none were fatal.

Seemingly out of the blue, Wettlaufer quit working as a nurse in 2016. She never touched a patient again. Both her mental health and her addiction problems were getting worse. A complete nervous breakdown was imminent. To add to her troubles, the murders and attempted murders she was responsible for had finally put her on the radar of law enforcement. While she was in another rehab facility, she told multiple people—both staff and patients—what she had done, and even went so far as to write a narrative account of the murders.

The more she admitted, the more she wanted to admit. A dam began to break, until Wettlaufer no longer cared who knew about her murderous past. Detectives examined her claims and found them to be valid. There was more than sufficient evidence to arrest her and charge her with the murder of eight former patients. There would also be charges leveled with regard to the attempted murders of patients who had received insulin overdoses and survived.

> Seemingly out of the blue, Wettlaufer quit working as a nurse in 2016. She never touched a patient again. Both her mental health and her addiction problems were getting worse.

During her 2017 courtroom appearance, Wettlaufer pleaded guilty to all eight murder charges leveled against her. She also accepted responsibility for four more attempted murders. This meant that the judge was able to skip trial and go straight to sentencing.

She offered a few words of remorse, which did little to answer the questions that the families of her victims deserved. Elizabeth Wettlaufer was sentenced to life imprisonment. The soonest she could conceivably be paroled will be sometime after the year 2040.

There are many reasons people give for committing murder. There is the infamous "the Devil made me do it," for example. In the case of Elizabeth Wettlaufer, the opposite was true—she claimed that her anger at the world, paired with instructions from God, drove her to kill.

Following her sentencing to life in prison, Elizabeth Wettlaufer is escorted by police from an Ontario courthouse.

Taking into account her childhood in an exceptionally strict, fundamentalist household, which indoctrinated her with a very specific set of religious beliefs, this is not a difficult explanation to accept—up to a point. But it isn't the complete picture.

Ever since she was a teenager, and possibly before, Wettlaufer fought against her feelings of attraction to the same sex. Her religion declared such feelings to be deeply sinful and fundamentally wrong. This clashed with her God-fearing nature and set up an existential conflict, which was temporarily controlled but never entirely mastered.

A professional psychological evaluation diagnosed her with borderline personality disorder and noted that she had extremely poor impulse control—particularly when provoked. As with so many of the other serial killers covered in this book, there was also the ever-present sense of anger and rage. These factors, coupled with the voices she began to hear, combined to push her over the edge. Harming helpless men and women (Wettlaufer admitted to sometimes selecting them because they would be least capable of fighting back) provided a sense of catharsis that she was unable to obtain elsewhere.

One of the most disturbing aspects of the Elizabeth Wettlaufer case is the sheer number of people she confided in about the murders she was guilty of committing. Her girlfriend, her pastor, and other friends and exes were all presumably shocked to hear her confess, but not one of them reached out to the police. A phone call from any one of them, just one anonymous tip, could have prevented Wettlaufer from ever killing again. Upon consideration, it appears as though she did have some kind of conscience after all, and it may well be the case that each of these confessions was a thinly veiled cry for help. It is entirely possible that on some level, Elizabeth Wettlaufer knew that what she was doing was wrong and that she secretly wanted to be stopped.

It must also be pointed out that had she been scrutinized in greater depth by the nursing authorities and her employers, fewer lives might have been lost. This would also have been the case if just one of her confidantes had come forward and spoken up. Wettlaufer had been written up and disciplined on numerous occasions, many of them for the misdosing and abuse of insulin. Only a significant systemic fault can explain the fact that she was able to cover these up for so long. In the wake of the revelations concerning the Wettlaufer murders, several of the organizations involved would institute a review of their policies and procedures, focusing on ways to close the loopholes through which she had slipped undetected.

It can only be hoped that the Canadian nursing system never again sees a serial killer like Elizabeth Wettlaufer within its ranks.

# TORONTO'S GAY VILLAGE MURDERER BRUCE MCARTHUR

It is a sad historical truth that members of the LGBTQ community have never been strangers to persecution. Along with the blatant prejudice and oppression that they have suffered throughout history, the most unfortunate of these men and women have also found themselves targeted for murder.

In the United States, the so-called I-70 Strangler, Herbert Baumeister, haunted the gay clubs of downtown Indianapolis under an alias, seeking out vulnerable gay men who would not be missed and luring them back to his home, where they would be murdered in his swimming pool. Baumeister was a married man, though it would later emerge that he preferred other males as his sexual partners. Baumeister found the facade of married life and the perception of being a family man to be a useful smokescreen for his homicidal tendencies.

The case of Canadian citizen Bruce McArthur bore similarities to those of Baumeister. He murdered at least eight victims, all of them males, beginning in 2010 and ending in 2017. All were gay, as was McArthur himself, and most were posed and photographed while either unconscious or dead.

Up until his forties, Bruce McArthur was also a happily married man—to outside appearances, at least. He was a father and grandfather, but after concealing his attraction to men for many years, he eventually decided to come out. The most likely reason for this taking so long is that he was a child of the 1950s, when homosexuality was generally seen as being something to be ashamed of. It is likely that as a youth or young man, McArthur learned to suppress his urges, or at the very least keep them hidden.

McArthur's parents liked to foster other children, and it wasn't unusual for them to have a house full of kids at any given time. Young Bruce grew up on a farm, part of a family that was devoutly religious and headed by a patriarch named Malcolm—probably not the sort of environment in which a gay man could flourish. Yet the family also had a reputation for living in a wholesome and stable environment. As far as we know, other than some altercations over religious differences between McArthur's parents, there are no allegations of serious abuse or misconduct.

His parents were dedicated churchgoers and passed that on to their son. For many people, faith can be a source of great comfort and clarity. Not so for Bruce McArthur, who found it to be the cause of internal conflict and confusion.

At the age of 23, McArthur married Janice Campbell, and the pair began to raise a family. The Christian faith remained a key part of his life, and just like his parents, McArthur was a regular church attendee. His desire for men grew, however, and he began sleeping with them without his wife's knowledge. Finally, the marriage broke down and the couple separated.

After leaving his wife, McArthur relocated to Toronto around 2000 and immediately gravitated toward its vibrant LGBTQ community. Ten years later, his first known murder took place on September 6, 2010, when he picked up Sri Lankan–born Skandaraj Navaratnam in a bar. The 40-year-old was said to have been friendly, but he kept his personal life private. He was last seen leaving a gay bar named Zipperz in the company of an unidentified male, now believed to have been McArthur, late at night.

Toronto's LGBTQ enclave, the Church and Wellesley neighborhood, was the home of popular gay bar Zipperz, which has since closed.

McArthur would wrap his naked victims up in a fur coat—the same one every time—and pose them in a variety of different positions before taking photographs as souvenirs. Some were also made to wear a hat, and McArthur had cigars jammed into their mouths. Officers also discovered a bondage kit in McArthur's apartment, materials such as zip ties and duct tape that had obviously been used to restrain his victims prior to their murders.

McArthur used his work van to pick up many of his victims. Three months after committing his first murder, on December 29, 2010, McArthur killed 44-year-old Abdulbasir Faizi. Faizi was a printer, and he liked to spend time socializing at Zipperz. After he went missing, officers later found Faizi's car parked in a neighborhood in which he did not live—close to the house where McArthur disposed of his victims' bodies. The vehicle had been abandoned.

It should be noted that homicide investigators did not classify the first two murders as being sexual in nature, but they did for the six that followed. On October 18, 2012, McArthur killed 58-year-old Afghani immigrant Majeed Kayhan, carefully staging the body and taking pictures with his digital camera. Kayhan was another regular at Zipperz.

Members of the LGBTQ+ community realized that some of their friends had disappeared without a trace, and they raised the alarm. In response, the police department launched "Project Houston" in November 2012 to discover the cause. Was there a serial killer working Toronto's gay village, preying on some of its men?

Apparently not, or so they thought. Project Houston was wrapped up in April 2014, after investigators found no compelling evidence to suspect a murderer was at large. The spotlight this increased police activity brought to the situation had succeeded in achieving one thing: driving Bruce McArthur underground. For the duration of the project, and more than a year afterward, he stopped killing.

Almost three years had passed with no further murders, and the sense of alarm some people felt had begun to abate. Then, on August 15, 2015, McArthur struck again, picking up 50-year-old Iranian-born Soroush Mahmoudi. Mahmoudi had a wife and a stepson but frequented the gay village on a regular basis. He made his living as a painter and was known for being a man with a big heart.

In a change to his former modus operandi, Bruce McArthur had now begun to use a ligature with which to strangle his victims. A ligature works on the same principle as a tourniquet but serves exactly the opposite purpose when employed by a killer. Tourniquets are progressively tightened around a limb to prevent blood loss from a wound. Ligatures are placed around the throat and are used to compress the blood vessels in the neck, effectively strangling the victim.

Mahmoudi's DNA would later be found on a coat McArthur kept in the back of his van. The police would later determine that this was the same coat in which other victims had been posed and photographed.

In addition to McArthur's victims' sexual orientation, there was another common factor. McArthur was already beginning to display a preferred "type": men of Middle Eastern or Indian descent, with dark skin and facial hair, ranging from beards to mustaches or goatees. He often chose men who were not openly gay.

Five months after murdering Soroush Mahmoudi, McArthur stuck to this newly established ligature pattern when, on January 6, 2016, he killed 37-year-old Kirushna Kanagaratnam. Kanagaratnam had come to Canada as an asylum seeker, hoping to establish a new life in a country that wasn't being torn apart by war and bloodshed. Canadian authorities, however, denied his request. Afraid of being deported, he felt his only option was to spend life on the run, making money wherever he could by doing odd jobs.

On April 23 of that same year, McArthur murdered 47-year-old Dean Lisowick. After surviving a difficult childhood spent in and out of foster homes, Lisowick experienced protracted homelessness as an adult. Despite the challenges life had thrown his way, those who knew him remembered him as a respectful, friendly, and polite man. He stayed out of trouble, spending his nights sleeping in homeless shelters and missions, wherever he could get a bed. He supported himself by doing manual labor when the opportunity presented itself.

It is a sad truth that nobody ever reported Kirushna Kanagaratnam or Dean Lisowick missing. In the first case, Kanagaratnam's family in Sri Lanka thought that he was trying to keep a low profile to avoid

McArthur's sixth victim, Dean Lisowick, was a decent citizen, though his lack of ties to the community meant few noted his disappearance. His name appears on the Toronto Homeless Memorial.

being sent back there. In the case of Lisowick, there were no immediate family members to notice that he had simply vanished. Their status as social outcasts may well have been the reason Bruce McArthur targeted the two men, on the assumption that they were less likely to be missed and draw the attention of the police.

After killing twice in the space of three months, the serial killer is believed to have gone dormant, resurfacing on April 16, 2017, to murder 44-year-old Turkish immigrant Selim Esen. Those who knew him described Esen as a thoughtful, kind, and, above all, loving man. Esen was bound with rope prior to his death before being fatally strangled with a ligature.

Fortunately, another of McArthur's intended victims was able to get away. In 2017, Sean Cribbin arranged for a sexual liaison with the serial killer, agreeing to participate in BDSM fantasy scenarios at the latter's apartment. McArthur drugged him, and a disoriented, bewildered Cribbin regained consciousness to find the killer on top of him in the bedroom. It was only after detectives reached out to him that Cribbin was told that photos they had confiscated from the crime scene showed him unconscious, posed in a sexualized position, tied up, and with Bruce McArthur holding a ligature at his throat. Had it not been for McArthur's roommate returning home unexpectedly, there is no doubt that Cribbin would have become the next in the long string of murder victims.

McArthur's eighth and final murder took place two months later, on June 26, 2017. Andrew Kinsman, aged 49, was also bound and strangled by ligature. Kinsman's disappearance would ultimately lead to the capture of his killer. Unlike other victims of Bruce McArthur, Kinsman had a network of family, friends, and colleagues from the Toronto HIV/AIDS network who not only missed him but also went out and actively searched for him. Once he was declared missing and an official police search was launched, detectives looked for clues inside his home. A single calendar entry for June 26 read simply "BRUCE."

> Had it not been for McArthur's roommate returning home unexpectedly, there is no doubt that Cribbin would have become the next in the long string of murder victims.

They had a name. Now, the police had to get a description of their quarry. Officers went door to door in Kinsman's neighborhood, looking for any building equipped with CCTV security cameras. They scored a lucky break with one camera setup. It had captured footage of Kinsman getting into a red 2004 Dodge Caravan with an unidentified male driver. After cross-checking with official transportation records, detectives found just five such vehicles registered to somebody named Bruce.

That was all they needed to trace the van back to its owner, Bruce McArthur. To solidify matters further, McArthur was already known to police because he had been reported for trying to strangle a man in the back of his van in 2016. He had even been interviewed as part of the investigation into the men's disappearances and had ultimately been discounted as a suspect.

Although McArthur had sold the van for scrap, detectives were able to track it down and sweep it for DNA evidence. They found enough of it to justify a search warrant on McArthur's apartment, which was carried out in secret in order to avoid alerting him.

Unbelievably, as late as December of 2017, the Toronto police were still publicly denying the possibility of a serial killer being responsible for some of the men's disappearances. At the same time, they had already launched "Project Prism" in response to the disappearance of Selim Esen and Andrew Kinsman but claimed that it had nothing to do with the aforementioned Project Houston.

Unfortunately, they were wrong—and detectives were slowly closing in on the man in question.

On January 18, 2018, Bruce McArthur was set on killing his ninth victim, whose name has not been released to the public. The unidentified male went up to McArthur's apartment, stripped naked, and allowed himself to be handcuffed as part of a sex game. Taking no chances, police officers entered McArthur's apartment, interrupting the serial killer's attempt to further restrain his intended victim.

Finally, after eight years of killing with impunity, Bruce McArthur was taken into police custody.

McArthur worked as a landscaper and used his chosen profession to help dispose of his victims' remains. After dismembering the bodies, he concealed body parts in the garden of a house belonging to some of his unsuspecting customers. The house was an ordinary residence in an ordinary neighborhood. Its owners had no idea that their landscaper was quite literally planting evidence of his crimes on their property. Sometimes, he would mix and move the body parts around, for reasons known only to himself. McArthur also abandoned the remains of another victim in a ravine located nearby.

McArthur's day job as a landscaper offered fertile opportunity to bury the evidence of his less horticultural hobby.

The owners of the home had given the landscaper free, long-term use of their garage, in which he kept most of his gardening equipment and (unbeknownst to them) used it as a secure place to dismember the bodies of his victims. In return, they received free yard work. It seemed like a good deal on the face of things, and there was nothing about Bruce McArthur to ring any alarm bells. To all appearances, he was just a hard-working, blue-collar kind of guy making a living. At no time did his behavior or his demeanor suggest he might be anything more than that. They were stunned and horrified when police officers knocked at their door and explained the reason why they needed to go over the house and grounds with a fine-tooth comb. The planters filled with flowers that Bruce McArthur had so carefully placed in their back garden now appeared in a much more sinister light.

A search of McArthur's apartment turned up personal effects from some of his victims, which he presumably retained as keepsakes. There were also syringes, implying that he might have used drugs to incapacitate them. Forensic analysis of his van turned up DNA evidence, further linking the missing men to him.

Experts in digital forensics went through McArthur's computer hard drive and found numerous photographs of his carefully staged victims. Methodical by nature, he had created a separate file folder for each of the eight dead men.

As time goes on, cyberspace is becoming an increasingly important domain in the hunt for not just serial killers but also criminals of various other stripes. Bruce McArthur contacted his intended victims via social media platforms, dating sites, and apps such as Growlr, maintaining a back-and-forth conversation with them, luring them in, and then setting up a meeting in person. Law enforcement information technology experts found photographs of his anonymous ninth would-be victim on his hard drive and determined that he had been cyber-stalking the man on social media. Armed with this information, they were able to prevent his murder just in the nick of time; a ninth folder was found on the hard drive, ready to be filled with images of his intended victim.

In 2019, at the conclusion of his trial, the 67-year-old Bruce McArthur pled guilty to having committed eight murders. Inevitably, questions were asked regarding how he could have gotten away with murder for at least eight years. McArthur's relatively advanced age and grandfatherly manner helped him successfully lead a double life for years. Indeed, he even spent a spell working as a mall Santa, bouncing hundreds of children on his knee and asking them what they wanted for Christmas.

Those who grew up with Bruce McArthur recalled him as a clean-cut boy, one who sought the good favor of his teachers and was not beyond ratting out his schoolmates if he thought it was in his best interests to do so.

With the benefit of hindsight, there were some red flags, the most obvious of which came on Halloween of 2001, when the 50-year-old McArthur launched a savage and completely unprovoked attack upon a man named Mark Henderson. Interviewed by CTV news journalist Avery Haines, Henderson recalled the day McArthur battered him about the head with a metal pipe, fracturing his skull. The assault was severe enough that Henderson could easily have sustained brain damage or even been killed.

Difficult as it is to believe, Bruce McArthur was never sent to prison for this brutal crime. Instead, he was sentenced to probation and house arrest. Not only was this far too lenient a penalty for almost killing a complete stranger, but McArthur was also able to obtain a pardon 13 years later. This helped keep him off the radar during the police manhunt for Toronto's gay village murderer—and that may well have cost some of his victims their lives.

**In 2019, at the conclusion of his trial, the 67-year-old Bruce McArthur pled guilty to having committed eight murders.**

As part of his sentencing, McArthur was evaluated by a mental health professional in 2003, who declared with respect to his release: "We are confident to conclude that the risk for violence is very minimal." In terms of his mental status and potential for re-offending, he was given a completely clean bill of health.

Considering that this evaluation took place seven years prior to his first act of homicide, we can only conclude that either Bruce McArthur was an incredibly good actor, effortlessly pulling the wool over the eyes of a seasoned clinician, or that something changed significantly in his psychological makeup sometime between 2003 and 2010. The first conclusion seems the most likely.

Yet things aren't quite that clear-cut. Rather than try to escape police attention, McArthur turned himself in after the attack and admitted to it. While he couldn't say why he had committed the crime, the soon-to-be-killer at least had the moral fortitude to confess, hardly the action of a man trying to evade justice.

One of the most troubling aspects of Bruce McArthur's case is the unsolved question of exactly how many victims he killed. Although he was sentenced for murdering eight men, it must be pointed out that he began murdering very late in his lifetime—56, if he is to be believed.

Bruce McArthur (fourth from left) stands trial in Toronto for the murder of eight men.

It's unlikely that McArthur is telling the truth, however. Few serial killers start murdering in their fifties. The vast majority begin in their thirties, though there are outliers on either side. It's entirely possible that there are other victims that the police were never able to connect with him. Homicide detectives can only wonder: just how many others are there?

From McArthur's point of view, there would be no benefit to confessing and coming forward with the details of further murders. Yet there would also be no detriment. Now in his seventies, McArthur is guaranteed to die in prison. There is no possibility of parole or reduction of sentence. In short, he has nothing to gain and nothing to lose by confessing. Some people, if put in his position, would take the opportunity to clear their conscience. But if the crimes of Bruce McArthur teach us anything, it is that their perpetrator almost certainly *has* no conscience.

There is, at least, one small glimmer of light to be found, in the form of the owners of 53 Mallory Crescent, where the remains of McArthur's victims were recovered. In September 2018, its owners, Karen Fraser and Ron Smith, held a ceremony of cleansing and blessing at their home. The idea was to honor the memories of the dead men and to wash away the stain of Bruce McArthur's heinous acts as best they could. One can only hope that this service may have helped them finally rest in peace.

# AS GREEDY AS A PIG
# ROBERT "WILLIE" PICKTON

As with so many different lifestyles and professions, farmers have a common stereotype associated with them. Rising long before the sun and toiling hard in the fields all day long, theirs is a hard-working existence, the hallmarks of which are clean living, fresh air, and an affinity for agriculture. Often, farmers are credited with having great wisdom regarding the workings of nature, particularly the land, animal welfare, and the weather. (It's not for nothing that the *Farmer's Almanac* is still published and widely read, 230 years after it first appeared in 1792.)

Farmers also have a reputation for honesty, being completely upfront and forthright in their dealings. This was never less true than in the case of Canadian pig farmer Robert Pickton, who nonetheless used the image to his advantage when it came to covering up a string of horrific serial murders.

Robert Pickton was born in 1949, into a farming family. He was the middle child of three, with a sister named Linda born one year before him and a brother, David, one year after him. His parents, Louise and Leonard, were hard-working people and, by all accounts, fairly colorful individuals. As pig farmers, the Picktons were around dirt and manure all the time. Inevitably, they stank. The two brothers were mercilessly teased because of the way they looked and smelled. Kids can often be cruel, and it's likely that Robert developed a simmering resentment during his childhood that never went away. One is forced to wonder how much of the bullying he endured as a boy contributed to the brutal acts he would commit in later life.

Although they weren't desperately short of money, the Pickton family lived in relative squalor, wearing hand-me-down and homemade

Now considered a suburban part of the Vancouver, British Columbia, Port Coquitlam was a primarily agricultural area when the Picktons moved in. The Pickton Pig Farm sat near the scenic Pitt River, about a 35-minute drive from Vancouver's Downtown Eastside.

clothes. Robert struggled academically from an early age, another source of jibes and mockery from other children. He dropped out of school before graduation, choosing to work full time on the pig farm. The farmyard animals were, generally speaking, better company than children his own age.

The Pickton family moved to a new farm property in 1963, though they were fond enough of their original farmhouse that they took it along with them. The property, located in Port Coquitlam, would eventually be inherited by the three Pickton children, and operated by Robert and David. Growing up, they worked long hours on the farm, taking care of every aspect involved with tending to the pigs. This included butchery. Robert Pickton may have been many things, but squeamish was not one of them.

Everything in the Pickton household was covered in dirt and filth, including the kitchen surfaces where food was prepared. The family was just oblivious to it. Pigs wandered in and out of the house, urinating and defecating whenever and wherever the urge came upon them.

Author Stevie Cameron, writing in the *Toronto Star*, uncovered claims that Robert's father, Leonard, physically abused him during his formative years. If so, this violent treatment may have made an already difficult childhood even worse. As a youth, Robert Pickton (who went by the nickname "Willie") liked to keep to himself, and he had few friends. As he grew to adulthood, he also had little in the way of empathy for his fellow human beings—although he was better with children than he was with adults. Those who knew him recalled that he had an explosive temper when provoked.

Due to the combination of his smell and generally poor appearance, Pickton didn't have a girlfriend or long-term love interest. He did, however, use the services of prostitutes to meet his sexual needs. Hardly an attractive man, particularly when factoring in the pervasive smell of the pig farm that clung to him wherever he went, he also used money as a means of enticing women to come back with him to party. He paid for drugs and liquor, using both judiciously to get what he wanted. Robert Pickton wasn't interested in earning the love of a woman. He simply wanted to control them, use them, and when he was finished, discard them—sometimes permanently.

Like so many serial killers before and after him, Robert Pickton chose sex workers as his primary victim type. In his case, they were exclusively female, which matched his sexual preference. He picked up many of his victims in one of the poorest districts of the Downtown Eastside neighborhood of Vancouver, but he committed the actual murders back on the pig farm, away from prying eyes. The farm offered him privacy and a convenient means for disposing of the evidence. Most were coerced there with the promise of cash, getting drunk, getting high, or all three.

The Pickton pig farm, an expansive estate located on Dominion Avenue, would ultimately become the scene of Canada's largest and most expensive murder investigation.

The women Pickton targeted were always vulnerable in one way or another, either living on the streets, working in the sex trade, addicted to drugs or alcohol, or sometimes, all three at once. Some had a criminal history, which led them to avoid contact with the police whenever possible. Many were indigenous women, of Aboriginal descent. Throughout the 1990s, they began to disappear in increasing numbers, and they continued to do so in the early 2000s.

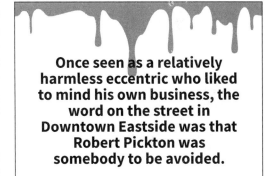

**Once seen as a relatively harmless eccentric who liked to mind his own business, the word on the street in Downtown Eastside was that Robert Pickton was somebody to be avoided.**

Inevitably, the women who made their living working the streets began to talk about the disappearances. Rumors of a possible serial killer stalking the area began to circulate among them. Some of the stories even mentioned the Pickton pig farm specifically. A few of the women had been known to have gone to party there before vanishing without a trace.

Then there was its proprietor. Once seen as a relatively harmless eccentric who liked to mind his own business, the word on the street in

Downtown Eastside was that Robert Pickton was somebody to be avoided. He was filthy, smelly, aggressive, and extremely erratic—the kind of john who one should only do business with as a last resort. But some of the sex workers continued to go with him, most likely because they were desperate. Hunger and addiction can often be sufficiently powerful motivators to overrule fear and good sense.

For several years, Robert Pickton was murdering the women who worked the Downtown Eastside sex trade. Pickton liked to strangle his victims after having had sex with them, though he wasn't above shooting them or cutting their throat with a blade. Another method he favored was injecting his victims with chemical solutions such as antifreeze and windshield washer fluid, which caused fatal cardiac dysrhythmias. Once they were dead, he would hang their body from a chain and saw it up, as he would a slaughtered pig, draining all of the blood in the process and removing some of the organs. The leftovers were fed to the pigs.

Robert Pickton killed with relative impunity until March 23, 1997. Taking one sex worker back to his farm, as he had done so many times before, Pickton got significantly more than he bargained for. It is likely that the serial killer had grown complacent and lazy, because he failed to anticipate that this particular lady might put up a fight.

Female sex workers throughout the region were all too aware that their friends and coworkers had been vanishing without a trace over the last few years. A law enforcement task force was convened to investigate the disappearances but came up empty-handed. Most of these women were now on their guard—but still, some continued to take Pickton up on his offers.

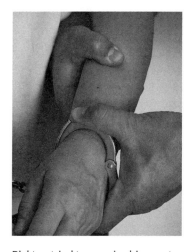

Pickton tried to surprise his guest with a little unannounced bondage, who surprised him in return by fighting back.

Shortly after he and his hired companion arrived at the farm, the pair had sex. Pickton was no stranger to her. They had already traded sexual favors for drugs. What she did not expect was for him to produce a pair of handcuffs and snap one of the cuffs on her wrist. She resisted, causing an enraged Pickton to pull out a kitchen knife and stab her repeatedly in the stomach. Despite what must have been excruciating pain and significant internal blood loss, she nonetheless put up a fight, snatching up a knife of her own and turning it on her attacker. Swinging the knife wildly, she scored a lucky hit with the blade, slicing his throat open with the blade. He began to bleed out.

With Pickton now wounded himself, the tables had truly turned. The serial killer saw no choice but to seek medical care. Every gunshot wound and stabbing that is treated in a hospital must be reported to the police, which left Pickton with some difficult questions to answer after the physicians in the emergency department stabilized him. His intended victim had gotten away and screamed for help, somehow making it out onto the street. Two passing motorists stopped to help the blood-splattered, seminaked woman, horrified to see that one of her wrists had a set of handcuffs dangling from it.

As fate would have it, she was treated for her severe injuries in the same hospital as Robert Pickton. The police soon made a connection between the two stabbings—particularly when they found a handcuff key in his possession, which just happened to open the cuffs that were still locked onto the wounded woman's wrist.

> **His defense attorney was prepared to cast the victim as the attacker, asserting that Pickton had in fact been the one to be assaulted....**

One would think that this would be the very definition of an open and shut case. Instead, as is seen so often with serial killers, Robert Pickton appeared to have the luck of the devil. His defense attorney was prepared to cast the victim as the attacker, asserting that Pickton had in fact been the one to be assaulted—after he had given a crazed hitchhiker a ride, from the sheer goodness of his heart. The fact that the true victim in the case had a history of drug use and arrests would have damaged her credibility in the eyes of the judge. She was also so afraid of her attacker that she was unwilling to testify. Pickton's version of events ultimately won out in the courtroom, and he was allowed to walk free—free to kill again.

Law enforcement and the legal system had several opportunities to end Robert Pickton's long string of murders. In addition to the botched opportunity to jail him after his 1997 knife attack, an acquaintance of Pickton's told a friend that she had seen a human body hanging from a chain in the slaughterhouse (although she refused to talk about it with the police at first). Another of Pickton's "friends" (to use the term loosely) knew about a stash of illegal guns he kept in his trailer and took that information to the police. It would ultimately prove to be Pickton's undoing.

It was February 2002, and the police finally had sufficient grounds to obtain a warrant to search the pig farm, due to the serious firearms allegations. In the same way that the gangster Al Capone was finally brought down due to tax evasion, in the end, serial killer Robert Pickton was collared because of his penchant for keeping guns.

Once detectives started searching the farm, it didn't take them long to locate the weapons their informant had told them about. Yet these were the least shocking of the discoveries they made at the pig farm. Their search turned up articles of clothing and personal effects of women that the police officers knew had gone missing over the past few years. Some of the items were even marked with the names of their owners. Amongst the jumbled mess, they also found a plethora of sex toys, restraints, and bloodstained handcuffs, suggesting that something sinister was going on. What had started out as a firearms bust had now become something more, and it would require a painstaking search of the entire farm property. It was to become a massive undertaking.

As the days-long search turned into weeks and then months, investigators found large numbers of blood stains spread across various surfaces, in places both obvious and hidden. DNA testing showed that the blood belonged to a number of missing women. Blood was also discovered on many of the victims' personal items, which Pickton had foolishly kept, either as trophies or because he was simply too lazy to throw them out.

There is a common fallacy, made popular by movies such as Guy Ritchie's *Snatch*, that claims that pigs will completely devour a human body, leaving not a single trace. The character of Brick Top, a crime lord played by Alan Ford, delivers this memorable speech: "You need at least sixteen pigs to finish the job in one sitting. They will go through a man that weighs two hundred pounds in about eight minutes. That means that a single pig can consume two pounds of uncooked flesh every minute. Hence the expression, 'as greedy as a pig.'"

This tends to be the part of the speech that viewers remember long after having seen the movie, but many forget that Brick Top also advises that the teeth must be pulled out and the hair sheared off first.

Teeth, hair, and bones were part of the biological evidence Vancouver Police found at the pig farm.

That wasn't all. When officers looked in the freezer, they found a bucket containing a frozen human head. Shortly after, they found a second head. Each head had been sawn in half, as though an anatomist had been creating a display specimen. Pickton had almost certainly used a power tool to make the cuts.

Alongside the two heads were two pairs of hands and feet. Subsequent forensic examination would confirm that these were the partial remains of two of the missing women, and that each had been shot in the back of the head with a .22-caliber bullet.

The vast majority of pigs on this planet are destined for human consumption. Given the chance, they're more than happy to return the favor.

At the very least, two of the missing women had now been found, and detectives had their confirmation that murder had indeed taken place at the Pickton pig farm.

One of the more disturbing facets of the Pickton case is that he supplied pork meat to the general public … meat that was almost certainly tainted with the remains of some of his victims. We can only wonder how many unsuspecting customers ate contaminated food without knowing it.

The capture of Robert Pickton may have brought closure to some of the families of the missing women, but many of them were angered by the way the Vancouver Police Department had conducted their investigation. Rumors had been circulating for years among members of the sex worker community about a farm in Port Coquitlam that had plenty of drugs and alcohol available if you went there. The existence of the pig farm as a place to go and party was well known, and despite its reputation as being dilapidated and creepy, there had been no shortage of women willing to go there to get high and unwind. The general feeling was that police should have intervened sooner.

Once detectives had gathered all the forensic and crime-scene evidence they could from the farm—they ultimately found DNA from 33 different women—the property was demolished and fenced off. Today, it is virtually unrecognizable, bordered by several business and housing developments.

Robert's brother David, the co-owner of the pig farm, strenuously denied all knowledge of the murders being committed on their shared property.

Initially, Pickton denied knowing anything about the disappearances and proclaimed himself totally innocent of any of the murders. Uncertainty exists over the number of women that Robert Pickton killed. Although he was initially charged with 26 murders, he claimed to a prison cellmate that he was responsible for 49, adding smugly that his target was an even 50. (Pickton, hardly the smartest of individuals, had no idea that his cellmate was in fact an undercover police officer who was subtly encouraging him to confess.)

It is certainly feasible that Robert Pickton could have killed 49 women. This may be one of those cases in which a captured serial killer

Robert Pickton is depicted in the prisoner's box during his trial during the presentation of evidence.

was actually telling the truth about his crimes, although he slyly refused to make a formal confession.

At the culmination of his trial in 2008, the 56-year-old Pickton was convicted on six counts of second-degree murder and was sentenced to life imprisonment. The remaining 20 murder charges were not pursued.

Yet Pickton contradicted himself in 2016 in a book he wrote and sold entitled *Pickton in His Own Words!* The manuscript was smuggled out of prison, sent to the United States, and published by a small press based in Colorado. The book, which might more charitably called a confused, jumbled work of fiction, claims that Pickton was innocent of the murders. Instead, he cast himself as the victim once more (just as he claimed to be after his would-be stabbing victim escaped), wrongly accused and persecuted by the police. Once again, he fails to accept a shred of responsibility for the atrocities he committed over the span of almost three decades. Shortly after the book went on sale, it was pulled from the catalog by the online retailer Amazon.

Allegedly abused by his father as a boy, Robert Pickton was continually ridiculed by other children. He found himself ostracized from everyone but his siblings, an outcast during the years in which every child desperately needs healthy social interaction. How much did this contribute to his becoming a serial killer?

Even so, many children are raised in similarly difficult environments and do not go on to become serial killers. What was it about Robert Pickton that drove him to commit the vile, depraved acts that he did? If he had been raised under more stable, nurturing conditions, would he still have developed a penchant for sadism and murder, or would things have turned out differently?

To make an already terrible case worse, under the terms of his sentencing, Pickton could conceivably walk free on parole in 2027. However, he is so greatly reviled by the Canadian people that his chances of doing so are remote. He would also be in his 70s by that time, and Pickton would likely have much to fear from those who harbor a desire for retribution. Any chance at freedom would mean, at the very best, a life spent looking over his shoulder for the past to catch up with him.

# SLAY AT RANDOM
# ISRAEL KEYES

I t isn't difficult to understand the fascination so many of us have for the serial killer. It's not that we admire them. We recognize the abhorrence, the sheer repugnance of the things that they do. So, why do we find their stories so compelling on a primal, visceral level?

One possible reason is that we seek to understand them, because in understanding, there is often safety. In an increasingly uncertain world, one that seems less stable with every passing week, we naturally crave that safety and the feeling of security that accompanies it. If we can comprehend the serial killer as completely as we possibly can, we tell ourselves, then we can learn how to spot them, anticipate them, and avoid them. We can figure out how they select their victims, the techniques they use while stalking them, and understand the ways in which they strike.

Unfortunately for us, all too many serial killers are not that predictable. While they may act in a rational way—according to their own sense of internal logic, no matter how twisted it may be—some of their number lash out at random. They follow no easily discernible pattern. It is this sheer randomness that is most frightening, because there is no real defense against it.

Enter Israel Keyes.

Israel Keyes was born in Utah in 1978 to Mormon parents. The Keyes family was large, consisting of ten children. Mormonism is a family-centric religion, but Keyes's parents, John and Heidi, ultimately grew disillusioned with the faith and converted to a rather more militant branch of Christianity instead.

Fundamentalist beliefs prompted the elder Keyeses to disconnect from modern society and move their ten children to remote Washington State.

Whether it came to politics, religion, science, or any number of other subjects, it's fair to say that John and Heidi Keyes held somewhat radical beliefs. The conveniences of modern living that we all take for granted, such as electrical appliances and other forms of technology, were anathema to them. They believed in living simply, and after relocating from Utah to Washington, they raised their family in a compact little cabin in the woods.

The Keyes family moved from state to state several times during Israel's formative years. All ten children were educated by their parents. Although home schooling has a certain stigma associated with it, subsequent evaluation of Israel Keyes revealed that he was of above average intelligence.

For entertainment, Israel and his siblings spent many hours hunting in the woods around their home. If his account is to be believed, young Israel was a talented hunter, relishing the process of stalking his prey before moving in for the kill. It was a skill set that he would one day turn upon human beings. Israel also had a taste for torturing animals, which was very clearly a portent of things to come.

As a teenager, he developed a taste for petty crime, primarily theft and vandalism. Some may write this off as being little more than a case of "boys will be boys," but Israel's misadventures all seemed to have one thing in common: guns.

Like many an outdoorsman, he was fascinated by guns. He was skilled with a rifle, an adept shot. He honed his marksmanship skills by taking pot-shots at the homes and property of his neighbors. Keyes took great delight in shooting out windows. As he got older, he also grew more daring, and he graduated from using the homes of strangers for target practice to breaking in and burglarizing them. This was how he added to his ever-expanding cache of guns.

It is entirely normal for a child to rebel against their parents, and in that regard, Israel Keyes was no exception. His parents' hard-core Christian beliefs had grown even more firmly entrenched as they grew older, and that became a big point of friction between them and their son. The religion that the Keyes subscribed to advocated the tenets of white supremacism; indeed, the sect, known as "Christian Identity," really wasn't Christianity at all, in anything other than name. It could better be described as a fundamentalist, racist cult, and one whose influence is currently on the decline.

Israel not only renounced his parents' chosen religion, but he actually went one better: Keyes began to express a belief in Satanism, though how serious this conviction was is open to debate. He may simply have been a dabbler, rather than a serious student, but in any case, it did begin to inform his manner of thinking.

The only real source we have for gleaning information on Keyes's state of mind and thought process is the comments he made to detectives and FBI investigators after his capture. As such, they should be treated with caution. It is fair to say, however, that during his interviews, Israel Keyes came across as blunt and forthright, a man with no real reason to lie to his interrogators. Indeed, he would even come forward and confess to murders that he might otherwise have gotten away with.

> **Israel Keyes's MO was a bizarre mix of random victim selection, in-depth planning, and thorough preparation.**

Israel Keyes's MO was a bizarre mix of random victim selection, in-depth planning, and thorough preparation. The men and women he killed meant nothing to him personally. They had no more of a meaningful connection to him than did the average person passing by in the street. For Keyes, it was simply an exercise in cold-blooded killing, and the identity of the victim or victims was secondary to the nature of the crime itself.

Keyes worked as a general contractor, moving from state to state from one employment opportunity to another. Yet he also had a secret life as a bank robber, the proceeds from which he used to travel around the United States. No matter what else he was doing, his mind was always focused upon murder, which for him equated to the meaning of life.

As he traveled to new parts of the country, Keyes put together kidnap and murder kits, which he would then stash in secluded places, where they were unlikely to be discovered. They contained zip ties, pistols, silencers, duct tape, and sometimes tools used for the disposal of bodies. There were also rolls of cash, which would allow him to make a rapid getaway from the area once his victims were dead—and be much harder to trace than credit card receipts would have been.

As previously mentioned, although he may have outwardly seemed like an unsophisticated individual due to his nontraditional upbringing and education, Israel Keyes was both smart and cunning. He did everything within his power to avoid detection and capture while committing his murders. He would often fly into a major airport, then hire a rental car and drive long distances to reach his next victim. This prevented him from ever establishing a geographic pattern, which would have allowed his movements to be plotted by law enforcement. The technique was remarkably successful.

Israel Keyes became used to killing animals in the great outdoors and began to fantasize about the possibility of doing the same thing to a human being. By the late 1990s, he had read about occult ritualistic killings and had developed a desire to carry one out for himself.

If Keyes is to be believed, he came close to killing his first victim in Oregon. She was floating down the Deschutes River on a tube. Heedless of the fact that it was broad daylight, Keyes splashed out into the water and snatched the unsuspecting young woman. This was a brazen kidnapping, one that could very easily have resulted in Keyes being seen and captured in the process. Had this been the case, a spell behind bars may have dampened his taste for abduction, rape, and murder. We can only speculate.

Keyes raped his teenage victim in a toilet, bound her, and prepared to kill her in a ritualistic way. Somehow, she managed to convince him not to go through with the murder, and incredibly, he ended up releasing his captive. He would later tell investigators that he regretted his initial lack of ruthlessness and would never make that mistake again.

It was around this time that he enlisted in the U.S. Army. He did a three-year hitch as an infantry soldier, assigned to the 25th Infantry Division as a mortar team member. He did not see combat but did spend one deployment overseas in Egypt.

The time Keyes spent in the military undoubtedly helped him refine his natural killing tendencies with discipline and new techniques.

His period of military service was unremarkable, and he returned to civilian life in much the same state that he had entered the service—with perhaps one exception.

All branches of the military place great emphasis on paying close attention to detail, and this quality is something that is trained into every service member during their initial and continuation training. It is possible that the meticulous planning with which Israel Keyes carried out his murders was instilled, or perhaps simply sharpened, during this period of his life.

By 2007 Israel Keyes had settled down to life in Anchorage, Alaska, with his girlfriend and his daughter from a former relationship. To all appearances, he seemed like a hard-working man trying to provide for his family.

He ran his own small business, working as a handyman and contractor. He took care of odd jobs, repairs, and low-end construction projects. Keyes had a reputation for being a hard worker who was reliable, dependable, and would get the job done for a fair price. Several of his clients were affluent, living in large houses. If any of them noticed that there was something strange about their hired contractor, they never came forward.

**The police officer in question had no idea just how close to death they had been while out on a routine patrol.**

His murderous impulses remained as strong as ever, but Keyes knew when to rein them in. During an interview with federal investigators, he recalled having come within a hair's breadth of shooting a police officer in an Anchorage park. He lay in concealment and was drawing a bead on the cop when a second officer arrived on scene. Not liking the odds of gunning them both down and being able to make a clean getaway, Keyes chose to slip away instead. The police officer in question had no idea just how close to death they had been while out on a routine patrol.

This survival instinct is by no means unique to Israel Keyes, but it does illustrate the fact that, despite his willingness to take coldly calculated risks in order to fulfill his lust for murder, he also knew when to step back and live to kill another day.

Based on retroactive tracking of his movements and statements that he would later make while in custody, it is believed that Keyes killed 11 or 12 victims in different parts of the United States before he was finally captured. We know the details regarding only three.

In 2011, Israel Keyes committed a double murder in Essex, Vermont. This was not his first time visiting the area. In the spring of 2009, he had flown there and concealed a murder kit, burying it in the ground at a marked location. It was nothing fancy: a plastic bucket from Home Depot, containing a silenced pistol plus ammunition, zip ties, and duct tape. The lethal cache sat undisturbed for two years, until Keyes returned on June 7, 2011, and dug it up.

Keyes made the journey in stages, flying into Chicago's busy O'Hare Airport, renting a car, and driving hundreds of miles to Vermont. He had the option of flying from O'Hare into the nearby Burlington International Airport but preferred to travel by road instead. His rationale was that when the murders he was about to commit were investigated, the police might well scour the passenger manifests of all flights that had come in and out of Burlington in the days before and afterward. Detecting somebody driving alone in a car, however, would be a much more difficult task. The long drive also gave Keyes an opportunity to turn the plan over in his head, looking for potential weaknesses and vulnerabilities.

Once he arrived in the area where he had buried his kill stash, he checked into a budget hotel and got some rest. The following evening, the former soldier went on a reconnaissance mission, scouting out potential targets. After sauntering around and getting the lay of the land, Keyes made his choice. The victims he selected were a married couple named Bill and Lorraine Currier, both of whom were in their fifties.

The Curriers were well-liked by their neighbors, two friendly and loving people about whom nobody seemed to have a bad word to say. They did not have any enemies, which made their disappearance a puzzling one for detectives to investigate. As things turned out, the only reason Israel Keyes targeted them was the location of their house. It was set apart from others, with no neighboring homes close by. Keyes reasoned that this would reduce his chances of being seen coming or going from the property and that any struggle would be less likely to be heard.

On the night of June 8, Keyes watched the house carefully. He waited for the lights to go out, suggesting that the occupants had gone to bed. He would have seen both Bill and Lorraine return home from work earlier that evening and deduced that the middle-aged couple were the only occupants of the house. There were no children for him to contend with. After dark, Keyes cut the landline to the house, ensuring that nobody would be able to call 911 unless they had a cell phone.

Sometime after midnight, Keyes broke into the garage and, from there, made entry into the house. Just as he anticipated, the couple were asleep in their bed. They were taken completely by surprise when he

charged into their bedroom, wielding a silenced handgun. He was able to overpower
and restrain them both, then used their own
car to drive them to a deserted farmhouse
several miles away.

Once inside the house, Keyes battered the struggling Bill Currier with a
shovel, then shot him several times with the
pistol he'd recovered from his kill cache.
Once Bill was dead, Keyes turned his attention to Lorraine, raping Lorraine repeatedly
before fatally strangling her in front of the
dead body of her husband.

By the time both Curriers were dead,
it was almost sunrise. Keyes sealed both of
their bodies inside trash bags and left them
in the basement of the house, after using

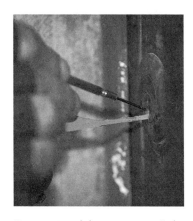

Keyes entered the property quietly
through the garage to sneak in on
the sleeping Curriers in their bedroom.

chemicals to burn off their faces and fingerprints to prevent identification when they were discovered—*if* they were discovered. In fact, they
never were. The farm was torn down, and no sign of Lorraine and Bill
Currier was ever reported by the demolition workers. By the time Israel
Keyes was in custody and confessed to the killing, the lot on which the
farmhouse had once stood was completely empty.

At the time of writing, despite the best efforts of the FBI, the
bodies of Bill and Lorraine Currier have never been located. It is highly
unlikely that they ever will be. Indeed, we only have the word of Israel
Keyes that he was responsible for their deaths. But his story had the
ring of truth about it, and the FBI agents who quizzed him were left in
no doubt that he bore full responsibility for their murder. The devil, as
always, was in the details. Keyes told them matter of factly that he had
tossed the pistol used to murder the Curriers in a lake and gave them
the location. Sure enough, when police divers searched the lakebed, they
found it exactly where Keyes had said they would.

If Keyes had stuck to his modus operandi, maintaining his habit
of traveling long distances to procure a murder victim, it is highly likely
that he would have continued to fly under the radar of law enforcement
for a long time—possibly for many years (and therefore, many victims).
When he was finally caught, it was due to the serial killer's classic neme-
sis: sloppiness.

While going about his daily routine in Anchorage, Keyes encountered a barista named Samantha Koenig. The 18-year-old was working

at a coffee stand when she caught the serial killer's eye on February 1, 2012. Koenig was not chosen as a victim based upon her physical appearance, her age, or any factor other than the particular stand at which she worked. Keyes had scoped out several other coffee stands as potential abduction sites before settling on that one. It was truly a case of being in the wrong place at the wrong time.

It was late in the evening when Keyes made his approach. The fact that he was wearing a ski mask would have alarmed some, but then again, this was Alaska in February—it was cold. When Samantha had finished making his coffee, Keyes kidnapped her at gunpoint. He stole what cash there was in the register, stuffing it into his pockets while keeping his eyes on his victim.

> **His plan was to use Koenig's own car as a getaway vehicle. The one problem with this was that she didn't have one.**

His plan was to use Koenig's own car as a getaway vehicle. The one problem with this was that she didn't have one. He had brought zip ties with him and used them to bind her hands together. Now he had no choice but to make his victim walk.

Knowing that this was her one chance for freedom, Samantha bolted out into the street and ran for her life. Unfortunately, Keyes was faster. He overpowered her and once again threatened her with the pistol. Had she truly suspected that she was in the hands of a killer, it is likely that Samantha Koenig would have run, screamed, or tried to fight back. Knowing this, Keyes lied to her, telling her that she was being taken hostage and would be released once her family paid him a ransom. Forced to choose whether to run or fight while looking down the barrel of a gun being held by a masked man is almost no choice at all. Koenig would have wanted to believe her abductor was telling the truth, and so, she did.

Plan B was for Keyes to use his own personal vehicle for the abduction. It was an anonymous-looking Silverado pickup truck. He had taken the precaution of unscrewing and removing the vehicle's license plates earlier that day, which made it next to impossible for any potential onlookers to identify the truck but did increase his chances of being stopped by the police if they noticed the lack of plates. He decided that it was worth the risk and bundled Samantha inside the cab.

The next part of Keyes's master plan was to convince Koenig's nearest and dearest that there was nothing wrong with her disappearance. Using her own cell phone, the killer sent texts to her boyfriend and to her boss, claiming that she was just going away for the weekend.

There was some truth to Keyes's story about wanting money. His murder trips were partially funded by theft, after all, and now he saw an opportunity to make more cash with minimal effort. Demanding his victim's ATM card, Keyes was surprised to learn that Koenig had left it in her truck at home. Going there to retrieve it would be an extremely risky thing to do, but that's exactly what he opted for, while Koenig was left tied up in Keyes's own tool shed.

It was an uncharacteristically foolish move on his part, but it paid off—financially, at least. He was able to get the ATM card, but he was interrupted by the appearance of Koenig's boyfriend, who was shocked to find a masked stranger rummaging around in their truck. Keyes fled, taking the card with him. He had already forced Koenig to give the PIN for it, and Keyes used the card to make a cash withdrawal from a nearby ATM. The cash machine's camera snapped a picture of a masked and hooded male taking out money from Koenig's account.

Keyes's victim was still there in his shed when he returned home to check on her. Keyes sexually assaulted Samantha Koenig and then strangled her, locking her body inside the shed. He had somewhere to be: a cruise ship, to be precise. Collecting his suitcase from inside his home, Keyes headed for the airport and caught a flight to New Orleans.

For the next two weeks, Israel Keyes enjoyed a luxury vacation, living the high life on the high seas. This was partially funded by the money he had stolen from Samantha Koenig's checking account. When he returned, her body was still exactly where he had left it. It was February 17. Despite Koenig's having been dead for 14 days, Keyes carefully positioned her body in such a way that it appeared she was still alive. He sewed open her eyes and positioned a copy of the *Anchorage Daily News*, dated February 13, alongside her. Then he took a photograph, which was intended to be a "proof of life" image designed to reassure her family that she was still among the living.

While his latest victim languished in death, the killer sailed off to live the high life.

With the benefit of hindsight, the knowledge that the young lady in the picture had been violated and murdered long before it was taken is gut-wrenching. Yet it is easy to see how people could have been conned into thinking that Samantha Koenig was still alive. The glassy-eyed stare and deadpan expression on her face is totally understandable when taken in the context of somebody who was taken hostage and held against her will.

The photograph formed the basis of a ransom demand for $30,000, which Koenig's parents promptly paid. At her kidnapper's insistence, the money was placed into Koenig's own bank account. Keyes had no further use for Samantha Koenig. He cut up her body and disposed of the dismembered remains in Matanuska Lake. The lake was frozen over, and Keyes dropped the body parts through a hole in the ice. Law enforcement operatives would recover her remains six weeks later, after her killer used a digital map to indicate the area in which they should search.

Now that the balance of Koenig's account was significantly boosted, Keyes used her ATM card to make cash withdrawals. This was now a federal kidnapping case, and the FBI had gotten involved. Practically all ATMs are fitted with cameras, which are triggered when the machine is used—particularly to withdraw money. FBI agents tracked withdrawals as they were made from different locations across the United States, beginning in Alaska and then moving to states such as New Mexico, Arizona, and Texas.

Despite his methodical behavior when it came to committing murder, Israel Keyes slipped up when he made an ATM transaction in Texas. He had rented a Ford Focus, which was partially visible in the ATM camera's field of vision. This gave law enforcement their first major clue as to who they should be looking for. A keen-eyed Texas police officer, who had been primed to be on the lookout for a white Focus, spotted Keyes driving along the highway and pulled him over to the side of the road.

A search of the Ford turned up Samantha Koenig's phone and ATM card. There was also a makeshift face mask, suitable for disguising Keyes's face whenever he made a cash withdrawal—or carried out a robbery. The game was finally up. Israel Keyes was taken into police custody and flown back to Alaska.

Keyes was held behind bars in Anchorage, where he showed a surprising willingness to talk about certain aspects of his crimes—but only to a point.

FBI agents who interviewed Keyes in an attempt to uncover the true extent of his murder spree were struck by how nonchalant he was when discussing them. Some criminals like to feign remorse, usually to generate sympathy on the part of both the authorities and the public. Not so Israel Keyes, who wasn't the least bit sorry about what he had done. He told his interviewers that if he had not been caught, he would simply have kept on killing for as long as he possibly could.

When asked what his intentions were in the event that he had not gotten caught, Keyes claimed that he was getting ready to leave Anchorage and begin traveling across the United States on a prolonged, long-distance journey—one that would have seen him commit widespread murder along the way.

With the FBI eager to question him in depth about his exploits, it would not be long before the captured Keyes found a way to permanently disappoint them.

In custody, Keyes walked a fine line between effusively talking about the three killings that law enforcement could definitely pin on him and slyly alluding to other potential murders, while providing little in the way of specifics. We can only speculate whether this was because it gave Keyes a feeling of empowerment knowing things that the FBI and police did not (quite likely, now that his freedom was going to be permanently taken from him) or because he planned to use that information as a bargaining chip for a possible future plea deal.

The FBI was denied the opportunity to learn more from Israel Keyes when, on December 2, 2012, he strangled himself with a bedsheet inside his cell. To improve his chances of the suicide attempt being successful, he also slit his own wrists. It worked. By the time corrections officers found him, he was dead. He was 34 years old, and although law enforcement had him down as a solid suspect for a minimum of three murders (and there were almost certainly many more), he had been convicted of none. He was due to be tried for murder in March 2013.

A search of Keyes's cell revealed several pages of scribbled notes and attempts at poetry, all written on the same blood-soaked notepad. This included lines such as:

VIOLENT METAMORPHOSIS,

EMERGE MY DARK MOTH PRINCESS,

COME OFTEN, AND WORSHIP ON THE ALTAR OF YOUR FLESH,

YOU SHUDDER, AND TRY TO SHRINK FAR FROM ME.

I'LL HAVE YOU TIED DOWN AND BEGGING TO BECOME MY SWEETIE.

I LOOKED IN YOUR EYES,

THEY WERE SO DARK, WARM, AND TRUSTING,

AS THOUGH YOU HAD NOT A WORRY OR CARE.

THE MORE GUILELESS THE GAME, THE BETTER POTENTIAL TO FILL UP THOSE POOLS WITH YOUR FEAR.

While not nearly as graphic as the writing of killers such as Gerard Schaefer, who is covered elsewhere in this book, Keyes's attempts at literary penmanship follow similarly dark themes. The writings of Israel Keyes offer a window into a diseased and dangerous mind.

It is impossible to say for sure when Israel Keyes first began to kill, though most experts agree that the murders began in his early twenties. He admitted to having killed eight victims, but the FBI agents who investigated his case suspected that this number may have been low. Following his death in jail, the FBI lost its number one resource for gathering information on the Keyes murders. Any further breaks in the case, if there are any, will almost certainly take years to come to light and may require a significant stroke of good fortune to occur.

> The secret life of Israel Keyes lasted for approximately 14 years. He was able to successfully pull the wool over the eyes of those who knew him....

The secret life of Israel Keyes lasted for approximately 14 years. He was able to successfully pull the wool over the eyes of those who knew him, playing the part of a father, boyfriend, soldier, and blue-collar working man, while simultaneously being a cold, calculating rapist and serial murderer.

Israel Keyes killed for one reason, and one reason alone: he liked it. He enjoyed the thrill of the hunt, the adrenaline rush he got from taking an innocent human life, and the satisfaction that came with the knowledge that he had gotten away with it.

He really did lead a double life. One of the rules by which Keyes abided was an absolute refusal to abuse or murder children. He had a child of his own, and the idea of harming another child repelled him. On the other hand, he thought nothing of raping and murdering adults. By all accounts, he was a loving boyfriend and father, and while it may conform to a stereotype, those who knew him really were shocked when his murderous activities finally came to light. They had difficulty equating the hard-working family man with the sadistic psychopath brought to light by the media. Indeed, when he finally made a partial confession, it was on the condition that his daughter would be shielded as much as possible from learning about the killings for which he was responsible. Israel Keyes, the man who got his kicks by coldly raping, beating, and killing a stranger, could not bear the thought of his daughter thinking of him as a bad guy.

After his suicide, a private funeral was held for Keyes. His mother and four of his sisters were in attendance. When eulogizing the deceased, a pastor will traditionally deliver a message of forgiveness and comfort. Not so in this case. The pastor, chosen by Heidi Keyes (Israel's mother), stated: "He is not in a better place. He is in a place of eternal torment."

It is doubtful that the families of Israel Keyes's victims would disagree. Now that Keyes is dead and gone, we are left with the lingering question of just how many others he killed. If he is to be believed, seven or eight more victims are still to be discovered. Despite the best efforts of law enforcement agencies, who followed Keyes's trail across the United States and looked into unexplained disappearances and cold cases along the way, there is no way to be sure how many families are still waiting for closure that will never come.

# THE GREEN RIVER KILLER
# GARY RIDGWAY

To the south of Seattle, Washington, lies the Green River. Some 65 miles long, for many years this waterway was relatively unknown to all but those who lived in its vicinity. All that changed in 1982, when the bodies of murdered women started turning up there.

What came to be known as the Green River killings took place between 1982 and 1984. Although the first victims were found floating in the river, subsequent bodies were discovered in other locations. The killer's MO was fairly consistent: he left each body naked, or nearly naked. The cause of death was strangulation.

The murderer eluded justice for many years, and at the time, the Green River killings came to be known as the worst unsolved serial murder case in U.S. history.

Gary Ridgway was born on February 18, 1949. His family lived in Salt Lake City, Utah, at that time, and relocated to Washington State ten years later. He was the middle child of three brothers. Ridgway's father worked blue-collar jobs, often as a truck driver. Years later, his son Gary would work in the paint shop of a truck manufacturing company, where his exacting attention to detail made him a natural fit for applying the more finicky, detail-oriented parts of the paint scheme.

Ridgway's mother was a housewife, and much of her time was devoted to raising him and his two siblings. Theirs was, by all accounts, not a particularly happy marriage. The couple argued incessantly, and the ire of Mary Rita Ridgway was directed at young Gary every bit as much as it was his father.

Greg, Gary's older brother, tended to outperform him in most things. Through no fault of his own, Gary lacked his brother's level of natural intelligence, and he struggled to keep up with him. It was a losing battle, for the most part, but Gary dealt with it as best he could. He was never going to be the most popular sibling, and certainly not the smartest, but he seemed to get on well with other kids his own age.

In school, Ridgway struggled somewhat, partially because of a learning disability. He was held back twice, which he found both frustrating and stigmatizing, especially at such a formative age.

Many male serial killers have a problem relating to females, but Gary Ridgway found the opposite sex easy enough to talk to. Dating was no great challenge to him, and he had a girlfriend more often than not. When his schoolmates and girlfriends talked about him afterward, many noted that he never really stood out as being an awkward kid.

Under the surface, however, he was already showing some of the classic signs of the serial killer he would one day become. He was a chronic bedwetter, and after each nocturnal incident, he endured the humiliation of having his mother wash off his genitals with warm, soapy water. This went on into his early teens, long past the time when a child would have been expected to outgrow it. Interviewed by a forensic psychologist after his capture, Ridgway would profess to have hated his mother so much that he wanted to kill her, which may have contributed to his homicidal behavior in later life.

His fantasies about harming his mother were graphic, varied, and extremely detailed. He constructed a slew of scenarios inside his head, hypothetical situations in which he could cut his mother, stab her, burn her, and inflict the most painful torture imaginable. Conversely, he also had a bizarre sexual attraction to her that he could not ignore. The lust he felt for his mother was constantly at war with the rage he felt toward her. These two opposing forces were always at conflict within Gary Ridgway and almost certainly impacted the way he treated other women as he grew older.

The troubled youth took his anger out in many ways, from low-grade mischief to animal abuse to, eventually, attempted murder.

Despite his relatively normal-seeming exterior, young Gary had a private life that would have shocked those who knew about it. He enjoyed starting fires and got off on torturing or killing small animals, usually domesticated pets. By far the worst incident took place when he was 16 years old. Out for a walk one day, he encountered a six-year-old boy who was playing by himself. Ridgway asked the boy, who was dressed as a cowboy, if he wanted to go and build a fort. The pair went off into the woods together. Once they were out of sight, Ridgway took a pen knife out of his pocket and calmly stabbed the child in the upper abdomen, puncturing his liver.

The wound hemorrhaged significantly. Ridgway stood laughing, watching the blood pour out of his victim. "I always wanted to know what it felt like to kill somebody," he said, before walking off and leaving the boy to die. Fortunately, the boy survived. His attacker was never caught.

Gary Ridgway obviously meant to kill him but did not stick around to make sure that he was successful. Had the child bled to death, he would have been the first of many victims to lose their life at Ridgway's hands.

After leaving school, he enlisted in the U.S. Navy. The Vietnam War was still happening, and Ridgway was deployed there, coming under fire in combat on more than one occasion. It was while in the Navy that he first began to frequent prostitutes. This was not necessarily unusual behavior for a sailor deployed in a war zone, but he continued to do so once he was honorably discharged and returned to the civilian world. Presumably his new wife had no idea that he was paying for sex, and Ridgway must have worked hard to conceal the fact that several of them had infected him with STDs over the years. The issue would have been mitigated if he had used condoms, but Ridgway never wore them.

> Presumably his new wife had no idea that he was paying for sex, and Ridgway must have worked hard to conceal the fact....

Settling down stateside after the war, he found work painting trucks and would keep that job until his arrest and imprisonment. He would be married three times in total. After his capture, stories would emerge about his fascination with kinky sex, of his demands to have sex in public places, and other lurid activities that held a high risk of being caught.

Ridgway's first marriage broke up, not least because both parties committed acts of infidelity. His wife was the one to initiate the divorce proceedings, and Ridgway remarried in 1973. The marriage produced a son, but it, too, ended in divorce, in 1981. It didn't help that one night,

Ridgway took his wife by surprise and choked his wife out. Needless to say, she found the experience terrifying.

She would later tell police that her then-husband often used to spontaneously disappear for the night, never offering any explanation as to where he was going. He would return the following morning, sweat-stained, dirty, and covered in mud, looking as if he had been digging or doing landscape work. Ridgway had also threatened to sew up her vagina, he claimed, in order to somehow stop her seeing other men behind his back—a decidedly warped solution, to say the least.

He stored industrial-sized rolls of plastic sheeting in the back of his pickup truck. While Ridgway made his living as a painter, this was nothing to do with his livelihood. He used the plastic to contain the bodies of his victims, and fragments of it would be discovered in several of their graves.

Interviewed by *Time* magazine's Terry McCarthy in 2003, Ridgway's neighbor, Clem Gregurek, recalled that the serial killer "was one of those quick, hyper people. He was always nervous. He was fast in everything he did. He was even fast mowing the lawn."

Other neighbors revealed that Ridgway had been an extremely vocal opponent of prostitution encroaching on the area. He was living close to the SeaTac Strip at the time, and while he was condemning the sex workers and their trade one minute, he was sneaking off to partake of their offerings the next.

The SeaTac Strip runs just along the near side of the Seattle-Tacoma International Airport tarmac, bracketed by Ridgway's childhood neighborhood.

Ridgway went from having a casual interest in the Christian faith to suddenly being obsessive about it. He and his wife went to church services every Sunday. The Bible became his new favorite read, and he was able to cite chapter and verse, which he tried to inflict on his neighbors by knocking on their doors uninvited and attempting to preach to them or convert them.

Gary Ridgway abducted many of his victims from the so-called SeaTac Strip, a long stretch of Highway 99 that ran alongside the bustling Seattle-Tacoma International Airport. The Strip had a shady reputation, derived from the fact that it had numerous strip clubs, dive bars, and low-rent motels. It was a favorite hangout for sex workers. The Strip was re-nowned for being a hotbed of vice and prostitution, making it an obvious hunting ground for the Green River Killer. It was the kind of place where a man picking up a woman in his car would not raise many eyebrows, and the sheer volume of johns cruising along the Strip created a natural smokescreen that Ridgway could blend into.

Like many johns, he made regular, slow drive-bys to check out the girls who were offering their services on a given evening. Sometimes he would find a spot to park and took the time to check them all out, looking for one who appealed to him. It wasn't just the Strip itself, but the smaller, quieter streets surrounding it that served as a place of business for the sex workers. Some serviced their clients in cars that were parked in quiet spots, but Ridgway—a man who often had murder in mind—preferred to drive a distance away from the Strip and all of its potential eyewitnesses.

After his second divorce, Ridgway bought a house that was just a stone's throw from the SeaTac Strip. There are suspicions that he had begun killing women earlier than the first of the Green River murders (Ridgway said as much himself on at least one occasion), but with a new home available and no wife around to ask awkward questions, he began murdering in earnest in the summer of 1982.

Bringing sex workers home was one method Ridgway used to lull them into a false sense of security. He shared custody of his son with the boy's mother and made a point of showing female visitors his room, which was replete with toys and games. He was playing the "hey, you can trust me, I'm a good dad and just a stand-up, everyday guy" card, and he had some success with that approach. His target usually found out differently in very short order.

Ridgway was nothing if not pragmatic. Once the front door to his house was shut and locked, he requested that his soon-to-be victim go to the restroom prior to intercourse taking place. Sometimes, in the throes of death, they would void bowel or bladder, creating a mess that repulsed him.

He had strangled his first victims with his hands or forearms but soon grew frustrated with how hard some of them fought back. He progressed to using an improvised ligature, such as electrical jump leads or an article of clothing, wrapping it around his victim's neck from behind. This happened immediately after sex, which he insisted happen with the female kneeling on her hands and knees in front of him. Once the act was completed, Ridgway attacked before she even had the chance to get off the bed. He would later tell investigators that he found the act of choking and strangling women "more rewarding" than he would shooting or stabbing them and did not stray from this modus operandi throughout the entire string of murders.

He was not a big man, nor was he particularly strong. Many victims fought until they were unconscious, refusing to believe Ridgway's lie that if they just stopped struggling, he would let them go. Some died only after he stood on their neck.

To the best of our knowledge, the first phase of murders began on July 15, 1982, when a pair of teenagers, who were out for a ride on their bicycles, discovered the almost naked body of a teenage girl bobbing up and down in the Green River. Because of a variety of tattoos spread across her body, she would soon be identified as 16-year-old Wendy Lee Coffield.

**Many victims fought until they were unconscious, refusing to believe Ridgway's lie that if they just stopped struggling, he would let them go.**

After his capture, Gary Ridgway was asked directly by investigators when he had first begun to kill women. He claimed to be unsure but freely admitted that he "might have" started to murder prior to killing Wendy Coffield, during the 1970s. In all likelihood, we will never know for sure.

As the body was found floating close to a bridge, it seemed reasonable to assume that her killer had dumped Wendy Coffield's body from the bridge into the river below. Detectives arrived on scene and examined the body as soon as it was pulled from the water by firefighters. There was no sign of a bra or T-shirt, but Wendy was still wearing her socks and shoes. Her denim jeans had been used to strangle her and were still wrapped around her throat.

An autopsy revealed that she had put up a fight against her attacker prior to her death, as evidenced by bruising, a broken forearm, and other signs of a struggle.

Despite being only 16, Wendy Coffield had already lived a sad and strife-filled life. She had come from a broken home and was admitted into foster care. After committing some petty crimes, Wendy had spent some time in juvie hall. According to her mother, from whom she was estranged, she had gotten into drugs and had engaged in prostitution as a means of making money. When she plied her trade as a sex worker, Wendy usually worked the Strip. She was the first of many young women who would disappear from there, only to turn up dead either along the Green River or in relatively close proximity to it.

On August 12, the body of 23-year-old Debra Lynn Bonner was found in the same river. Known to her friends as "Dub," she had been missing since July 25. Bonner had been traveling around, without a fixed address, and had gotten arrested a number of times on charges of prostitution. She, too, had been fatally strangled before being thrown in the water.

Rising in the Cascades southeast of Seattle, the Green River meanders generally northwest for about 65 miles before becoming the Duwamish River for the last 12 miles of its trip into Seattle's Elliott Bay.

Sometime between August 1 and 15, Ridgway killed Marcia Faye Chapman, a 31-year-old mother of three. She was a friendly and well-liked woman, nicknamed "Tiny" because she was short. The sex trade was her only means of supporting herself and her family. Chapman's body was found on August 15 in the Green River, just as Wendy Coffield and Debra Bonner had been.

The 15th turned out to be a very dark day indeed. In addition to the discovery of Marcia Chapman, the bodies of two other women were also found in the Green River. The nude body of 17-year-old Cynthia Jean Hinds was floating alongside Chapman. Both had been fatally strangled.

To make matters worse, a third body was lying in the tall grass along the riverbank nearby. Opal Charmaine Mills, 16, had been strangled with her own trousers. Opal had no connection with the world of prostitution but was friends with Hinds.

The coroner estimated that the young women had all been killed at different times, anywhere from one day to two weeks before their discovery. They were then dropped into the river or alongside it at about the same time, as their murderer disposed of his backlog of victims.

By this time, it was obvious that a serial killer was operating in the area. The similarity of the three murders was blatantly obvious, as was the fact that the perpetrator was growing bolder, killing three women in the space of just one month, and disposing of their bodies in public. This wasn't somebody who was trying to hide his activities by burying the remains of his victims in secret (though that would come later)—this serial murderer was leaving them along a heavily trafficked waterway, making little effort to conceal what he was doing.

It was from this first series of five victims that the unidentified murderer derived the nickname "the Green River Killer." After the triple discovery on August 15, Ridgway chose different sites at which to dispose of their bodies. He drove prostitutes to those locations and had sex on or around the graves of former victims. Sometimes, he killed the woman he was with and buried her in the ground next to the others.

Ridgway liked to bury the bodies of his victims in groups, or clusters (this was the term Ridgway used himself to describe each place of burial). The use of clustering was for mainly pragmatic reasons: as time went on, there were so many of them that this was the only way he could revisit all their burial sites. It also meant that when the remains were finally recovered, sometimes after a tip-off from Ridgway himself, the discovery of one victim would lead to the discovery of others.

> The serial killer took satisfaction from making repeated drive-bys of his various clusters, going back and forth past each one, while reliving the details of each murder over and over in his mind.

Each cluster was located close to some geographical or architectural landmark, a distinctive point of reference that would allow Ridgway to easily identify the location again in the future. The serial killer took satisfaction from making repeated drive-bys of his various clusters, going back and forth past each one, while reliving the details of each murder over and over in his mind.

He took the personal effects of each victim, not as a trophy or souvenir but primarily to make it harder for each woman to be identified if her body was ever discovered. Most of these items were simply discarded, but one exception was any piece of jewelry the victim may have been wearing. These Ridgway kept and took to work. He liked to slip into the women's restroom when nobody was looking and leave them there—a highly risky practice, but one that he got a kick out of because he loved to see female employees of the truck company walking around wearing jewelry belonging to women he had murdered.

A sometime necrophiliac, he had sex both before and after his victim was dead. Several of the deceased victims were significantly decomposed at the time intercourse took place. Ridgway claimed that sex with the dead was not something that he found particularly arousing, adding that it was more difficult for him to achieve climax with them than it was with a living woman, and that he soon gave up because he "preferred them fresh."

The pickup truck that Ridgway drove was used to take his victims back to his home. That house was the scene of many of the Green River murders, but Ridgway also killed a number of women in the truck itself, usually when it was parked in dark, out-of-the-way places. If neither of those two locations suited him, for one reason or another, then he would simply drive to the site where he planned to dispose of the body and commit the murder there.

Once word was circulating on the streets that the Green River Killer was targeting sex workers, the prostitutes became a little more cautious. Most of them were desperate, however, working to support themselves and their families in the only way they knew how. Ridgway was of relatively slight stature and did not come across as threatening. He was asked many times if he was the Green River Killer, and he laughed it off, asking rhetorically if somebody his size really looked like a murderer. More often than not, the prostitute agreed with him and got into his truck. Sometimes they came to no harm, but sometimes, they did not come back alive.

Although it would be a slow process, 1983 saw the beginning of Gary Ridgway's downfall. It began with him being caught by a police patrol, in flagrante delicto with a 17-year-old sex worker. They were having sex in Ridgway's truck, which he had parked close to a school. This would come back to cast suspicion on him later.

A little over two months later, on April 30, Ridgway picked up an 18-year-old waitress named Marie Malvar, who also worked in the sex trade. Malvar's boyfriend watched her get into the maroon pickup truck and leave. The truck was distinctive, and he had no trouble remembering or describing it later. A brief, stressful exchange took place between Malvar and the driver, as evidenced by their body language. Then the truck sped off. This, by itself, was un-

Ridgway was arrested for a prostitution-related charge in 1982 but did not become a murder suspect for another couple of years.

usual. Men who were picking up prostitutes never wanted to draw attention to themselves and tended to pull slowly away from the curbside once they had a passenger in their vehicle. Gunning the engine was an odd thing for the driver to do.

Her boyfriend, fully aware that Malvar was a prostitute, was sufficiently concerned about the john's odd driving that he hopped into his own car and followed the truck. Although he didn't get a good look at the man, he was able to make out that he was somewhere in his 30s and that he had dark hair. After tailing the vehicle for a while, he lost sight of it at a busy intersection. He would never see his girlfriend again.

When Malvar subsequently disappeared without a trace, her boyfriend and father looked for her, trawling the neighborhoods close to the Strip. They looked at every truck sitting in a driveway or on the street. Finally, there it was. The pickup was parked outside Gary Ridgway's home. The two men took down the address but did not go to the door to confront the driver of the truck.

> Marie Malvar's skeletal remains would not be found for another three decades. Her disappearance did put Gary Ridgway on the radar of law enforcement, however.

It would have made no difference if they had. By that time, Marie Malvar was already dead, murdered inside that very same house. Her skeletal remains were abandoned in a ravine near Auburn, in King County, in 2003.

After they reported Malvar's disappearance to the police on May 4 and supplied them with the address where the vehicle was parked, officers paid a visit to the house in question. The man who answered the door, Gary Ridgway, was in his mid-thirties and had dark hair, just as Malvar's boyfriend had described him. He politely insisted that he knew nothing whatsoever about a missing 18-year-old. This was now a "he said/she said" situation, and the officers had little option but to take him at his word and leave.

Marie Malvar's skeletal remains would not be found for another three decades. Her disappearance did put Gary Ridgway on the radar of law enforcement, however. Although he wasn't yet identified as the Green River Killer, the cloak of anonymity behind which he hid was beginning to fray. Soon, it would be in tatters.

In 1984, Ridgway, then aged 35, agreed to undertake a polygraph test. He came to the attention of the police because he had tried to pick up a sex worker and had creeped her out enough that she felt compelled to report him. He was hooked up to the machine and, after a baseline was established, was asked questions about his potential participation in the Green River murders.

He passed the test.

The polygraph is quite rightly controversial, and the technique has seen a marked decrease in popularity in the twenty-first century. Gary Ridgway is not the only serial killer to have successfully fooled the so-called lie detector. Ted Bundy was able to achieve the same thing, and for the same reason—a pathological personality felt no shame at his acts and not a shred of remorse for other human beings.

Ridgway might have beaten the polygraph and walked free, but he lacked the self-control to lie low. A few months later, officers questioned him again after a different female sex worker claimed that he had choked her. Somehow, he managed to talk himself out of being charged, and the matter was dropped for the time being.

He was still a viable suspect, but there was no tangible evidence against him, and certainly not enough to press charges, let alone secure a conviction.

Detectives staffing the task force that was set up in January 1984 to bring the Green River Killer to justice followed up on every possible lead that came their way. There were tens of thousands, almost all of them well-intended but utterly meaningless. Inevitably, this led the detectives down a number of blind alleys as they searched in vain for the man behind the murders.

One dead-end lead came in the form of William J. Stevens, a law school student who lived in the vicinity of the murders and had allegedly expressed a hatred for sex workers on more than one occasion. An anonymous tip led the task force to start investigating him.

Ridgway handily passed a polygraph test, or so-called lie detector. The American Psychological Association cites a lack of evidence supporting the use of such tests.

Initially, Stevens seemed like a promising suspect. It was theorized that the killer might be posing as a police officer, to entice the victims more easily into his vehicle and get them to do what he wanted. Stevens collected police memorabilia, including badges, uniforms, handcuffs, and other similar items. In this, he was hardly alone. Williams went a little further than most, driving around in a repurposed former police cruiser. Some of his collection had been stolen, a crime for which Stevens had already served time in prison.

There are many law enforcement aficionados and wannabe cops out there. Not all of them express a desire to cut up sex workers, however. Stevens liked to tell stories to his friends, and some of them strongly suggested that he was the man police were looking for. Whether he did this to make himself appear more interesting than he actually was, or simply for his own amusement, is impossible to say. The tall tales came back to bite him when those stories reached the ears of the police.

Much like the actual killer, William Stevens frequented the local prostitutes, but there was no evidence to suggest that he had ever harmed, let alone killed one.

On being questioned, Stevens insisted that he was innocent, and he steadfastly refused to be part of the investigation when he was arrested in 1989. Investigators found that Stevens went by at least 30 different aliases at various points in his life and kept a stash of fake Social Security numbers. After scrutinizing his life in minute detail, detectives finally concluded that, although he had a shady background and had served jail time, he was not the Green River Killer. By the time he was crossed off the list of suspects, the members of the Green River Task Force were exhausted and even more frustrated. They seemed further away than ever from catching the man who was terrorizing the communities they had sworn to protect. To make matters worse, their funding was slowly but surely cut, depriving them of the money and resources they needed to bring the killer to justice.

Despite his having passed the polygraph test, the name of Gary Ridgway never disappeared completely from the minds of the detectives. What finally broke the case wide open was a technological advance in DNA analysis.

In 2001, because of the samples Ridgway had given 14 years before, DNA-matching technology was able to tie him to semen deposits sampled from some of his victims. He was arrested on November 30. His third wife, Judith, who had married Ridgway in 1988, was absolutely blindsided to learn that the man she loved was a serial killer. She was stunned, she told investigators, because her husband had treated her like a newlywed, and she found it difficult to square his behavior as a loving spouse and father with the atrocities he had inflicted upon female sex workers.

Likewise, the rest of his family were equally shocked. Even though he had once been listed by the police as a suspect in the Green River murders, they had supported him and offered their sympathy. Gary Ridgway had successfully pulled the wool over all their eyes for years. He had compartmentalized his life into two separate and distinct halves. One was the domesticated family man, the churchgoer, the solid employee; the other was a sadistic rapist and murderer. Somehow, both of these diametrically opposed lives coexisted within the same man—a man who, between the years 1982 and 1984, had assaulted and murdered at least 43 girls and women.

One reason that the hunt for the Green River Killer took decades was because, unlike some serial killers, Gary Ridgway had no deep-seated longing to be caught. If he had had his way, he would have continued to kill with impunity for as long as possible. This was a man who was capable of keeping his mouth shut about practically anything, with the exception of religion.

He was adept at hiding in plain sight, holding down a job, a marriage, and to some degree, a social life. The fact that he had almost fatally stabbed a six-year-old boy was known only to him and the victim and did not become common knowledge until after his arrest, when the victim, then in his forties, realized that the serial killer on the front page of the newspapers had also been his assailant.

Rarely did he get reckless and slip up. He made a point of cutting the fingernails of the dead women if they had scratched him, to remove any of his DNA from underneath them. However, in the earlier cases, leaving semen samples for forensic analysts to find was a critical blunder, and one that would ultimately prove to be his undoing.

In the spring of 2003, forensic investigators were able to identify tiny flecks of paint that were found on the bodies of several Green River murder victims. They traced the specific type of paint to the kind

Time caught up with the Green River Killer, as forensic technology and techniques continued to evolve and create new potentials to match old samples.

used at the workplace of Gary Ridgway, where he spray-painted trucks for a living. Some of the paint came from the jeans of Wendy Coffield, believed to have been his first victim. There was no reason why paint from a commercial trucking company's premises should have ended up on the pants of a murdered 16-year-old, and the only connection between the two was Gary Ridgway.

The real slam dunk, however, was the DNA evidence that proved that bodily fluids from Ridgway were present in some of the earliest Green River victims. It had taken years for technology to reach the point where it could prove, beyond all reasonable doubt, that the same man who provided his DNA samples had also engaged in sexual activity with the murdered girls and women.

Law enforcement finally had the evidence they needed to press murder charges.

Later in 2003, the case went to court. Initially, Ridgway tried to plead not guilty. As the stack of evidence against him continued to mount up, he and his lawyers both realized this was an untenable position, and Ridgway's attorneys struck a deal with prosecutors. The terms were that he would confess to the Green River killings, be incarcerated for life, and in return, the death penalty would be taken off the table.

> The real slam dunk, however, was the DNA evidence that proved that bodily fluids from Ridgway were present in some of the earliest Green River victims.

The judge gave him 48 life sentences, one for each of the victims he was known to have killed. Each sentence was to be served consecutively, thus guaranteeing that the serial killer would never walk free from prison. A 49th and final one would be added later.

In addition to pleading guilty, an agreed-upon part of this process involved him cooperating with the police, who were struggling to identify some of his victims. It provided strong motivation for Ridgway to tell the truth: if he was caught in a lie, the deal could be declared null and void—which meant that the death penalty would now be a possibility.

As the investigation progressed, Ridgway provided what details he could, but he openly admitted, "I killed so many women, I have a hard time keeping them straight." This statement was almost certainly true.

By the time of his capture, some of the victims had been dead for more than 20 years. It is also fair to say that when a john picks up a sex worker, he is usually given a fake name (if he asks for it at all) and is unlikely to learn anything about the worker's background. The best Ridgway could do, in many cases, was direct detectives to a cluster and give a physical description of the victims he had buried there.

Gary Ridgway's youngest victim, a girl who was just 14 years old, remained unidentified for decades. Kept in storage, her unearthed remains were referred to as "Bones-10." Finally, her identity was established in 2021, thanks to the hard work and persistence of the King County Sheriff's department. DNA testing and a process called genetic genealogy determined that the previously unnamed victim was Wendy Stephens. Wendy had disappeared from her home in Denver in 1983 and was never heard from again. It took 38 years for her family to finally gain closure.

In the courtroom, Ridgway stood before the family members of some of his victims and cried what were almost certainly crocodile tears, claiming, "I have tried for a long time to keep from killing any ladies." He expressed sorrow for having murdered each of the girls and women.

The serial killer's newly found contrition did not impress the bereaved next of kin who were present that day. Understandably, many threw Ridgway's words back in his face. Showing an almost unfathomable degree of forbearance, others openly forgave him.

It was initially believed that Ridgway was active as a serial killer between 1982 and 1984, before going dark until his capture. Yet, as we have discussed elsewhere in this book, it is rare for a serial killer to simply stop killing once they have developed a taste for murder. They may slow down, particularly if they feel that the heat is on, and they may stop entirely if they are imprisoned for some other crime, fall ill, or die—but they very rarely just decide to quit.

The fact is that Gary Ridgway did continue killing after 1984 but at a vastly reduced rate—or so it is believed. At the time of writing, even with his cooperation, detectives believe he may be responsible for

The full extent of Ridgway's killings may never be known, but more recent forensic work has helped identify victims from as far away as Denver, Colorado.

far more than the 49 victims he was convicted of killing. The real number could very easily be twice that.

Although there is much uncertainty regarding possible murders that took place in the 1990s, he did confess to "falling off the wagon" and killing "a couple of times."

Most of the women Ridgway killed were sex workers. He had paid for sex throughout most of his adult life, starting with his time in the military and continuing even through the most devout years of his religious faith. The paradox of Ridgway going to church and renouncing the sinful life, while simultaneously engaging in prostitution and committing a string of brutal murders, shows that he was able to compartmentalize his mind in a manner of which few other human beings are capable.

Why did he kill? If we are to believe Ridgway himself, he killed sex workers because he hated them. Before his trial, he confessed to prosecutors, "The plan was: I wanted to kill as many women I thought were prostitutes as I possibly could."

He went on to admit: "I picked prostitutes as my victims because I hate most prostitutes and I did not want to pay them for sex."

Ridgway was a regular client of the prostitutes who worked the SeaTac Strip. His pathological hatred seemed directed at the fact that they would dare sell their sexual services to him, and he felt totally justified in taking their lives after the deed was done. In his warped view of the world, Ridgway resented each woman for giving him something that he desperately craved, and he killed them for meeting his need.

In May 1982, two months before his first confirmed murder, Gary Ridgway was arrested on charges of prostitution. He was cruising the Strip and asked a woman he thought was a prostitute to get into his car. Instead, she was an undercover police officer. The shame and anger Ridgway, to all outside appearances a respectable family man, must have felt would soon be directed against the real sex workers. It is notable that this interaction with law enforcement did not scare him away from soliciting other women for sex in the future. His sexual urges were stronger than his fear of being publicly shamed.

In a well-established pattern among serial killers the world over, Ridgway also targeted sex workers because he assumed—correctly— that it would be easier to stay one step ahead of the police. As a group living on the fringes of society, sex workers often keep to themselves, and it is a sad truth that, when one of them disappears, their loss often takes days or weeks to be discovered—if their absence is even noticed at all. By that time, the killer has already moved on and the trail has gone cold. Those who engage in prostitution, whether they are selling or purchasing sex, generally do not like talking about it with police officers and, therefore, tend to be less than forthcoming about the illegal activities taking place around them.

"I thought I could kill as many as I wanted without getting caught," Ridgway admitted, in a moment of uncharacteristic sincerity. On this point, at least, we should absolutely take him at his word. Not all his victims were engaged in sex work, however; Ridgway also murdered runaways, strongly implying that his story about being motivated by hatred of prostitutes either only goes so far or should be largely discounted. The great likelihood is that, like so many other male serial killers, Gary Ridgway simply got off on abusing and murdering females.

Ridgway has also told detectives that he is responsible for killing more victims than he is currently being held accountable for. This does seem likely, and there is sadly no shortage of missing women and Jane Does who could fit the profile of Ridgway victims. However, the serial killer likes to play mind games with the police, not least because this is the only form of personal power he has left in the world. It goes without saying that he is not a man to be trusted.

"In most cases, when I murdered these women, I did not know their names," Ridgway confessed in his guilty plea document. "Most of the time, I killed them the first time I met them, and I do not have a good memory for their faces."

At the time of writing, the remains of two more victims of Gary Ridgway still await identification. They bear the temporary identifiers of "Bones-17" and "Bones-20." We can only hope that some day, the dogged investigators who have never

A frequent customer on the Strip, Ridgway was nonetheless not savvy enough to tell a prostitute from an undercover cop.

stopped working on behalf of the victims and their families will finally be able to restore their names.

Ask pretty much any ordinary human being, and they would probably agree that Gary Ridgway was an evil man. He did not see himself in that same light, however. A detective asked him candidly to rate himself on a scale of being evil, with one being not evil at all, and five being the evilest person on the face of the planet. Ridgway thought about it for a moment and decided that he was a three, rationalizing that, despite the huge number of females that he had murdered, "I didn't torture 'em. They went fast."

This is true, as far as it goes. He did not inflict torture upon any of his victims prior to their deaths. Gary Ridgway gained gratification from the power he exerted over his victims and from the act of murdering sex workers, which he considered to be his life's work.

"I'm good in one thing," he declared during an interview, "and that's killing prostitutes."

# THE KEN AND BARBIE KILLERS
## PAUL BERNARDO AND
## KARLA HOMOLKA

O n the outside, they looked like the perfect couple. Attractive, blond, and clean cut, Paul Bernardo and Karla Homolka looked like the stereotypical couple next door—and indeed, that's what many people took them for. Just as their nickname suggested, they evoked images of the Barbie and Ken dolls that countless girls have played with over the years. A number of reporters have described the duo as having the looks of Hollywood movie stars, which perhaps goes some way toward explaining why the Canadian public still remains fascinated by them, decades after their crimes took place.

Bernardo and Homolka seemed to have plenty of money (although in truth, they were smuggling to fund their lifestyle), and to the casual observer they seemed to be a successful young couple. They lived in an upscale, affluent Toronto neighborhood, populated by other young professionals. They were also wannabe social climbers, friendly enough to those they knew or people who could do something for them. Beneath the surface, however, lay a very different story. Bernardo and Homolka harbored sick and twisted tendencies, which led to them leading a secret life of rape, torture, and murder.

Karla Homolka was born in 1970. Raised in Ontario, she had two younger sisters. Those who knew her during her school years remembered an argumentative girl, one who tended to stick to her guns whenever there was conflict. Predictably, she also had a temper, particularly when she didn't get what she wanted. The same is true of many children, and so her parents found little cause for worry about their daughter's new beau.

It is a well-known red flag that some serial killers hurt and murder animals as a precursor to killing human beings. Homolka was inclined

Karla Homolka's work at a veterinary clinic allowed her to pilfer substances to help her and her husband carry out their loathsome deeds.

in the opposite direction. She seemed to love animals, or at the very least liked them enough to find work at a veterinary clinic. Prior to that, she had worked in a pet store. Subsequent events would show that her empathy for animals did not extend to her fellow human beings.

Paul Bernardo was born in 1964. His home life was a less than happy one. Unknown to him at first was the fact that the man he thought of as his dad, Kenneth, was nothing of the kind. Bernardo's mother had had an affair and became pregnant by her lover. When he found out about his true parentage, young Paul flew into a rage. He hurled a torrent of abuse at his mother, much of it directed at her sexual morality—or the perceived lack thereof. Furthermore, Kenneth Bernardo, the primary male role model in his son's life, beat his wife when the mood took him and would later be convicted of sex crimes.

As a boy, Paul Bernardo was a Boy Scout. He made friends easily and was never seen as a problem child or a troublemaker. As he grew to adulthood, Bernardo's ambitions began to crystallize. He wanted to be rich, successful, famous, and above all, powerful. He devoured the works of countless business and self-help gurus, choosing business and finance as his major when he enrolled at the University of Toronto. His long-term goal was to make a name for himself in the business world—to become a high-flying executive, living a champagne lifestyle.

As he grew older, Bernardo's dislike of women deepened into outright disgust. Although he was outwardly a polite and respectful young man (most of the time), he began to see females as something to be humiliated and degraded. They became, at best, living objects of his sexual fantasies, which were of an increasingly sadistic and perverse nature. Girlfriends never stuck around for long after they broached the surface image and got a glimpse of Bernardo's true nature. He was manipulative, controlling, and narcissistic, obsessed with himself, his image, and his personal wants and desires. Bernardo took to making sexually explicit, abusive phone calls to women he knew. This earned him a restraining order and was a sign that his behavior was becoming increasingly erratic.

Bordering on Lake Ontario, the Scarborough suburb of Toronto is a large and colorful district of this major Canadian city. During the late 1980s and early 1990s, it was plagued by a serious of vicious rapes. The perpetrator, an unidentified male, estimated to be in his late teens or early twenties, was dubbed the Scarborough Rapist. His real name: Paul Bernardo.

The first rapes occurred in 1987. Bernardo targeted young women in their teens and early twenties, with one victim being just 15 years old. He spent time hanging around at bus stops and other isolated places, waiting for an opportunity to catch an unsuspecting female alone.

No matter the circumstances, rape is a vicious and sadistic crime. As the number of attacks carried out by the Scarborough Rapist increased, so did the physical violence he inflicted upon some of the victims. One target of Bernardo's fought him off, but he pulled a knife and inflicted multiple stab wounds in the process.

> **The first rapes occurred in 1987. Bernardo targeted young women in their teens and early twenties, with one victim being just 15 years old.**

Paul Bernardo had already committed several rapes when he met Karla Homolka in the fall of 1987. Aged 17 when she first encountered the man who would become her husband, Homolka was six years Paul Bernardo's junior. The two soon entered a relationship, spending hours talking on the phone and driving to meet up on a regular basis.

At first, Bernardo seemed like a respectable, clean-cut young man. As an accountant at the big city firm of Price Waterhouse, he had strong career prospects. Small wonder that Homolka's parents approved of him. Yet all was not as it seemed. Although most young men are driven by their libido, Paul Bernardo took this to an entirely new level.

He soon developed an unhealthy interest in Homolka's younger sister, Tammy, and became a Peeping Tom, staring in through her bedroom window in the hope of seeing her naked. When Homolka found out about this, she could reasonably have been expected to go berserk. Incredibly, she instead began to help Bernardo by doctoring her sister's blinds so that he could get a better view. Homolka had found out her future husband was sexually interested in her own 15-year-old sister and was very consciously choosing his side over her sister's well-being. From this development alone, it becomes obvious that the relationship between Bernardo and Homolka was a meeting of two warped, pathologic personalties.

Benardo was a domineering boyfriend, taking every opportunity to batter Homolka's self-esteem and humiliate her behind closed doors. He insisted upon having absolute control over her life, making decisions both large and small for her. He dictated what she could and could not wear. Sexually, he got a thrill from acts of bondage and restraint.

Homolka later claimed to have been held fully in the thrall of her lover. Bernardo had her at his beck and call, she insisted, and took full advantage of her willingness to cater to his sick peccadilloes. He addressed her with the most degrading names imaginable, making her crawl at his feet and declare him her absolute master in all things. Auto-erotic asphyxiation—the choking of an individual during sexual intercourse—was one of Bernardo's kinks, and he applied it remorselessly to Homolka.

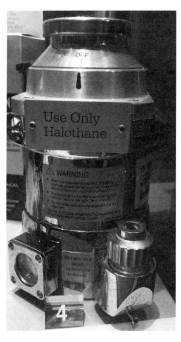

In the skilled hands of a medical professional, halothane is safely administered using a machine that mixes the anaesthetic in low concentrations with a mix of oxygen and atmosphere.

As Bernardo's obsession with Tammy Homolka grew, he made her older sister dress up in Tammy's clothes prior to having sex with her and pretend to actually be Tammy during intercourse. Interviews conducted after Tammy's death, however, suggested that Karla had a real motivation for wanting her sister dead: she saw Tammy as a very real threat to her relationship with Bernardo. When Bernardo made it clear that he reciprocated, the seeds were sown for tragedy.

On December 23, 1990, Paul Bernardo and Karla Homolka concocted a scheme for Bernardo to rape Tammy. Karla's job at the veterinary clinic gave her access to a variety of controlled substances, including anesthetics and sleeping pills. Smuggling some of them out of work, she drugged her unsuspecting sister by spiking her eggnog, rendering her unconscious. The pair held a rag over their victim's mouth to keep her from waking up. The rag had been dipped in halothane, a general anesthetic commonly used during surgery. Unlike many other anesthetics, halothane is not injected—it is inhaled, in the form of a gas. When the rag was removed, the chemicals that had soaked into the rag had left a stark burn injury on Tammy Homolka's face.

Then, Bernardo sexually assaulted Tammy, with Karla not only in the room but also as an active participant. In the days leading up to the assault on her sister, Karla had purchased a video camcorder, which Bernardo used to document his rape of the unconscious teenager. Once he had finished, Karla took her turn. She would later claim to have been forced to do so, though every statement she made should be treated with great skepticism. As events would show, she possesses a manipulative and extremely cunning personality.

One common side effect of unconsciousness is that a person loses the involuntary reflexes that protect the airway. The tongue and soft tissue inside the mouth go floppy, due to the lack of muscle tone. There is also a tendency to vomit and to aspirate the contents of the stomach, including potent stomach acids, down into the throat and lungs. Some sedative drugs also knock out the body's respiratory drive, slowing and sometimes stopping the rate of breathing.

After the assault, Tammy's killers panicked when she would not wake up. Later, they would claim that neither of them ever intended for her to die—that it was a tragic accident. By the time the police arrived, they had cooked up a cover story. Because it was the holidays, they said that Tammy had drunk too much alcohol and passed out while they were all watching a movie together.

Paramedics were called to the scene and did their best to resuscitate Tammy, intubating the unresponsive young woman and breathing for her with a bag valve mask. With lights and sirens running, they rushed her to the hospital, but the damage had already been done. Tammy had suffered a severe loss of oxygen to the brain and died in the hospital the next morning.

Karla Homolka would later claim in court that Paul Bernardo had bullied and coerced her into doing this, blatantly ignoring the fact that she could have gone to her parents and the police at any time before aiding and abetting the murder and stopped it from happening.

It's difficult to understand why the presence of an obvious burn on the dead girl's face didn't prompt more questions regarding her death. Her murderers brushed it off as a rug burn, claiming that they had

Paramedics rendered care at the scene and transported Tammy to the hospital, where she died.

dragged Tammy across the carpet to try and save her life. Years after the murder took place, several medical experts looked at photographs of the burn and declared it highly unlikely that a rug or carpet could have been responsible. Even as a lay person, taking a cursory look at photographs that were taken of Tammy's cheek wound and surrounding areas makes it blatantly clear that this was no carpet burn. It was far too severe in nature to even be considered as such.

Although an autopsy was carried out, the presence of illicit sleeping drugs in Tammy Homolka's bloodstream was not detected. However, the medication in question—Triazolam, a potent muscle relaxant and sedative also known as Halcion—is not picked up on a general toxicology screen. A pathologist would need to suspect its presence first and then would have to look for it intentionally with a targeted test. It was only three years later, when a second autopsy was performed after the arrest of Bernardo and Homolka, that this was done. This time, the results registered the presence of Halcion, a drug that Tammy Homolka had not been prescribed.

As the Christmas and New Year holidays came and went, Bernardo and Homolka slowly came to the realization that they had gotten away with murder. Although the police acknowledged that there were still lingering questions about her death, little in the way of meaningful follow-up was performed. The official story became that Tammy Homolka had died in a tragic, alcohol-induced accident. The case was closed—for the time being.

Emboldened by the knowledge that they had gotten away with murder, Bernardo and Homolka started planning their next crime. Homolka teased her lover with the possibility of abducting "some 13-year-old virgins" to rape. Bernardo loved the idea, and the pair agreed to implement it as soon as possible.

Meanwhile, Bernardo continued his string of sex assaults as the Scarborough Rapist. Despite the police posting "wanted" posters throughout the district, each one containing an artist's rendition of the perpetrator that was an accurate likeness of Bernardo, he continued to sexually assault women. Such was his arrogance that he kept a journal describing each and every sex attack he had committed, which would come back to haunt him in the courtroom after his capture.

In the early morning hours of June 15, 1990, they abducted their next victim: a 14-year-old girl named Leslie Mahaffy. She had spent the night with friends and had stayed out for hours longer than her parents would allow. Leslie was worried about going home and getting into trouble, but at three o'clock in the morning, she didn't have many other options.

Arriving at her house, she was surprised when a man approached her out of the darkness. That man was Paul Bernardo. Despite the early hour, the two began chatting. Bernardo could be charismatic when he chose to be, and he lured Leslie into his car with the promise of a smoke. What she got instead was the blade of a hunting knife being held against her and the threat of being killed if she didn't keep quiet. The teenager was abducted right outside her own house, where her parents were sleeping.

Bernardo and Homolka had a house of their own. Bernardo drove his terrified victim back there, arriving before sunrise. He sexually assaulted her alone, then woke up Homolka to participate. The evil duo videotaped the prolonged, horrific sex attack on Leslie Mahaffy, all of which took place while she was blindfolded. Bernardo knew that Leslie had seen his face prior to her kidnap, however, and knew that she could identify him. Ignoring Leslie's desperate pleas to be allowed to live, to be let go on the promise that she would never describe his appearance to the police, Paul Bernardo strangled her until her heart stopped.

Once she was dead, Homolka helped him carry her body downstairs to the basement. Then, her two killers calmly ate dinner with Homolka's family, who came over to the house to celebrate Father's Day.

Paul Bernardo used a power saw to cut up Leslie's body, encased the parts in concrete, and tossed them into a lake. They would be found two weeks after the murder by fishermen, who immediately alerted the police. In a grim twist of fate, the date was June 29, 1991.

On that same day, Paul Bernardo and Karla Homolka were married. It was a no-expense spared, fairytale wedding ceremony, of the

There may be parts of the world where a lake is a good place to hide a body, but Canada is not one of them.

sort that so many young girls dream, complete with an expensive white dress for the bride and a fancy suit for the groom. Karla positively glowed, beaming radiantly and posing for pictures with her new husband. They had chosen to get married near Niagara Falls, and they pulled out all the stops to make it a day to remember.

Nobody would ever have guessed that the bride and groom were responsible for the deaths of two young girls and that the handsome, charming Paul Bernardo was also a serial rapist.

Their perfect married life was not quite the success story that they liked to portray it as. The couple smuggled cigarettes to make extra money, demonstrating that they had no qualms about breaking the law if it suited their purposes. They also doubtless got off on the thrill of committing a crime and getting away with it, over and over again.

Behind closed doors, it did not take long for the honeymoon period to come to a jarring end. Bernardo was physically abusive, punching Homolka whenever the mood took him. One assault, in which Bernardo battered her with a flashlight, was severe enough to send Homolka to the hospital. She sustained two black eyes and other significant bodily injuries.

Also in 1991, the couple ensnared a 15-year-old girl who came to be known publicly as Jane Doe. She was a colleague of Homolka's at the pet store, and when the latter began to befriend her, she went along willingly, not suspecting what the older woman's true motives were.

On June 7, 1991, Bernardo and Homolka took Jane Doe back to their residence and plied her with a drink that was laced with sedative drugs. Once she passed out, Paul Bernardo repeatedly raped her, recording the awful act on videotape. When she awoke the next day, Jane had no recollection of the assault. She would be made aware of it later when police obtained the tape and introduced it as evidence.

To make matters worse, the same thing happened again two months later. This time, Jane Doe was drugged so severely that she came close to respiratory arrest. Fortunately, she survived the incident, but it is clear that neither Bernardo nor Homolka cared about the risks of killing another victim. The value of human life was nothing when compared to their need for sexual gratification.

After ten months of matrimony, Bernardo and Homolka were ready to rape and murder again. Their victim was a 15-year-old girl named Kristen French. On April 16, 1992, Kristen was on her way home from school when she was abducted. She was trying to be helpful, approaching Bernardo in his car when he asked if she could give him driving directions. He kidnapped her, drove her to the home he and Homolka

**The value of human life was nothing when compared to their need for sexual gratification.**

shared, and raped her repeatedly. The pair tortured Kristen mercilessly, recording the abuse so that they could enjoy a replay later. Bernardo played the recording they had made of their assault on Leslie Mahaffy.

Despite the horrific treatments she endured at the hands of her captors, Kristen French did not cower. Video footage recovered from the Bernardo residence backed up Homolka's testimony that the captive schoolgirl had verbally stood up to Bernardo several times, giving him a piece of her mind. This inability to break her spirit only served to enrage Paul Bernardo, who upped the level of abuse he and his wife were inflicting on Kristen. Bernardo got a big kick out of verbally humiliating his victims, but his fragile, hyper-inflated ego was incapable of tolerating even the slightest perceived insult in return. Although she finally broke down and apologized to Bernardo, stroking his ego with false praise, Kristen French displayed an incredible amount of courage throughout her ordeal—almost certainly more bravery than Paul Bernardo has shown in his entire life.

After brutally abusing Kristen for almost three days, Bernardo fatally strangled her with an electrical cable. It was Easter Sunday. After the murder, the pair blithely drove over to visit Homolka's parents for dinner. They left Kristen's body unattended in their home, and when they returned, Paul Bernardo had apparently given some thought to covering their tracks. Together, they put the dead body into the bath and washed it thoroughly. An attempt was made to wash away traces of Bernardo's semen from her vagina. Kristen's personal effects, including her hair and clothes, were burned.

Rather than dismember the body, this time the Bernardos left it in a ravine. They made a half-hearted effort to cover it up with tree branches and leaves. It can have been no coincidence that the remains of Kristen French were left just a few hundred feet away from the cemetery in which Leslie Mahaffy lay buried.

Her body was discovered on April 16, two weeks after she was killed.

In the weeks after their deaths, Karla Homolka dressed up as each of the three murdered girls, role-playing as if she really was them, for the sexual gratification of Bernardo, and perhaps even herself. Bernardo frequently handcuffed her and used Homolka as an outlet for his fantasies, although he reserved the fulfillment of the most twisted and extreme for the victims of his abductions.

Paul Bernardo came close to being caught several times. As artist's renderings of the Scarborough Rapist began to circulate, a former colleague of his recognized its almost uncanny likeness with that of Bernardo and tipped off the police. After others who knew Bernardo contacted them, detectives interviewed him and even obtained his consent to take DNA samples, which languished in evidence storage for several years before being matched with the DNA of the perpetrator they were looking for.

It was not until 1993 that the samples led police officers once again to the front door of the Bernardo home. They took Bernardo into custody. At the same time, Homolka felt that she had endured one beating

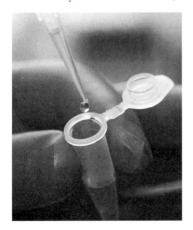

too many from her husband and pressed charges against him. Detectives strongly suspected that the Scarborough Rapist was the same criminal who was responsible for the murders of Leslie Mahaffy and Kristen French. Testimony obtained from interviewing Karla Homolka only solidified those suspicions, and Paul Bernardo was arrested on suspicion of serial rape and murder.

Though investigators took DNA samples from Bernardo in 1990, they were not tested until two years later.

After examining the sordid story of Paul Bernardo and Karla Homolka in detail, one is forced to wonder just what, exactly, made them carry out the horrific crimes that they did. One thing is clear: we are not dealing with stupidity or a lack of mental capacity.

While both killers are undeniably intelligent, Karla Homolka is remarkably so. In a 2005 *Whitehorse Star* newspaper article on the case, journalist Mark Bonokoski notes that she has "an IQ of 134, a score that MENSA [the society for people with a very high intelligence quotient] describes as belonging only to people of 'very superior intelligence'—the world's top two percent." If this is indeed the case, then Karla Homolka serves as a textbook example of just how widely disparate an individual's intellectual capability and capacity for sound judgment can be. Alternatively, if her psychologist is to be believed, her intelligence could not counteract her susceptibility to the influence of a controlling individual such as Paul Bernardo.

Due to her medical work with animals, Homolka not only had access to veterinary drugs, but she also possessed at least a working knowledge of their side effects. Testifying in her own defense, Homolka told the court that she had never intended to kill her sister, wanting only to incapacitate her to facilitate the rape. However, one of the drugs she obtained—halothane, which had caused the burn injury on Tammy Homolka's face—had a very narrow therapeutic window. This means that it is easy to inadvertently overdose the patient with that particular drug. Clinical professionals always treat such medications with great caution, calculating the dose and the rate of infusion carefully. Not so Karla Homolka, who soaked a rag in halothane and held it over her sister's face for so long, it burned away the skin tissue. Although there was no easily accessible Internet in 1990, it would have taken her just a few minutes to flip through one of the medical textbooks at her place of employment to review the drug profile of halothane. If she had, she would have learned that a halothane overdose can easily be lethal, particularly when it is not given as a gas.

Unless, of course, murder was her intent all along.

No matter how clever, no matter how cunning, no matter how manipulative she was, Homolka did get caught in the end. Despite her best efforts, she was unable to excuse her way out of the criminal charges.

She did, however, contrive to get off rather more easily than most people would like. Homolka and her legal counsel cut a plea deal, which would buy her a degree of leniency in exchange for her testifying against Paul Bernardo. She was therefore tried first.

At the conclusion of her trial, the 23-year-old Homolka pled guilty, not to murder but to manslaughter, in a deal arranged with prosecutors. This gave her a lesser sentence of just 12 years, which she served to completion, and she was released from prison in 2005. Despite the heinous nature of her crimes, she was not considered to be at serious risk for reoffending, and Canadian law therefore mandated she be given her freedom. Understandably, there was a public outcry. The Associated Press dubbed her "Canada's nightmare cover girl."

The center of a media frenzy, Homolka attempted to return to something of a normal life, changing her name and trying to keep a low profile. She married the brother of her lawyer and had three children. Despite changing residences several times, it didn't take long for the public to figure out that "Leanne Teale" was actually the infamous serial killer whose face had stared back at them from so many newspaper front pages and TV news reports.

In 2016, there was a public outcry when it was revealed that Homolka was living close to a school, where her own children were pupils.

Shown at her family home sometime after arraignment and before commencing her prison sentence, Homolka got off easy compared to husband Bernardo.

No matter how frequently she and her family move, her identity and address wind up getting published. Quite understandably, many of her neighbors react with disgust and horror when they find out who she really is. At one stage, the woman who was convicted of helping to torture and kill three girls was somehow able to get a volunteer position at a local school.

Was Karla Homolka truly forced into participating in the rapes and murders by Paul Bernardo? This was certainly the narrative that her legal team adopted. (Bernardo's lawyers took the diametrically opposed view: that she was a willing and very active participant.) The mental health professional who profiled her agreed that she was very much under the control of her husband.

Public opinion on the matter was split. Some pointed out that, as an abuse victim herself, subject to regular pillorying by her husband, Karla Homolka had little choice but to go along with Bernardo's demands. The alternative would have been to risk being murdered herself, which seems like a reasonable fear—particularly as she knew all her husband's criminal secrets. Paul Bernardo was undeniably unhinged. It's no stretch of the imagination to think that, with little or no provocation, he was capable of turning on his own wife.

> **Paul Bernardo was undeniably unhinged. It's no stretch of the imagination to think that, with little or no provocation, he was capable of turning on his own wife.**

On the other hand, the counterargument holds that she had ample opportunity to call the police. Homolka knew she was, at the very least, an accomplice to rape and murder. She must have wondered which version of events a jury would believe.

The truth will, most likely, never be known. She appears to have turned away from past events, preferring to focus on raising her own children. It is a privilege that the parents of her victims—including her own mother and father—shall forever be denied.

After ghoulish souvenir hunters broke off pieces of the Bernardo home as keepsakes, the property was demolished in 1995, doubtless to the relief of the entire neighborhood surrounding it.

Paul Bernardo was found guilty on all counts by a jury of his peers. Imprisoned for life since 1996, he has spent much of his time behind bars in solitary confinement, not least for his own protection. Placing him amongst the general population would be tantamount to giving him a death sentence. There are few things a prisoner hates more than a rapist, pedophile, and torturer of the innocent.

Despite blaming his then-wife for the murders, Bernardo needed a different excuse to explain the serial rapes he committed. He claims that after having given the matter much thought, his violent sex crimes all stemmed from a lack of self-esteem and were fueled by alcohol. There may be some truth to this; it would go some way to explaining his compulsion to degrade and humiliate members of the opposite sex, seeing them as being inferior to himself in every possible way. Be that as it may, it does not constitute a defense for the appalling acts he committed.

Bernardo was sent into solitary at the Kingston Penitentiary, a longtime maximum-security prison in Ontario. When the aging prison was decommissioned in 2013, he was transferred to the Millhaven Institution.

Paul Bernardo continues to submit applications for release from prison, but at the time of writing, he has yet to be successful. In the summer of 2021, he attempted to convince his parole board that he was no longer a danger to the public. He classified himself as being a "low risk" of reoffending. (Note that he did *not* say "*no* risk.") The prison system, on the other hand, has afforded him the status of "dangerous offender."

Paul Bernardo shows little in the way of contrition or remorse for his crimes. Neither does he seem to accept any real responsibility for them, although he does pay lip service to the idea that he is in some way reformed. In a parallel with the case of British serial killing couple Fred and Rose West, while Bernardo has been sentenced as the dominant (and therefore more culpable) party, he maintains that his wife at the time—Homolka — is more responsible for the crimes than the court recognized.

The next of kin of some of his victims attended the hearing and spoke out against him, in impassioned pleas. They argued, quite understandably, that a level of mental depravity such as that shown by Paul Bernardo can never be cured. Mental health professionals concur: after conducting an in-depth assessment, they diagnosed Bernardo as a psychopath—one with perverse and sadistic sexual tendencies to boot. The parole board dutifully listened, and Bernardo's request for release was swiftly rejected.

Far from being rehabilitated, as would be hoped of somebody seeking release from life imprisonment, one is in fact forced to wonder whether Bernardo is putting in any kind of effort at all. His own parole officer recommended against release, adding that Bernardo appeared to have made "no progress" since his last hearing in 2018. He is eligible to apply for parole again in 2023. It is fair to say that his chances of being successful are not good.

# MURDEROUS REALTOR
# TODD KOHLHEPP

Todd Kohlhepp was born in Fort Lauderdale, Florida, in 1971. Few of those who knew him as a child remarked upon his intelligence, but he was relatively bright, with the potential to do well in school and achieve success when he graduated and began to build a career. Unfortunately, he was also cunning, vicious, and savage, and he had these negative characteristics throughout his childhood and early teenage years.

Renowned for his poor, sometimes nonexistent impulse control, the future serial killer was prone to unprovoked outbursts of anger. Most such episodes were also physically destructive in nature. Kohlhepp vented his rage on anything and everything around him, be it his personal property or that of others; the location he happened to find himself in; and most ominously of all, helpless animals and pets, which he took a sick delight in torturing.

By all accounts, he behaved this way from a very early age. His parents' marriage broke up when he was two years old, and Kohlhepp harbored a deep resentment of his father because of it. His mother recalled that Kohlhepp was difficult, if not impossible to control, an absolute parental nightmare when he did not get his own way. One neighbor recalled him as being "a devil on a chain." Perhaps in an attempt to mollify him, Kohlhepp's mother brought him a brand-new bedroom set one day. The boy smashed it to pieces with a hammer.

While growing up, Kohlhepp attended counseling sessions and even spent several months in a mental health institution, but none of the care he received seemed to make much of a difference. He was a bully and enjoyed intimidating and beating up other children. During one fit of pique, he threatened to murder his own mother. This was the final straw, and he went to live with his father in Arizona.

There was clearly no shortage of warning signs that Todd Kohlhepp would grow up to be a monster. In 1987, at the age of 15, he sexually assaulted a 14-year-old girl at gunpoint. She and her family were neighbors of his. Kohlhepp brazenly went over to her home in broad daylight and asked her to come outside. He produced a pistol, held it to her head, and made her go over to the house Kohlhepp shared with his father, who was out at the time. Once there, he taped her mouth shut, tied her up, and raped her.

When he was finished, Kohlhepp escorted the girl back to her home and threatened to murder her family if she told anybody what he had done to her. Despite his threats, Kohlhepp was soon found out. Officers arrived at his house and found the teenager casually holding a rifle. He was arrested, tried as an adult rather than as a juvenile, and sentenced to 15 years' imprisonment. Upon his release, at the age of 30, he was a registered sex offender. While in prison, he had managed to suppress his resentment of authority to some degree and mostly kept his nose clean. He worked a series of menial tasks and showed an interest in operating and programming computers. On his release, Kohlhepp enrolled as a student at a local community college, ultimately earning a degree in computer science. His grades were good, and his instructors recalled him as a motivated and diligent student. Afterward, he would go on to obtain a second degree with a business major.

Although Kohlhepp was listed as a sex offender, he managed to build a thriving and successful career as a Realtor. He worked as a broker-in-charge for a real estate company in South Carolina. He purchased his own home in a solidly middle-class neighborhood, drove a pair of BMWs, and earned a pilot's license.

Kohlhepp racked up two bachelor of science degrees, in computer science and in business administration-marketing, paving the way for his success in the world of real estate.

He was also antisocial, according to those who knew and worked with him. His neighbors were aware that he was a registered sex offender, which they found understandably disturbing. They kept a close eye on him but never saw anything out of the ordinary taking place at his home. Although Kohlhepp mostly kept to himself, he could be seen working in the yard on occasion. Other than his legal status, he seemed like nothing more than an average, everyday Joe.

The adult Todd Kohlhepp who emerged from the Arizona correctional system was, in some ways, different from the teenager who had been incarcerated in 1987. That is only to be expected. He could be incredibly personal, even charming, according to some of those he dealt with in the world of real estate. He fooled many with his nice-guy persona. Yet underneath it all, there was still the rage, ready to instantly lash out whenever the mood took him.

Not everybody bought into his act. Some clients and colleagues got a look at the real Todd Kohlhepp, perceiving him as boorish and arrogant, egotistical to a fault. He could brag and boast along with the best of them, lacking modesty and empathy. Those he couldn't charm sometimes found him to be something of a "creeper."

In business terms, Kohlheep was a raging success. He built up his real estate company to the point where he was overseeing multiple different Realtors. It was lucrative work. He used some of his profits to buy a parcel of land in Spartanburg County, which he promptly fenced off and posted "no trespassing" signs around the perimeter. This seemed odd to local residents, who couldn't understand why he would pay tens of thousands of dollars to secure what was essentially a mix of farmland and wasteground.

Nobody suspected that Todd Kohlhepp would soon have a very good reason to value his privacy.

On November 6, 2003, Todd Kohlhepp had walked into the Chesnee, South Carolina, Superbike Motorsports store. By the time he walked out again, everybody inside was dead. He had fatally shot them all, putting one bullet in each of the victims' foreheads. The four victims were the owner of the store, Scott Ponder; his mother, Beverly Guy; and employees Chris Sherbert and Brian Lucas.

The bodies were discovered by a shocked visitor to the store, who immediately called 911. Police launched an investigation. No motive for the killing was ascertained, and despite the best efforts of detectives, the case went unsolved for the next 13 years. After running down every possible lead, no prime suspect was identified. During most homicide investigations, suspicion usually first falls on the close family members of the deceased. Detectives interviewed the spouses and next of kin of the victims, but after a protracted investigation, they finally ruled them out as suspects.

Todd Kohlhepp wasn't on their radar. He congratulated himself on having gotten away with murder—at least, for the time being.

It is believed that his motive for carrying out the killing spree was the fact that some of the Superbike Motorsports staff had laughed at him once while he was at the store. He was unable to forgive the perceived slight, and four people died because of it. Kohlhepp had earned himself a reputation as an "angry customer," which he proved was well-deserved.

On November 3, 2016, Spartanburg County sheriff's deputies executed a warrant to search Kohlhepp's property, located in Woodruff, South Carolina. Officers heard repeated banging sounds coming from inside a large metal shipping container, which was secured with a padlock. As they got closer, a woman's voice began calling out for help.

Inside the container, they found 30-year-old Kala Victoria Brown trapped in a makeshift cage. Thankfully, she was still alive. A thick metal chain was looped around her neck, preventing her from moving far. Her left ankle was secured in place with a set of handcuffs. Her captor had provided her with paperback books to read and plastic bottles of juice.

While most of Kohlhepp's victims were buried on his property, officers followed the sounds of banging to discover a missing woman chained inside a shipping container.

In an interview with ABC Columbia's WOLO-TV, Anderson detective Charlynn Ezell recalled that Kala Brown's first words were: "Thank you so much for finding me."

Brown and her boyfriend, 32-year-old Charlie Carver, had been missing for two months, and many had feared the worst. After their sudden disappearance in August, all attempts to locate them had failed, and foul play was suspected. Their dog had been left alone, without any food in its bowl or water to drink. The couple failed to keep a dinner date with friends, instead seeming to simply vanish into thin air. Attempts to trace their cell phones failed. The devices had both been switched off. Kohlhepp had made a crucial mistake, however: he allowed the phones to make contact with a cell tower located near the piece of land where he had taken his victims. Those final cell phone pings revealed the last known locations of Brown and Carver to the police.

Things took another turn for the bizarre when Carver's Facebook page continued to post status updates. Unbeknownst to the world, which followed the unfolding story with horrified fascination, Todd Kohlhepp had hacked their pages and was acting as if he was Carver. Instant messages were sent to those who knew Carver, but his friends and family members were not reassured, finding the impersonator's turn of phrase unconvincing. This feeling of unease was only bolstered when Carver's Facebook account started sharing the official missing persons reports for the couple. Over time, the whole thing began to take on the air of a sick and twisted game.

When a Facebook friend posted "Where the hell is Kala Brown?" Carver's account replied with "Kala is with her huband [sic] Charlie." Even ignoring the typo, the format of the sentence did not ring true. Who refers to themself in the third person?

"Why can't she have any contact with us?" the commenter asked. The reply: "She dosent [sic] want to."

With the benefit of hindsight, the big clue to their whereabouts was the fact that Kala Brown had a side job working for 45-year-old Todd Kohlhepp. She did a little cleaning work on some of his properties. This was how he had groomed her as a potential victim.

Deputies worked to free her from her restraints. As they talked with Brown, a grim picture began to emerge. She and Carver had driven to the farm to meet her erstwhile employer. Kohlhepp had shot Carver dead right in front of her, then imprisoned her in the shipping container. She had been trapped there for months. She had been fed regularly, though only once per day. It was almost as if her abductor could not decide what to do with her and had not yet decided to kill her.

Brown's time in captivity was appalling. She was kept in conditions of near-total darkness for much of the time, allowed out only on

**Had her whereabouts not been discovered in time, it is likely that Kala Brown would have met the same fate as her boyfriend.**

rare occasions, and under the direct supervision of her captor. She would later reveal in an interview that Kohlhepp had sexually molested her twice a day, every day. Had her whereabouts not been discovered in time, it is likely that Kala Brown would have met the same fate as her boyfriend. There had been no possibility of escape because of the chains and the cage, and if even if she had been willing to take the risk, Brown was terrified of the potential consequences. Kohlhepp had shown her the shallow grave of her boyfriend and two other murder victims, telling her that if she tried to get away, she would end up dead and buried alongside them.

Deputies fanned out to search the entirety of the 95-acre lot. They found a vehicle that was registered in Charlie Carver's name. It had been resprayed and had been covered in tree branches, in a half-hearted attempt to conceal it. The day after Brown's rescue, the search turned up a set of buried human remains. The body was Carver's and bore multiple bullet wounds. Brown's story was proven right. Todd Kohlhepp had murdered him in cold blood.

Shortly after Kala Brown was rescued from his shipping container, Todd Kohlhepp was arrested and brought in for questioning. Rather than bluster and obfuscate, Kohlhepp remained calm and polite throughout questioning by detectives. When requested to do so, the serial killer returned to the property and led detectives to the shallow grave in which two more of his victims were buried. They were later identified as being a missing married couple, 25-year-old Meagan Leigh McCraw Coxie and her husband, 29-year-old Johnny Joe Coxie. He also admitted to having committed the 2003 Superbike Motorsport murders.

For the families of those killed in the 2003 shooting, Kohlhepp's confession came as something of a relief, however. It provided them with a sense of closure that they had been lacking for the past 13 years. Also grieving, however, were the families of the Coxies. Meagan had been a waitress at a Waffle House that Kohlhepp regularly frequented. His reputation there was as a customer to avoid, if possible. Although he was a big tipper, he made regular passes at the waitresses, all of whom found his behavior creepy. Things got so bad that whenever he was seen entering the restaurant, a male waiter was dispatched to take his order.

Life had not been easy for Meagan and Johnny Joe. They had taken up Kohlhepp's offer to do some paid manual work on the land he owned. Johnny Joe Coxie apparently said something that Todd didn't like. Whatever it was, it must have tripped the realtor's hair-trigger temper. He shot both dead. Johnny Joe sustained multiple gunshot wounds to his torso, while Meagan died of a single shot to the head. After completing an autopsy on both bodies, the coroner determined that Johnny Joe had died on or about December 19, and his wife had been killed a week later, suggesting that she had suffered the same type of captivity as Kala Brown.

A nightmare regular at Waffle House, Kohlhepp had merely to walk in the door to send female servers running to send a male in their place.

South Carolina is a death penalty state. Avoiding the sentence of legal execution with a plea bargain, Kohlhepp accepted instead life imprisonment without the possibility of parole.

With the Motorsport Murders now solved, detectives considered other cold cases throughout South Carolina and Arizona, both locations where Kohlhepp had spent time. No definitive connections were ever drawn between him and other murders, but there are still rumors and suspicions that he may have killed more than the seven victims for which he was finally held accountable. Kohlhepp himself continues to insinuate that he was responsible for further murders, but at the time of writing, he has offered little more than cryptic hints to that effect.

Even before the murders, Todd Kohlhepp had gotten off on slyly taunting both the authorities and the world at large, leaving hints to the crimes he was committing. Hacking Charlie Carver's Facebook account was perhaps the most prominent example, pretending to be a man who had already died at his own hands. While it is possible that his instant messages and posts were a clumsy attempt to fool people into thinking that Carver and Brown were still alive, the increasingly darker tone assumed by those communications strongly suggests that it was simply Kohlhepp having fun at the expense of his victims and their loved ones.

Somewhat more cryptic were comments that he left for products on Amazon.com. This included a five-star review for a set of four master padlocks that Kohlhepp had ordered, which included the phrase:

"Now even my locks have locks … have 5 on a shipping container." That shipping container, of course, was used to imprison Kala Brown.

Kohlhepp had a fascination with guns and bladed weapons. In and of itself, that isn't necessarily a red flag, but as a convicted felon, South Carolina law expressly forbade him from owning firearms. The police officers who searched his property found a huge stash of weapons, a mix of handguns, shotguns, and semiautomatic rifles. His ownership of these guns was a serious criminal offense all by itself and showed yet again his willingness to flout the law whenever he felt like it.

One aspect of the case that drew a lot of media attention was Todd Kohlhepp's Amazon review history. A common thread runs through the items he purchased and chose to leave a rating for: their usefulness for committing acts of violence. He rates one particular tactical knife highly, adding that while he hasn't actually used it to stab anybody yet, he dreams of doing so "with a quality tool like this."

Perusing those reviews gives one a sense of darkness and barely restrained violence, yet if his murderous background wasn't known, most would simply dismiss them as the rantings of a blowhard. Some reviews extol the virtues of a particular weapon for harming another human being, whereas another talks about using a particular shovel to help dispose of a body. Taken in the light of the seven murders Kohlhepp was responsible for, these reviews are positively chilling.

The same can be said of his social media accounts. Kohlhepp was active on Facebook and had used the platform to contact Kala Brown to secure her services as a cleaner. His timeline contained a number of disturbing posts, including one that seemed to indirectly relate to the kidnapping and murders he was responsible for:

In a show of dark humor, Kohlhepp trolled the world by posting item reviews that hinted at his less conventional, off-label use cases.

"Reading the news … this person missing, that person missing, another person missing … oh, wait … that person just went to beach with friend, other person found with parole violation boyfriend … in the event I become missing, please note no one would take me. I eat too much, and I am crabby, they would just bring me back or give me 20 bucks for a cab ride. Most likely if I am missing, its because my dumb ass did something on that tractor again and I am too stubborn to go to the doctor.... I got 9 lives."

Nobody reading this diatribe was aware that it had been written by a man who was behind several of those very legitimate missing persons reports.

Kohlhepp's posts frequently bemoaned what he saw as the disrespectful and entitled attitudes of children and young people. He also had little time for humanity at large, as evidenced by the following comment: "We need ebola to come as a huge snowstorm, to wipe out half the population, and then melt away...."

In keeping with his self-centered, narcissistic nature, he seemingly gave no thought to the possibility that he might be in the half of the population that died. Neither did he think of himself as one of those disrespectful people he maintained were a large part of society's problems, although there was no shortage of Todd Kohlhepp stories that showed him in exactly that light.

He was also noticed exhibiting behavior that was simply bizarre. Addicted to pornography, he was caught watching it in his office at the realty business. As the boss, he could afford to simply laugh it off, but it caused his employees to give him a few sideways looks. Kohlhepp developed a reputation for being something of a sleaze, rarely missing an opportunity to slip a sexual innuendo into a conversation.

Perhaps unsurprisingly, the one person who stuck by Todd Kohlhepp and defended him to the bitter end was his mother, who claimed during an interview with CBS television that her son was "misunderstood, not a monster." His motivation for killing, she added, was not pleasure but rather simply the actions of a man who was lashing out because he had been hurt in the past.

This was how she rationalized the murder of Charlie Carver, and she added that Kohlhepp was forced to imprison Kala Brown because she had witnessed the killing firsthand and could not be allowed to contact the police.

The same mother that young Todd Kohlhepp had threatened to kill was trying to convince the world that he wasn't such a bad guy after all.

When it comes to her son's motivation for murder, however, she may be close to the truth. If there is one predominant driving force in

Todd Kohlhepp appears in court to plead guilty to a number of charges, including seven counts of murder.

the life of Todd Kohlhepp, it isn't sexual in nature; it is anger. Boyhood psychiatric evaluations noted that his defining characteristic was anger, and it was an emotion that he was never fully able to control.

In addition to the lifelong rage that consumed him, the teenaged Kohlhepp's probation officer also noted that he was basically devoid of any sort of conscience. He thrived on confrontation and didn't care about the consequences, so long as he came out on top. This, along with his clinical diagnosis of borderline personality disorder, made Kohlhepp the equivalent of a ticking human time bomb, just waiting to go off when the proper stimulus arose. Ideally, he should never have been released from prison in the first place, but his attorney had struck a deal to have the sexual assault charged dropped on the condition that Kohlhepp plead guilty to kidnapping.

Despite never having served in the military, he liked to claim that he had. Kohlhepp told wild stories about having supposedly machine-gunned entire villages from a helicopter. These were nothing more than fantastic tales, told to explain why he had been absent from society for 15 years and also to appease his inflated ego. They constituted a vain attempt to impress the person he was telling them to. In fact, the effect tended to be the opposite of what Kohlhepp intended, because none of the stories were remotely believable.

A common theme through his life was a refusal to accept responsibility for anything. He seemed to feel no guilt, whether for the crime of rape, murder, or kidnapping. The total lack of remorse he displayed was chilling, the mark of a true psychopath. Society is fortunate that Todd Kohlhepp is now locked up in prison and will spend the rest of his life there.

# THE HOOKUP APP KILLER
# STEPHEN PORT

The Internet can be a wonderful place. It holds the answers to any of a trillion questions we might have. It provides us with entertainment, education, and information. The Internet also allows us to stay connected with one another, even over great distances, and to make new friends and connect with new people that we might otherwise never have met.

There is also a dangerous side to the World Wide Web. Predators lurk in the dark, shadowy corners. Most portray themselves as decent, kind, everyday human beings, when in reality, they are the very opposite. Such a man was Britain's Stephen Port.

Port's childhood was unremarkable. There is no evidence of abuse or neglect in his family history, none of the obvious red flags that may betray the presence of a future serial killer.

After leaving culinary school with chef's qualifications under his belt, Port worked a number of different jobs in the food service industry. None of it was glamorous, but it was honest work, and it paid the bills. To all outside appearances, he seemed to be a respectable young man.

Stephen Port was well into adulthood when he came out openly as a gay man. This didn't come as a huge revelation to some of those who knew him, but it has been claimed that his parents were disappointed to see their hopes of having grandchildren dashed. With that aside, it seems that this particular aspect of his life was not the cause of great turbulence for him.

In 2006, he got his own residence, in the town of Barking, outside London. This brought with it a degree of freedom that he could never have enjoyed while living with his parents, but it also had a downside. Port began using drugs recreationally. His libido kicked into high gear, and so did his addiction to pornography—the violent kind, much of which included rape.

As the Internet continued to balloon throughout the mid- and late 2000s, Port discovered MySpace, Facebook, and various other digital platforms through which he could converse with other gay men. At one point, he was running multiple accounts on several different sites, some of them set up under fake names. He claimed to have graduated from Oxford, one of the United Kingdom's most prestigious universities, and to be a teacher who worked with children with special needs.

All his online activities were geared toward getting him as much casual sex as he possibly could. Stephen Port's sexual appetite was insatiable. As time went on, he cared less and less about obtaining consent and decided to simply take what he wanted.

Grindr is a phone-based app that is primarily used for gay men to connect with one another and to schedule sexual encounters. Once somebody installs the Grindr app, they complete a short bio regarding their sexual preferences—and can upload a photograph of themselves. The app uses the location tracking features of the user's smartphone to identify other Grindr users who are close by.

Conventional wisdom among Grindr aficionados holds that potential hookups should meet in a public place first, to scope one another out. This is for reasons of safety. Stephen Port is the poster child for just how important this particular safety measure can be.

Grindr is a dating app popular among gay men looking for a quick, no-obligation hookup.

Port used the app to locate and meet up with potential victims. He brought them back to his flat, drugged them, and raped them. The cause of death was drug overdose. Port targeted men who were much younger than himself, usually in their early to mid-twenties, though some were teenagers. Some were not even half his age. All had a very similar body frame—slender but muscular. He did not like overweight men or those he considered to be unattractive.

A little after four o'clock in the morning on June 19, 2014, in the East London town of Barking, an unidentified male called the national emergency number 999. The man making the call told a bogus story about traveling along Cooke Street when he noticed the body of a male lying motionless. Could they please send an ambulance?

What the 999 dispatcher could not have known was that the anonymous caller was, in fact, the dead man's murderer.

The town's pubs, bars, and nightclubs had already closed their doors for the night. When the ambulance arrived, the EMT and paramedic crew found Anthony Walgate dead in the street. He was 23 years old. Bizarrely, he was sitting up and his legs were crossed. This posture was not consistent with a drunk who had simply passed out in the street or a postseizure patient, as had been proposed by the 999 caller.

Crouching down close to his body, the EMS crew quickly began to assess their patient. They soon realized that the young man was dead—and not newly dead, either. His body temperature was cold, particularly for a summer night in June. His pupils were nonreactive to light, and his skin had the pallid quality that is a hallmark of the deceased. Further clinical assessment revealed no signs of life whatsoever. The dead man had been that way for a while. He hadn't simply collapsed in the street—which 23-year-olds tend not to do most of the time.

A bag was also found at the scene, containing a small bottle with traces of liquid inside it. That liquid was the date-rape drug Gamma-Hydroxybutyrate (GHB).

Using the alias of Joe Dean, 41-year-old Stephen Port had rented the services of fashion student and part-time male escort Anthony Walgate. Back at his flat, Port dosed Walgate with gamma-hydroxybutyrate, better known as GHB. This potent sedative is commonly used as a date-rape drug. The levels of GHB in Walgate's bloodstream were sufficiently toxic to have killed him.

Port also used high doses of GHB to incapacitate his next two victims and to facilitate their rape. Their deaths took place in September, three weeks apart. Port was either too lazy or too inept to transport the bodies of 22-year-old Gabriel Kovari and 21-year-old Daniel Whitworth very far from his residence on Cooke Street, how-

Gamma-hydroxybutyrate (GHB) is a drug with some minor medical uses, known primarily for its off-label recreational use as a euphoric and aphrodisiac, and especially for its abuse as a date-rape drug.

ever, choosing instead to dump their remains in the same cemetery, not far from where he lived. The bodies of both young men were found sitting up, rather than lying down, just as Anthony Walgate had been, and in exactly the same spot in the graveyard of St. Margaret of Antioch's Church. One can only feel sympathy for the lady who was out walking her dog when she discovered both bodies.

Kovari had been staying with Port for a few days, ostensibly as a flat mate, though Port referred to him as his live-in "twink," a slang term for a young, boyish gay male. Twinks are usually physically attractive and can be much sought after by older men. Men such as Stephen Port. It didn't take Gabriel Kovari long to discover that his new landlord was a mean and twisted individual, and shortly before his death, he had texted a friend to tell him that Port was a bad man. Unfortunately, he had no idea just how bad.

Detectives had already discovered that Anthony Walgate's 999 caller and Stephen Port were one and the same man. Port lived in a flat at 62 Cooke Street, close to where Walgate's body had been found. Police officers paid Port a visit at home. He spun the police officers an implausible yarn about having returned from a late-night shift at work, only to find what he thought was a drunk passed out near his front door.

Investigators uncovered the fact that Port had been Walgate's escort client, and they knew he had lied to them. Under further questioning, Port's story changed repeatedly, twisting and turning awkwardly with each new question that was put to him. He tried to pin the blame for Walgate's death on an unspecified drug that Walgate himself had supposedly brought along and taken voluntarily. In reality, Stephen Port had given Anthony Walgate a massive dose of GHB.

Suspicious as the death was, for some reason the police did not pursue it as a possible murder. To make matters worse, they had a smoking gun in their possession in the form of Stephen Port's laptop, which they had confiscated as evidence. Not only had Port been sending his soon-to-be-victim hookup requests, but he had also neglected to clear his Internet search history of such terms as "rape and torture nude boy" and "date rape drug."

> Had they checked into Port's web browsing history and sent messages at the outset, he may have been deprived of the opportunity to kill again.

It's hard to see this as anything other than the police dropping the ball. Had they checked into Port's web browsing history and sent messages at the outset, he may have been deprived of the opportunity to kill again. Unfortunately, they neglected to do so. They had arrested Port prior to the murders of Gabriel Kovari and Daniel Whitworth, then let him go on bail to await trial for perverting the course of justice (i.e., giving false testimony to police in an active investigation). It was during this period that he killed them both. The police had missed an opportunity to prevent those crimes from happening.

There were also commonalities in the way in which the bodies of Walgate, Kovari, and Whitworth were found. All of them were discovered in the sitting position, rather than the supine or prone position in which most corpses tend to be found. Although all three were wearing clothes, their shirts had been pulled up toward the chest to expose their midriffs. All were young men, of a similar physical build and sexual orientation. None showed signs of traumatic injury. Their cell phones had all been taken.

Most damningly, all three of the bodies were discovered within a stone's throw of Stephen Port's flat on Cooke Street.

As the investigation into the death of Anthony Walgate progressed, Stephen Port was arrested—not for murder, but for having lied to police officers regarding Walgate's death.

In a clumsy attempt to explain away these two murders, Port had scribbled a suicide note that purported to be written by Daniel Whitworth. The note claimed that Whitworth was responsible for the death of Kovari three weeks earlier. Kovari had died of a drug overdose during sex, it said, and Whitworth couldn't bear it anymore. When Whitworth's body was discovered, police found the suicide note in his hand.

The note had a damning postscript, which read: "BTW Please do not blame the guy I was with last night, we only had sex then I left. He knows nothing of what I have done. I have taken what g [GHB] I have left with sleeping pills so if it does kill me it is what I deserve. Feeling dizey [sic] now as I took 10 min ago so hoping you understand my writing."

The investigating officers seemed to take the note at face value. The paragraph that suspiciously asks them to "not blame the guy I was with last night" refers to Stephen Port. It is a ham-fisted attempt on Port's part to deflect blame and attention from himself. Although Whitworth had a boyfriend, he had arranged for a meeting with Port and was never seen alive again.

Daniel's Whitworth's body was found sitting on a bed sheet that could have been linked to Stephen Port's apartment—if, that is, it had been forensically tested. It was not. Port's DNA was already on file, after the first police visit to his flat. A DNA match would have given the investigation a clear direction in which to go.

Apparently, nobody thought to ask why a suicidal young man, who was about to end his life, would have laid down a sheet to sit on first. With the benefit of hindsight, it seems obvious that the sheet was there to aid Port in carrying or dragging Daniel's body to the churchyard in the dead of night.

In January 2015, Stephen Port's court date came around. He had been charged with an attempt to pervert the course of justice and ended up being sentenced to eight months in prison. He was not tried for the murder of Anthony Walgate, however, and was back on the streets that summer, having served just two months of his sentence.

He was about to kill again.

In the early morning hours of September 13, 2015, 25-year-old Jack Taylor's phone pinged. It was a notification from Grindr, informing him that he had just made a match in the local area. He liked the look of his match enough to be willing to meet him just a few minutes later, in Barking. The Grindr hookup was, of course, Stephen Port.

Stephen Port stands trial in the Central Criminal Court of England and Wales, widely known as the Old Bailey.

The precise details of what happened next will almost certainly never be known; the only living person who could recount them is Port, and he is unlikely to tell the truth. What *is* known is that Port met up with Jack Taylor. Footage from CCTV cameras on the streets of Barking captured them walking together, a little after three o'clock in the morning. It is probable that the same scenario played out with Taylor that happened with Port's three other victims: a return to the flat on Cooke Street, a surreptitious overdose of GHB, nonconsensual sex, and ultimately, another tragic death. Port took Taylor's remains to his now-familiar churchyard dumping ground and left them there.

Even a casual glance at the position of the body made it apparent that he had been placed there by the same perpetrator as the year before. The body was found sitting up, leaning against a wall, with a bare abdomen. A search of the dead man's clothes turned up a small bottle of what had once contained GHB, plus a needle and syringe. The narrative Stephen Port was trying to spin when he abandoned Jack Taylor's body was the tried-and-trusted "he died of an accidental, self-inflicted overdose" story. Yet this was the fourth such death in the space of 15 months. All were young men, and all had been posed in precisely the same way.

Only an idiot would have thought he could have gotten away with it—and Stephen Port was that idiot. To make matters worse, he was almost right. No murder investigation was launched into the death of Jack Taylor. The police dismissed his death as being exactly what it looked like: a tragic, fatal overdose, with no foul play involved. Fortunately, members of his family weren't going to take no for an answer. They de-

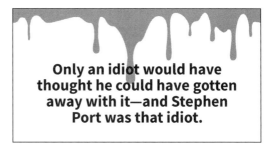

**Only an idiot would have thought he could have gotten away with it—and Stephen Port was that idiot.**

manded that the police make a photograph of Taylor and his unidentified male companion available to the public, along with a request for help in identifying him.

It did not take long before the name Stephen Port popped up on their radar. Finally, a murder probe would be launched. Arrested and detained for questioning, Port denied having any involvement with the four deaths, or going anywhere near the church where three of his victims' bodies had been abandoned. Detectives noticed that his stories were full of inconsistencies. Yet this blanket denial, rarely an effective legal tactic, was defeated when word of his arrest and suspicion of having committed rape and murder made the news.

Aghast at what they saw in the media, a multitude of Stephen Port's former sex partners came forward. They had some horrifying stories to tell. All followed a similar theme. They had met Port through a dating or hookup app and had found him to be fairly normal when they first set eyes on him. He was polite, pleasant, and accommodating. He would offer them a drink, which unbeknownst to them was laced with GHB.

Port had previously worked as an escort, reveling in the excitement that a life of promiscuity brought him. He engaged in orgies with multiple partners and even filmed some of his encounters to share with his friends and potential partners. He fantasized about drugging his lovers into a state of unconsciousness and then raping them without their knowledge. Eventually, Port started using the drug GHB as a means of turning his sick fantasy into a reality.

Port had begun recreationally abusing his chosen murder weapon, GHB, himself before using it on his victims. As a central nervous system sedative, the drug renders the person taking it unconscious and can knock out the respiratory drive if given in too great a quantity. Its colorless, odorless, and tasteless nature makes the drug easy to slip into an unsuspecting individual's drink.

At lower levels, however, GHB can induce feelings of extreme euphoria and can also make the person extremely open to suggestion. We all have inhibitions, to some degree. GHB smashes through those barriers, causing people to do things under its influence that they would normally only consider in their wildest dreams.

During the course of their investigation, detectives learned that Stephen Port had an addiction to drug rape porn that bordered on the outright obsessive. He collected gigabytes of such pornography on his laptop, spending practically every waking moment consuming it, fantasizing about it, and talking about it with other men. Port even appeared in some amateur porn that had been filmed at his flat, with both himself and other men videoed having sex with unconscious young males.

Some of Port's hookups watched the rape porn with him, perhaps as a prelude to being given GHB themselves. Whether they consented to partake or were given the drug unknowingly is uncertain.

An avid consumer of hardcore porn, Port would also video some of his own exploits.

Stephen Port found himself in court, charged with multiple counts of murder. In light of the avalanche of evidence and testimony stacked against him, the jury refused to believe any of his protests of innocence, which had rung hollow from the outset.

After the jury found him guilty of the murders of Anthony Walgate, Gabriel Kovari, Daniel Whitworth, and Jack Taylor, the judge sentenced him to a whole life order, guaranteeing that he will never be released from prison. Such a sentence indicates the judge's firm belief that the convicted offender can never be successfully rehabilitated and will remain a significant menace to his fellow human beings if his freedom should be restored.

A key question is: did Stephen Port know that he was committing murder? It might be argued that the very first time he administered a fatal overdose of GHB, he did not mean to kill. His intent was most likely simply to incapacitate his victim as a means to committing rape. But what about the second, third, and fourth killings? There were also a number of other men who went back to Port's flat and were given GHB, only to survive. Did he even care whether they lived or died, so long as he achieved sexual gratification? Certainly, the jury considered him to be a murderer. The nature of his whole life sentence means that he will never be a threat to the British public again.

# THE BUTCHER OF KANSAS CITY
# ROBERT "BOB" BERDELLA

**W**e often tend to believe that serial killers should be easy to spot. That they should appear a certain way—brooding, with a psychotic stare, perhaps—and live in the sort of run-down, ramshackle derelict building that would befit the lair of a monster. On occasion, this does turn out to be the case, but evil can be found among us. It hides in plain sight, wearing a friendly smile, and living in the same type of home as anybody else.

Such was the case with Robert Berdella, whose preferred victim type was always a young male, often an escort or sex worker. He enjoyed kidnapping them, often with the benefit of drugs to lower their resistance. This abduction was then followed by prolonged sessions of rape and torture. These sessions could last for days or even weeks on end. Finally, Berdella killed his victim and cut up the body into its constituent pieces. This earned him the nickname of "The Butcher of Kansas City."

Born in 1949, Robert Berdella grew up in the town of Cuyahoga Falls, Ohio, near the city of Akron. According to those who grew up with him, his early childhood was almost entirely unremarkable. He had a stable home life, with little in the way of drama or trauma. His parents were hard workers but made time for their son and showed him no lack of love and affection. The Berdella family was Catholic, attending church on Sundays, but there is no evidence that young Robert was particularly devout.

Berdella did well in school—a solid student, if not particularly academically gifted. He was the victim of some bullying, which made life difficult for him. His response was to become increasingly insular, turning inward and preferring his own company to that of others. Socially isolated and lonely, it's likely that the seeds of Robert Berdella's future pathologic behavior were sown at this point in life. The fact that he was beginning to feel attraction for other young men did not help matters, particularly as the Catholic Church insisted that such feelings were a sin. These conflicting forces likely caused him no small amount of emotional turmoil and angst.

Then, in 1965, everything changed for the worse. Berdella's 39-year-old father, Robert Sr., died of a massive heart attack, leaving the 16-year-old Robert shell-shocked and fatherless. To make matters worse, he was sexually molested by an older male colleague at the restaurant where he had taken a job as a cook. This line of work would sustain him financially over the next few years.

Berdella's mother remarried soon after the death of his father. Young Robert took this personally, growing a seething resentment toward her.

Berdella graduated from high school in 1967 and enrolled at the Kansas City Art Institute, in the hopes of feeding his creative side. Wholeheartedly adopting the student lifestyle, he began to both take and sell drugs. This backfired when he was caught attempting to make a drug deal with an undercover law enforcement officer. He was also busted for possession. Neither brush with the law saw him go to prison, although Berdella did spend a few days behind bars in the jail. This very brief period of incarceration didn't seem to have an effect on his drug dealing and abuse.

More disconcertingly still, it was in his capacity as an art student that Robert Berdella began to kill animals. Ostensibly, this was done as part of his performance art projects. In reality, it is safe to assume that this was the sadistic side of his psyche rearing its ugly head for the first time. This ultimately led to him exiting the Kansas City Art Institute and returning to restaurant kitchens to work for a living.

Free of his academic obligations, Berdella made no pretense at being heterosexual. Like most other major urban centers, Kansas City had its own thriving gay scene. What money he had left over from paying off legal fees accrued during his encounters with the criminal justice system was spent on socializing and the purchase of a house in the city's respectable Hyde Park neighborhood.

He began operating a business, named Bob's Bazaar Bizarre, at the Westport Flea Market, buying and selling obscure collectibles and curiosities. Some of his commodities were genuine historical artifacts, whereas others were little more than junk. Surprisingly, Berdella was a savvy collector and retailer, who knew a bargain when he saw one. At the very least, the Bazaar provided him with a livable wage and allowed him the freedom to live reasonably well and party whenever he was in the mood.

Between 1984 and 1988, Berdella tortured and murdered six men at his residence at 4315 Charlotte Street. After drugging them into a state of unconsciousness, he stripped them naked and tied them to a bed upstairs. Prior to the death of his victims, he indulged in lengthy sessions of torture and brutality, which were intended to inflict the maximum amount of pain possible. Berdella kept a log book of every vile act, assiduously noting exactly what he had done, at what time, and what the effects had been. He would later loftily declare this to be "experimentation," though in reality it was about little more than venting his rage upon helpless male captives.

In the style of a researcher, Berdella thoroughly documented his depraved endeavors on both paper and film.

On July 5, 1984, the national Independence Day holiday was over. It was a Thursday, and most Americans were going back to work, already looking forward to the weekend. Robert Berdella had a different focus for his attention: he was about to commit his first murder.

His chosen victim was 19-year-old Jerry Howell. The Howell family occupied a spot next to Berdella's at the flea market. They also lived directly across the street. The two men were out taking a drive, with Berdella behind the wheel, when the older man passed the younger a drink. Howell accepted it, not knowing that Berdella had added a secret ingredient: veterinary sedatives, mixed with Valium. Ostensibly friends, Howell had no reason to be suspicious of the driver's motives.

Within an hour, the drugs had kicked in. Howell found himself growing unaccountably drowsy. This was exactly the effect that Berdella had hoped to achieve. He turned for home, helping the almost somnolent young man inside the house and locking the door behind them.

As Jerry Howell began to wake up, Berdella sedated him again. He had stockpiled drugs for this very reason, and now that they were behind closed doors, he used a syringe to inject the tranquilizers directly into his victim's vein. Any medication given directly into the bloodstream has a quicker-acting and more potent effect, and it wasn't long before Howell was down for the count. Berdella stripped him completely naked and tied his wrists and ankles to the bed.

Psychologists familiar with the case believe that Berdella had long been nursing the desire to torture and molest a helpless male captive. Now, his dark fantasies were finally made manifest. He spent the rest of the day raping and abusing the helpless young man, taking sadistic pleasure in inflicting pain upon him at every opportunity. Berdella used different objects to sodomize Howell. In order to keep him from screaming, Howell had been gagged, and repeat doses of sedatives were injected whenever he began to return to full consciousness.

There were also physical beatings, a way for Berdella to vent some of the rage he had begun to feel. Jerry Howell died at ten o'clock on the night of July 6, after enduring repeated sessions of truly horrific torture. His cause of death remains unknown. It is possible that the sedatives knocked out his respiratory drive, causing him to stop breathing. He may also have choked to death on his own vomit, another side effect of being heavily sedated, or of cerebral hypoxia, a lack of oxygen to the brain caused by the gag. No autopsy would ever be performed because an intact body was never found.

> **Psychologists familiar with the case believe that Berdella had long been nursing the desire to torture and molest a helpless male captive.**

Berdella either dragged or carried Howell's corpse downstairs to the basement and suspended it by the ankles from a sturdy beam. Taking photographs as he went, he sliced open the major blood vessels, allowing gravity to drain the blood into a large container that he placed beneath the head. After the body was as bloodless as it was going to get, he set about slicing it up into multiple pieces. The process of dismemberment took many hours. When it was finally complete, Berdella placed the body parts into trash bags, sealed them up, and left the bags out for the city's waste disposal truck to pick up during the next scheduled garbage collection.

This method of disposal displays a level of confidence that verged upon sheer arrogance, a character trait for which Robert Berdella was well known. All it would have taken was for one bag to rip, revealing the contents, and his crime would have been discovered. Although he had taken care to double-bag the human remains, allowing the evidence of a murder to sit and decompose at the curbside was still an incredible risk to run.

The gamble paid off. The remains of Jerry Howell were collected and sent to the refuse heap without anybody being the wiser—apart from the young man's killer. Based upon his future actions, it is likely that Berdella intended to torture his victim for much longer than a single day. In all likelihood, Howell died accidentally, which was a very small mercy that future victims would not be granted.

For all the care Berdella put into dispatching his first victim, when it came time to get rid of the evidence, he took the easy road.

Nine months passed without any further murders. During this time, Berdella was busy making a living and no doubt contemplating the results of his first torture-murder. He had taken numerous photographs during the crime and had kept copious notes that he later referred to. Although he was not a medical professional, he had also documented the time and dose of each sedative injection. He did not want his next victim to die as quickly as Jerry Howell.

In April 1985, a house guest of Berdella's became the next to die at his hands. Robert A. Sheldon, 20, lived in California but had been hitch-hiking his way east across the country, intending to reach Chicago. Instead, his final destination became 4315 Charlotte Street in Kansas City.

Berdella and Robert Sheldon met two years before the latter's murder, when Berdella had thrown a party at his home. Sheldon was invited and spent the better part of a week sleeping at the house on Charlotte Street, sometimes using drugs to the point where he would pass out. The pair had an intermittent acquaintanceship over the two years that followed. The house was a convenient crash pad for Sheldon, a place to stay the night when he needed to, in exchange for a few bucks.

Robert Sheldon thought that 4315 Charlotte Street was a safe place. He was tragically wrong.

On the evening of April 10, 1985, Sheldon turned up at Robert Berdella's door once again. Berdella let him in and noticed that the young man seemed unwell. He bided his time, waiting for him to fall asleep on the couch. Once Sheldon had passed out, Berdella drugged him repeatedly. His plan didn't work, however. Despite having been tranquilized, Sheldon managed to regain consciousness. He now felt worse than he had when he first arrived at the house but had no idea that he had been injected with sedatives.

The following day, April 11, Berdella refrained from drugging his house guest further, but resumed it on the 12th.

Berdella tied Sheldon to the bed, gagged him, used a regular course of sedatives to control him, and subjected him to three continuous days of agonizing torture and rape.

On April 15, there was a knock at the door. An acquaintance had dropped by the house unannounced. This was cause for concern, if not panic. Unsure whether he could keep his victim quiet, the serial killer decided he had only one option. Stalling the friend for a moment, he quickly went upstairs to the bedroom where Sheldon was still restrained. He put a plastic bag over Sheldon's head and tied it off with a rope. Then he allowed the young man to slowly suffocate.

Once the visitor had left, Berdella went back upstairs and untied Sheldon's body. After draining it of blood and cutting it up, he decapitated the head and stored it as a keepsake before disposing of the remainder of the body's components. He used a chainsaw to separate the pieces.

A little over two months later, on June 22, Berdella found a young man hiding in the shed outside. It was 28-year-old Mark Wallace, a Marine Corps veteran who had since fallen on hard times. He was taking shelter from heavy rain. Sensing an opportunity, Berdella invited him into the house to dry off and rest. The two had met before, and Wallace saw no reason not to accept the offer. He had been drinking, and if Robert Berdella's testimony is to be believed, he allowed the serial killer to give him an injection in order to help calm his nerves.

Like a scene from a horror movie, Berdella used a chainsaw to dispose of his victim's remains.

The injection was, of course, a potent tranquilizer. Combined with the alcohol, it soon knocked him unconscious. By the time he came around, he was tied down and being jolted with an electric current from a portable transformer Berdella had installed in the bedroom.

Mark Wallace was dead by seven o'clock the following evening. Under questioning, Berdella claimed that he had died of suffocation, caused by a combination of the gag, which restricted airflow and oxygen into his mouth, and repeated doses of sedative drugs.

Robert Berdella had been getting away with his crimes for long enough that he had now developed a taste for them. The abductions were growing more frequent. In September, he chose Walter James Ferris to be his next victim. He survived for approximately one day, succumbing after having suffered a similar regimen of abuse to the other young men.

Photographs later recovered from the scene showed Ferris bound, gagged, and lying face down on the bed. Two large needles can be seen protruding from his upper back, still attached to syringes. Berdella was attempting to experiment with the human nervous system by applying needles to specific areas. Ferris's naked body clearly shows multiple injuries distributed across the skin, from being beaten, shocked, and injected.

> **Robert Berdella killed his final victim on August 5, 1987, after having taken another year-long hiatus.**

Berdella did not kill again until the following summer. On June 17, 1986, he drugged 23-year-old Todd Stoops. He was already known to Berdella, having spent some time as his roommate a couple of years prior. After breaking up a handful of tranquilizer tablets, the serial killer sprinkled the resultant powder into a drink and on a sandwich he was preparing for his guest. Shortly after consuming them, Stoops passed out.

Stoops suffered at Berdella's hands for not just days, but two weeks. In all that time, in which he was regularly subjected to vicious beatings and myriad other tortures, Berdella rarely fed him. He was electrocuted repeatedly. Berdella attached crocodile clips to his bare skin and used them to send thousands of volts through his body. He documented the process in numerous photographs. These same images showed him growing increasingly emaciated as time went on. Before his death, he was a shadow of his former self. He became infected, most likely due to one of the many injuries he sustained, finally dying on July 1 (most likely of sepsis, although severe hemorrhage is also a possibility).

Robert Berdella killed his final victim on August 5, 1987, after having taken another year-long hiatus. Larry Pearson, aged 20, of Wichita, had first met Berdella at the Bazaar. He had been on the streets and looking for a way out. They shared similar interests in occult artifacts.

Pearson was murdered the same way Berdella had killed others: a bag tied tightly over his head, inducing fatal asphyxia. This came at the end of a staggeringly long, 43-day marathon of torture and molestation—more than six weeks.

Sticking to his established MO, Berdella documented everything. Disturbing photographs taken by the killer show the helpless young man naked, with his wrists bound above his head. His neck is hyperextended, tilting the head back. Piano wire tied around his head serves as a makeshift gag. A needle and syringe poke out of his neck, directly inserted midline above the esophagus and trachea. One of Berdella's favorite sick "experiments" involved injecting drain cleaner directly into the throats of his victims.

For weeks, Larry Pearson had been tortured and starved into submission. Robert Berdella had set out to break his will and believed that he had succeeded. He was wrong. On August 5, while being forced to give his captor oral sex, Pearson bit down on his penis as hard as he could. Exposed to just a fraction of the pain he had inflicted upon others, Berdella went to the closest emergency room. Surveying the wound, a doctor told him that it would require admission to the hospital to be properly treated. Before checking himself in, the serial killer returned to Charlotte Street and murdered Pearson.

He saw it as simply tying up a loose end, telling detectives later that he had "put him to sleep." Berdella had no more regard for human life than he did for any of the objects in his collection at the Bazaar. Unbeknownst to him, however, a reckoning was on the horizon.

The rest of 1987 passed without any further killing. It would be the following year, on April 2, 1988, that Robert Berdella's luck finally ran out. His latest victim, who came close to becoming the seventh man to be murdered on Charlotte Street, made a break for freedom by jumping out a window on the upper floor of the serial killer's home. Wearing nothing but a dog collar, 22-year-old Christopher Bryson ran to the nearest house for help, where a Good Samaritan picked up the phone and called the police.

A squad car responded to Charlotte Street immediately. The officers were immediately struck by the fact that Bryson had red marks on his wrists and ankles, consistent with his having been forcibly restrained. His testimony was horrific. A sex worker by trade, Bryson had been kidnapped and held captive for the past five days, in the house from which he had just escaped. During that time, he had been repeatedly raped by his abductor. He had also been subjected to torture, which included being injected with several different chemicals, beaten, and electrically shocked over and over again.

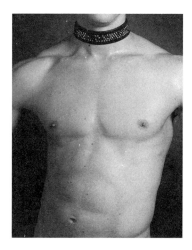

Investigators got a lucky break when one of Port's "pets" broke free from his sadistic kennel.

Bryson wasn't the first he had done this to, his captor told him, and if he didn't submit and go along with it, he was going to be killed—just like those who had gone before him. He then showed the helpless man photographs to prove it: pictures of other men, bound spread-eagled to the very same bed he now lay on.

Berdella had left Chris Bryson tied to his bed with ropes and headed off to work, confident that his victim could not escape from his bonds. Pain and the fear of near-certain death are both powerful motivators, however, and Bryson was somehow able to snag a book of matches from close to the bed. He struck a match and used it to burn his way through one of the ropes, before freeing himself entirely and making his escape.

Berdella wasn't home when Bryson made his desperate escape. He was at work. Word soon reached him that there were multiple police cruisers parked outside his home. Rather than go on the run, he made the surprising decision to return and turn himself in. He was arrested on the spot and charged with multiple felony crimes.

Once law enforcement personnel gained access to 4315 Charlotte Street, they found a house of horrors within its walls. The skull of an unidentified male was sitting on a shelf in a closet. Subsequent forensic investigation would prove that it belonged to Robert A. Sheldon.

Robert Berdella had meticulously documented every act of cruelty and torture that he had inflicted upon his helpless victims. He noted everything on looseleaf paper, upon which the media would later confer the title of "torture logs." (Berdella took exception to this term, complaining that his notations could hardly be described as "meticulous." Yet they were detailed and extensive.) A search of the house on Charlotte Street eventually put those documents into the hands of police and helped make the legal case against him all but watertight.

In addition to the logs, detectives found hundreds of photographs, many capturing a grisly scene of brutality. The Polaroid images had been taken inside Berdella's makeshift torture chamber, right there inside his home. Not all were photos of his six known murder victims, however; many were pornographic images he had taken of naked young men in compromising sexual positions. Some were flaccid, their eyes closed, as though unconscious—or dead. Not all of them were identifiable, and to this day, an accurate accounting of Robert Berdella's victims remains virtually impossible.

One of the photographs showed the dead body of a naked young man hanging from a beam in the basement by his ankles. After close scrutiny, detectives concluded that it was likely Jerry Howell, subject of a missing persons case since his disappearance in July 1984.

Once the police search shifted to the yard of the residence, more human remains began to be unearthed, including another male skull. Syringes and needles were scattered around the house, something for which Berdella had no medical need. There were also veterinary-grade sedative and tranquilizer medications, which were supposed to have been used for the treatment of dogs. Instead, they had been injected into his victims.

Besides the detailed torture logs, investigators were greeted with plenty of other evidence, openly kept around Berdella's home.

Much like the Jeffery Dahmer case, which happened in the same part of the country, the Robert Berdella murder trial gained national notoriety in the media. The crimes were similar—the torture, rape, brutalization, and murder of young gay men—but there were also notable differences. Dahmer had lived in a crime-ridden, low-income area. Robert Berdella's neighborhood was the polar opposite, being inhabited predominantly by working professionals. There was a perception of respectability that made the revelation of Berdella's activities seem all the more shocking, a sense of "it couldn't happen here."

Surprisingly, rather than concoct a pie-in-the-sky story, Berdella admitted to the crimes of sodomy and murder. Berdella's legal team had negotiated a specific condition of his pleading guilty to all counts of murder: he would not be given the death penalty. In a decision that would prove unpopular with many of the victims' next of kin, the prosecution agreed to these terms. Upon accepting the defendant's guilty plea, the presiding judge imposed a life sentence upon Berdella. It allowed no possibility for parole. He was simply too dangerous to be allowed to walk the streets as a free man.

What drives a man like Robert Berdella to kidnap, torture, rape, and kill? Some pointed a finger at his alleged interest in black magic and the occult, which is said to have developed after the loss of his father and his turbulent late teenage years. Berdella fancied himself a devil worshipper, the story goes, collecting numerous books on Satanism and the dark arts.

In this, he was far from alone. Other serial killers have demonstrated a fascination with the arcane, most notably Richard Ramirez, the so-called Night Stalker, who believed himself to be personally protected by Satan himself. (If this was true, then Ramirez must have somehow fallen out of favor with the devil, because he was identified in public and badly beaten, requiring rescue by the LAPD.)

Much has been made in some quarters of the supposed Berdella–Satanism connection, but it must be pointed out that the captive serial killer himself claimed he was not an adherent. Above Berdella's bed at the house on Charlotte Street hung a crucifix, perhaps indicating a reversion to his Catholic upbringing.

When asked about his motives during interviews, Berdella stated that he hadn't even the vaguest idea of what had motivated him to do the awful things that he did. Whether this was true or not is impossible to say. It's possible that he lived in a state of perpetual denial. The fact that the families of his victims had banded together to launch a $100 million civil lawsuit against him may also have influenced his willingness to speak candidly.

Those who knew Berdella—in a superficial sense, at least—had nothing bad to say about him. Almost all of them were surprised when the news came out that a serial killer had been living and working in their midst. Sure, he was weird—the man sold decorative human skulls at the local flea market, after all. That could easily be put down to mere eccentricity, the sort of thing one might expect from the proprietor of

"Bob's Bazaar Bizarre." But torture and murder? The people of Kansas City were understandably stunned and horrified in equal measure.

Berdella had successfully erected a convincing facade, which painted him as a solid member of the community. His neighbors had little inkling that he was anything other than normal. When there was a fundraiser, he was among the very first to donate his time, efforts, and money. He played a pivotal role in running the local neighborhood watch program, helping keep an eye out for possible criminal activity on his street. Ironically, the worst crimes that were committed on Charlotte Street were committed by Robert Berdella himself. They were inflicted upon six of the unsuspecting older boys and young men that he brought back to number 4315.

The constant stream of visitors to Berdella's home did not go unnoticed by his neighbors, but he deflected attention by earnestly claiming that he was simply looking out for vulnerable members of society—all of them male and under the age of 30. This explanation seemed to be adequate to satisfy those who made casual inquiries. While there might have been a little gossip floating around, as is the case with any neighborhood, nobody suspected that torture, rape, and murder were going on behind the closed doors of the unassuming looking 4315 Charlotte Street. Its occupant was polite and friendly enough to throw off all suspicion. After all, who would suspect that the nice man who cooked tasty treats for the infrequent neighborhood block parties was responsible for such heinous acts?

A member of Neighborhood Watch and well-liked by those who knew him, by all accounts Berdella was an upstanding citizen. (Except for, you know, the crimes.)

Was the fact that the curtains were kept drawn around the clock really all that big of a deal? Perhaps the tenant just really valued his privacy. It was only after Robert Berdella's crimes came to light that his neighbors realized there had been signs and red flags all along. Some had seen him digging in the garden at night and thought it just a little odd. The unearthing of human remains explained that he was more than just an overly enthusiastic gardener.

It should also be noted that at least one man *did* suspect Robert Berdella of nefarious activity: Paul Howell, the father of his first victim. Police officers searching for Jerry Howell after his disappearance questioned Berdella, who played innocent, and the case went cold. Without a body or evidence of foul play, the police had no concrete reason to suspect Berdella of having committed a crime. They did not even have solid grounds to get a warrant to search his house. But something about the sad-faced, mustachioed flea market trader seemed off to Paul Howell, who could never shake the feeling that he was involved somehow with his son going missing. It was not until 1988 that his worst fears were finally realized.

Robert Berdella claimed to have been heavily influenced by a movie named *The Collector*. The novel on which it was based was published in 1963 and marked the debut of acclaimed author John Fowles, who would go on to write such classics as *The French Lieutenant's Woman*. The plot involves a deranged man who kidnaps a young woman and keeps her captive in the cellar of a house located in the middle of nowhere. In order to kidnap his victim, the novel's protagonist drugs her with chloroform. The parallels with Berdella's MO are not difficult to see, up to this point. Yet in *The Collector*, there is no rape or torture—not in the physical sense, at least. Psychological trauma, yes, but no sexual component or violence.

While it's unclear whether Berdella ever read Fowles's novel, he admitted to having watched the movie as a teen in the mid-sixties. This may well have marked the beginning of his obsession with the idea of kidnapping other human beings and keeping them prisoner, but his innate streak of sadism compelled him to brutalize them as much as he possibly could, documenting his abuses as he went along. His graphic Polaroids and torture logs were most likely kept as mementos, allowing him to relive his experiences over and over again once the victims were dead. Alternatively, Berdella may have convinced himself that the act of documentation lent his twisted actions a perverse sort of legitimacy, that it allowed him to tell himself that this was all for "research," rather than to fulfill his own sick fantasies.

> **Berdella told detectives and attorneys that he bound and sedated Howell because he felt a compulsion to have sex in such a way that he had total and utter control over his victim.**

If his own testimony is to be believed, the primary motivation behind Berdella's first murder (that of Jerry Howell) was not that he enjoyed the prospect of killing; instead, it was all about control. Berdella told detectives and attorneys that he bound and sedated Howell because he felt a compulsion to have sex in such a way that he had total and utter control over his victim.

This need for absolute dominance is seen with other sexual killers too. There are, once again, parallels with Dahmer, who sought to make his own totally compliant "sex zombie" by injecting chemicals directly into the brain. Berdella's statement has the ring of truth. Rape is, primarily, a crime of control and violence. Even if Berdella's victims had survived, Berdella could hardly allow them to go free afterward. As such, once he had vented his rage and lust upon them, there could only ever have been one outcome.

Berdella claimed that the acts of torture and rape he committed allowed him to feel that he was "no longer weak and helpless."

Even after his conviction and sentencing, in the light of a mountain of evidence stacked up against him—much of it documented by himself—Robert Berdella tried to downplay some of his culpability for the crimes he had committed. He maintained that the police and television news media had made him out to be far worse than he actually was, a prospect that would be laughable if it wasn't also such an insult to his victims and their families.

This tendency to dismiss or downplay the severity of the brutal acts they have committed is a common trait among serial killers. Sometimes, it grows to become outright denial. It may be a psychological defense mechanism, a means of living with having committed something that the perpetrator knows deep down is truly heinous. On the other hand, it is often simply the sign of a diseased personality, one that is irreparably callous and indifferent to the suffering of its fellow human beings. Whichever is the case, it cannot be cured.

In 1988, Robert Berdella's personal effects were auctioned off in a public event that many found distasteful. He had amassed an extensive collection of historical artifacts and curios over the years, and it was no longer something he could enjoy while he was sitting behind bars. There was also, as professional appraisers pointed out, a lot of worthless junk for them to sift through to find the valuable nuggets that held true market value. There were artifacts dating back to the era of ancient Rome, thousands of years old, mixed in with odd-ball items that were worth next to nothing. Over a thousand boxes had to be searched through and catalogued.

The killer's estate of oddities went up for auction. From behind bars, the killer participated in the process of valuing and disposing of the items.

Virtually the entire contents of Bob's Bazaar Bizarre went under the auctioneer's hammer. Rather than being divorced from the proceedings, Berdella was allowed to make as many phone calls as he wanted from jail. He called the estate auctioneer over and over again, setting prices, offering advice, and making demands. Those familiar with this circus began to suspect that it was every bit as much about Robert Berdella stroking his own ego and feeding his need to remain in the spotlight as it was about making money. The end result was a little over $60,000.

Much of the collection was purchased by a wealthy businessman named Del Dunmire. Dunmire was a colorful character himself, being infamous for having robbed a bank as a young man, serving jail time, then going straight and turning his life around. As an industrialist, he made millions and was about to do the residents of Kansas City's Hyde Park neighborhood a genuine service.

Ever since the discovery of Berdella's criminal behavior, the house at 4315 Charlotte Street had been an open sore on the neighborhood. It served as an unwelcome, grisly reminder to the residents that they had had a serial killer living among them. Who, they reasoned, was going to want to live there, considering the property's grisly history?

Del Dunmire bought the property and had the house demolished, turning it into an empty lot. This prevented the possibility of Berdella's home becoming a ghoulish tourist trap, attracting the attention of those who sought to keep his name alive. Suspicions had been expressed that Berdella may have killed more than the six victims police knew about and might perhaps have concealed their remains inside or beneath his home. Dunmire said that the demolition process was carried out carefully, and no human remains had been discovered by the time number 4315 was reduced to nothing more than soil.

On October 8, 1992, Robert Berdella died in prison. He had developed a reputation among prison officials for being an inveterate complainer, constantly whining about the conditions under which he was being held. Little wonder, then, that when he began to complain of chest pains, some perceived this as being just another instance of "the boy who cried wolf."

Just as had happened with his father, Berdella's cause of death was a massive heart attack. He was 43 years old and had served just four years of his life sentence. Many felt that he had escaped justice in the end, failing to pay anything like the full price for his crimes. Most of the residents of Kansas City were simply glad to see him gone.

Today, he remains one of the United States' lesser-known serial killers. Whenever lists on the subject appear in articles, Berdella is rarely, if ever, mentioned. Perhaps those who were personally affected by his atrocities can take some small measure of degree in the fact that, in death, Robert Berdella has been denied the notoriety and fame that he so desperately craved.

# THE YPSILANTI RIPPER
# JOHN NORMAN COLLINS

**T**he unidentified suspect had many nicknames. The Ypsilanti Ripper was one. The Co-Ed Killer was another—coined because of the murderer's preference for victims who attended classes at Eastern Michigan University. Then there was the more pedestrian: the Michigan Murderer. Starting in 1967, John Norman Collins assaulted and killed seven female college students in the vicinity of Ypsilanti and Ann Arbor. From 1967 to 1969, he remained on the loose, striking fear into thousands of citizens.

Ann Arbor wasn't the kind of place where something like this should happen, people felt. New York or Chicago, perhaps, where murder seemed to happen all the time, but not a university town in the heart of Michigan. Ann Arbor was an affluent, or at the very least comfortable, place to live.

All that changed in the summer of 1967, when the killing started.

On July 9, 1967, 19-year-old Eastern Michigan University student Mary Terese Fleszar left her apartment in the university neighborhood of Ypsilanti to take an evening stroll. She almost certainly did not expect it to be the last walk she would ever take. One of her neighbors saw a car pull up alongside the young woman, its male occupant appearing to try and coax her inside. Whether she got in or not remains unknown. That neighbor was a man named Gregory Fournier, who would become an authority on the case and go on to write a book about it titled *Terror in Ypsilanti: John Norman Collins Unmasked.*

Fleszar's naked, decomposing body was found by a pair of teenagers one month after her disappearance, left on a stretch of farmland. Her chest and abdomen bore numerous stab wounds, the signs of a fren-

Tucked between metropolitan Detroit and the famously pleasant college town of Ann Arbor, Ypsilanti is home to Eastern Michigan University, where student Collins began his killing spree.

zied knife attack. She had also been struck with a blunt object multiple times. Her facial features had been all but obliterated. Evidence suggested that not only had her killer gone back to her body on more than one occasion between the murder and its discovery, but that each time, he had moved it from one place to another and also had inflicted more wounds upon the corpse.

By the time police closed off the crime scene, both of Mary Fleszar's feet had been amputated, as had a number of her fingers. Whether they were taken by her killer or by animals was impossible to tell. The body had been exposed to the heat and the elements for four weeks, and due to the state of decomposition, the pathologist who conducted her autopsy could not tell whether she had been sexually molested or not. Fleszar's clothes, which showed signs of having been forcibly removed, were found close by.

Shortly before Mary Fleszar's funeral, an unidentified male attempted to bluff his way into the undertaker's place of business with the express intent of photographing her one last time. He claimed to be a family friend, though nobody in the Fleszar family recognized his description—though it was consistent with a young man named John Norman Collins. With the benefit of hindsight, it seems likely that this was Mary's killer making a brazen attempt to admire his handiwork one last time before her burial. Fortunately, he was denied permission and left in a huff.

There were no obvious suspects, and the police investigation soon hit a brick wall. The concept of a serial killer had not been crystallized by the late 1960s, and when months went by without any additional murders, the public's attention turned elsewhere. The rest of 1967 passed quietly, and the murder of Mary Fleszar began to seem like a tragic and reprehensible anomaly. It faded into the background, drowned out by the hustle and bustle of everyday life—until the killer struck again.

After the murder of Mary Fleszar, John Norman Collins did not kill for another year. We can only speculate as to why he took such a relatively long break. It may simply be that he was processing the enormity of his first murder, wondering whether he would be caught by the authorities. Finally, it would have dawned on him that he had literally gotten away with murder and could probably do so again.

Eastern Michigan University student Joan Elspeth Schell, 20, was murdered sometime at the end of June 1968. She was last seen hitchhiking, with the intent of meeting up with her boyfriend. Schell was spotted accepting a ride in a car with a driver and three passengers, none of whom have ever been identified, although once again, one of them fit the description of John Norman Collins.

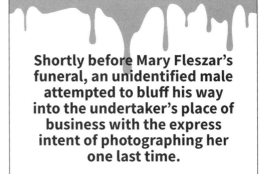

**Shortly before Mary Fleszar's funeral, an unidentified male attempted to bluff his way into the undertaker's place of business with the express intent of photographing her one last time.**

Schell never arrived at her boyfriend's place. On July 5, her naked, savagely traumatized body was found by construction workers a few feet from the side of the road, close to the place in which Mary Fleszar's remains had been abandoned the summer before. She had been stabbed more than 20 times on her upper body, both front and back, and the neck, after which she had also been strangled with her own skirt.

An autopsy would show that she had been raped. There were marked similarities between her murder and that of Mary Fleszar, and detectives soon came to the conclusion that both women had been killed by the same perpetrator. Neither victim had been killed in the same place that their body was discovered. The murders had taken place elsewhere, and the remains transported and dropped off postmortem. The question was: where?

There was also the university connection. Was the killer enrolled as a student at Eastern Michigan, or was he simply using the university as his hunting ground? Seeming to target dark-haired young women, he found no shortage of them on campus or in the surrounding area.

Several different suspects were questioned in the wake of Joan Schell's murder. One of them was John Norman Collins, who was interviewed after he was heard talking about the condition of Schell's body with a coworker. He appeared to have an almost insider level of knowledge. After speaking with detectives and offering up an alibi, however, he was dropped as a potential suspect. The fact that his uncle was a state trooper may also have helped avert suspicion.

For most people, popping up on the police radar as a potential homicide suspect would have served as a cold dose of reality. Not so with Collins, who, rather than keep a low profile, soon went back to killing.

His third victim was 23-year-old Jane Louise Mixer, a law student at the University of Michigan. Mixer did not have her own car, but rather than hitchhike, she put up a flyer on a bulletin board at the university, requesting a ride share. A man who went by the name of David Johnson responded. This was clearly a pseudonym, as police officers tracked down the only David Johnson enrolled at the university and confirmed that he could not have committed the murder, as he was at a public event at the time it took place. He had taken to the stage and performed in a play, in front of an audience—about as solid an alibi as anybody could have asked for.

Mixer wasn't to know that she was being set up, however, and she probably didn't ask too many questions about her driver's identity. After all, who wants to look a gift horse in the mouth? Tragically, failing to do so cost her her life. On March 21, 1969, her body was found in a cemetery, her head and shoulders leaning up against one of the graves.

This time, the killer had changed his MO—if, that is, John Norman Collins truly was the man responsible. Jane Mixer had been shot twice in the head, which rested on top of a folded towel. Unlike Joan Schell, she had not been raped, although she was found with her pantyhose pulled down to expose her genitalia. A single stocking had been used to strangle her. Unlike other victims, she had not been stripped of her clothing. The place where she was found inside the cemetery looked very different to that of the Mary Fleszar and Joan Schell crime scenes. A raincoat was draped across her body, protecting it somewhat from both sight and the elements.

Jane Mixer's body was found in Denton Cemetery, in nearby Van Buren Township.

The subsequent autopsy would find no traces of molestation, although evidence suggested that Jane Mixer had been menstruating at the time of her murder. Could this have deterred the killer from carrying out a sexual assault?

Although police believed that Jane Mixer was killed by John Norman Collins, the case developed an unanticipated twist in 2004 when DNA evidence suggested that she had been murdered by somebody else: fellow Michigan resident and retired nurse Gary Leiterman, who had submitted a saliva swab to police for an unrelated charge. When entered into the DNA database, Leiterman's sample popped hot for a match with DNA found on the panties worn by Jane Mixer at the time of her death.

Leiterman did live in the vicinity of the murder scene but had no real motive, and questions were raised about the integrity of the DNA evidence handling. There were concerns about possible contamination having occurred while storing or processing that evidence. Despite having had drug issues in the past, Leiterman had no history of violence, and though he had owned a .22 caliber pistol, it was never proven to have been the weapon used to murder Jane Mixer.

Everything hung on the DNA, and it must be pointed out that the DNA of another criminal (one who *did* have violent offenses in his criminal past) was also picked up on Jane Mixer's body—yet this "suspect" would have been just four years old at the time of the murder and would not enter the criminal justice system until years later. Nobody is sure how this third-party DNA ended up where it did.

Expert witnesses testified that the amount of Leiterman's DNA found on the pantyhose was significant enough that it could not be easily explained away as an error. The jury ultimately sided with the prosecution and convicted Leiterman of murder. He was sentenced to life imprisonment and will never be eligible for parole. He maintains his innocence, and his family and supporters insist that he is the victim of a miscarriage of justice.

> Everything hung on the DNA, and it must be pointed out that the DNA of another criminal (one who *did* have violent offenses in his criminal past) was also picked up on Jane Mixer's body....

Certainly, the crime scene did not look like the others that were attributed to John Norman Collins. Those victims had been savaged and then their bodies were abandoned with no more thought for their dignity than one would give to a piece of trash. Jane Mixer's body was positioned carefully and the scene around it looked neater, less haphazard, as if the killer showed some small degree of remorse for what he had done. The fact that she had been covered up after her death and was found mostly clothed also set Mixer's murder apart from the others. Nor did her body bear the multitude of stab wounds that had been inflicted upon both of the previous victims.

Is it possible that neither John Normal Collins *nor* Gary Leiterman killed Jane Mixer? Absolutely. It is likely that we will never know the an-

Pantyhose, stretchy but surprisingly strong leggings usually made of shear nylon weave, were in wide use during the late sixties as an expected part of most women's wardrobes.

swer definitively. Leiterman died in prison on July 4, 2019. He maintained his innocence until his dying day.

On March 23, 1969, John Norman Collins struck again. This time, his target was not a college student, but 16-year-old Maralynn Skelton did have friends at Eastern Michigan University and was on her way to the campus to socialize with them when she ran into her killer.

Her naked body was found two days later by a road survey team, dumped in the woods outside Ann Arbor. No attempt had been made to cover up the body this time. Her clothes were scattered haphazardly around her body.

Maralynn's killer had gagged her to muffle her screams. She was killed by means of severe blunt force trauma to the head and face. She had also been strangled. Her body bore the marks of multiple contusions, which pathologists believed had been inflicted with a leather belt. In a final act of desecration, a tree branch had been forcibly inserted into her vagina.

Collins's attacks were increasing in frequency and becoming more brazen. On April 16, less than a month after the murder of Maralynn Skelton, he killed his youngest victim, 13-year-old Dawn Louise Basom. Dawn's boyfriend had escorted her most of the way home from a get-together at Eastern, but she had walked the last few blocks by herself. It is likely that John Norman Collins was tailing her, looking for a moment of vulnerability. When he saw his window of opportunity, he struck, just a stone's throw from Dawn's home.

The specifics of what happened next are not known. Was Dawn snatched into a vehicle, or was she lured there with the promise of something she may have found enticing? Either way, assuming that Collins stuck to his familiar pattern, she would have been taken somewhere private to be subdued, tortured, and murdered. Then her body was transported to a remote location and left there.

While not rendered completely naked, Dawn had been positioned with her breasts and genitalia exposed. Yet again, John Norman Collins's latest victim had been strangled—with wire, this time, rather than nylon—and gagged. He had also returned to his habit of repeatedly stabbing her with a knife.

A search of the immediate area turned up pieces of clothing and wire matching that used to kill Dawn Bascom, in a nearby barn and farmhouse, both of which were long abandoned. The property was isolated enough that it could easily have been the site where the murder took place, prior to Dawn's body being transported and dumped in public.

In what may or may not have been a coincidence, a month later, the barn was burned to the ground. Fire investigators declared it to be an act of arson, though there is no evidence to suggest that Collins had any involvement in the matter.

Alice Elizabeth Kalom was 21 years old at the time of her death. She was no longer a student, having already obtained her degree at the time of her murder. On her last night alive, she had been partying in Ann Arbor. Late in the evening of June 7, 1969, or in the early hours of the following morning, an assailant had stabbed Kalom repeatedly in the heart. He also shot her in the head several times at close range with a .22 caliber rifle and went on to slit her throat. Any one of the three wounds, taken on its own, would have been fatal. The killer was doing more than simply making sure that his victim was truly dead. There was a savagery at work that implied a personal hatred for the young woman he had murdered.

Her partially clad body was found two days later by three young men walking along a rural trail. Continuing with his established pattern, Collins had used another derelict farm as his body disposal site and had left Alice Kalom's body in a place where it would easily be found by somebody taking a walk.

When questioned by detectives about the brutal murder, John Norman Collins denied responsibility for killing Kalom and said that he had never even met her. Yet

Collins preferred to transport his victims' bodies to abandoned farms.

years later, when he met with police officers again, in the light of fresh evidence, he changed his story, claiming to have taken her for a ride on his motorbike shortly before she was killed. This about-face on the part of Collins understandably led them to ponder what other lies he might have told them during the course of his initial interrogations.

John Norman Collins's final victim was 18-year-old Karen Sue Beineman. In an almost unbelievable turn of fate, Collins decided for some unfathomable reason to murder her in the basement of his uncle's house. That uncle, David Leik, was a trooper with the Michigan State Police. As such, he had been part of the manhunt for the serial killer on the loose around Ann Arbor. Never in his wildest dreams could he have imagined that his own nephew was responsible for the sadistic acts that he was investigating. But that's exactly what happened on July 23, 1969, when she disappeared without a trace.

As soon as the young woman was reported missing, the police launched a massive, multiagency search that covered hundreds of miles. They knew the serial killer's MO all too well by now. He liked to kill his victims at a location of his own choosing and then dump the bodies of his victims in places that were relatively secluded, but at the same time, not *too* far from civilization. Places such as ravines, fields, farms, and riverbanks were the obvious places to start.

The police had been keeping an eye on Collins, and even before the body of the missing woman was discovered, officers brought him in to answer a few questions. Collins understandably lawyered up.

The Leiks had a dog, and when David Leik took his family on a two-week road trip, Collins had been tasked with coming over to the house and feeding it. He also brought the unsuspecting Karen Sue Beineman back with him and killed her. Yet for an intelligent man, he did a poor job cleaning up after himself, and the Leiks realized things were out of place shortly after they returned home. Drops of blood were later found in the basement by crime scene evidence technicians. There had been no bloodstains before the Leik family had left for their vacation, and John Norman Collins had been the only person with access to the property. He had also made a ham-handed attempt to cover up other bloodstains with black paint, something that Mrs. Leik noticed right away. The blood in the basement of the Leik residence would later be confirmed to match that of Karen Sue Beineman.

Other markings found suggested that there had been some sort of struggle inside the house and that Collins had tried to cover it up after the fact.

Beineman's body was dumped in a ravine. She had been severely beaten and fatally strangled. The physical assault had fractured her skull and facial bones. In a disturbing new development, a chemical had been used to inflict severe burns upon her upper body,

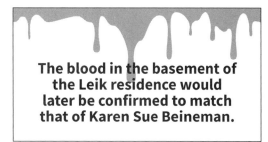

**The blood in the basement of the Leik residence would later be confirmed to match that of Karen Sue Beineman.**

most likely while she was alive. The killer was exhibiting a new layer of sexual sadism and hatred of the feminine that was heretofore unseen. Karen's semen-stained panties had been inserted into her vagina post-mortem.

After a lengthy investigation, in which hundreds of leads were pursued and countless law enforcement personnel hours were spent, the killing of Karen Sue Beineman was the only one of the Michigan murders that detectives felt was sufficiently strong enough on which to convict John Norman Collins.

When questioned, Collins flatly denied ever having had any contact with Karen Sue Beineman, let alone killing her. Yet at least one eyewitness, the owner of a wig store, recalled having seen the two of them together, getting off a motorbike outside. Beineman came into the store alone. The owner sold her a wig and remembered the transaction later when the unfortunate young woman turned up dead, because she had made comments about regretting buying a wig and "accepting a motorcycle ride from a stranger."

That stranger, of course, had been John Norman Collins.

At trial, Collins's legal defense team refused to put him on the stand, which was probably a wise idea. Collins not being allowed to testify did not, however, save him in the end.

At the culmination of his trial in August 1970, Collins was found guilty of one single count of murder, that of Karen Sue Beineman. He was sentenced to life imprisonment without the possibility of parole. With nothing left to lose, he was permitted to speak at his sentencing, which he described as being "a travesty of justice."

In letters written to his cousin years after his conviction, Collins did a U-turn on the "I never even knew her" story. Rather than confess to Beineman's murder, however, he blamed it instead on his roommate, Arnie Davis. Collins claimed that after giving her a ride to the wig store, he made out with Beineman at his uncle's home, then left for a while,

Clean-cut Collins showed off his bad-boy side when cruising around on his motorcycle.

only to return later that night to find her naked and dead at Davis's hands. Davis's supposed reason for killing her was, Collins said, that she spurned his sexual advances.

We are expected to believe that, after finding out that his roommate had just murdered a casual acquaintance in cold blood, a shocked John Norman Collins then managed to regain his composure and, being such a good buddy, helped him dispose of the corpse rather than report him to the police. He also laid blame for the murder of Alice Kalom at Davis's door, but conveniently failed to provide a good reason for failing to report that murder to police either.

Canadian by birth, Collins came to the United States with his American mother, following her divorce from his father.

John Norman Collins did a great job at hiding in plain sight. He went to a Catholic high school and appeared to fit in well with its many rules and regulations. He was athletic and excelled at a wide variety of team sports, particularly football, where he rose to become captain of the team. No stranger to the gym, he liked to keep himself in good shape, and young women often gravitated to him. By all accounts, he was the kind of boyfriend who treated his partners with respect. Nobody could fault his manners, which leaned towards the old-fashioned.

Collins was an intelligent young man and charismatic to boot. Those who knew him found him to be charming, and he was popular among his peers. The fact that he was handsome also did not hurt his prospects, as he found out when he was approached to appear shirtless in the pages of a bodybuilding magazine. He wore leather jackets and jeans, rode a succession of motorcycles, and developed an image that contrasted the "clean cut" and "bad boy" looks.

Delving into Collins's background evokes comparisons with the better-known serial killer Ted Bundy. In both cases, beneath the polished and erudite exterior lurked an ever-present sense of anger and emotional instability that was never too far from the surface. Personal letters written by Collins suggested that he liked to treat women roughly and held them in little regard—if not outright hatred. This is further borne out by the severe facial trauma that he inflicted upon his female victims.

In a 2019 interview with reporter Rob Wolchek of Fox News 2 Detroit, a former Eastern Michigan University student named Pam recalls the time Collins pulled his car over alongside her and tried to offer her a ride. At first, he was charming and tried to coax her. When she demurred, saying that she only lived a short distance away, he suddenly became enraged and spat: "You motherfucking cunt, aren't you going to get in the car with me?" He then floored the accelerator and sped off.

It's an unnerving window into the man's psyche. Nobody of sound mind would expect such an expletive-laden phrase to actually work. The sheer speed of Collins's flip from seemingly good-natured nice guy to crude and profane jerk is suggestive of deeper issues.

All the victims were females, young (in their teens or early 20s), and had brown hair. It has been pointed out that Collins's mother, Loretta, also had brown hair. Was there some degree of hidden maternal resentment at play, leading

**Delving into Collins's background evokes comparisons with the better-known serial killer Ted Bundy.**

him to project it upon young women who reminded him of her? If so, he would hardly be the first serial killer to take anger he felt at his mother out on innocent female victims.

John Norman Collins was also suspected of the murder of 17-year-old Roxie Ann Phillips. This killing took place in Salinas, California, rather than Michigan, on or about June 30, 1969. Collins had been visiting California at the time of the murder, and his appearance was consistent with that of a man seen in Phillips's company shortly before her death. She was spotted getting into an Oldsmobile that was the same color as the one owned by Collins's mother—a vehicle with Michigan license plates, which would have looked out of place in California. Roxie's killer battered her with a blunt object, strangled her with the belt of her own dress, and left her body in a canyon. Only later, with his arrest and charging, would the murder of Roxie Ann Phillips be attributed to Collins.

Generally considered attractive and charming, Collins could change his temper in a flash.

At the time of writing, John Norman Collins remains imprisoned for the murder of Karen Beineman. Although he has changed his story on more than one occasion, he continues to deny responsibility for any of the murders of which he is suspected and does not speak publicly about the crimes. Yet can it really be a coincidence that, after he was apprehended by police and sent to prison in 1970, the string of Michigan murders suddenly stopped, never to resume? Rarely does a serial killer simply stop killing. Usually, the murders cease because of some outside circumstance being imposed on their perpetrator. They move elsewhere or are arrested for their crimes (in some cases, they are arrested for entirely different crimes). Occasionally, they die.

In a 2019 email written to the *Detroit Free Press*, who sent multiple requests for an interview, Collins reiterated his demand to be left alone.

The murders of Jane Mixer and Karen Beineman are officially solved, but none of the other homicides linked with John Norman Collins have closure yet. They remain open cases, which begs the question: is the serial killer responsible sitting behind bars, or is he still out there, having evaded justice for more than half a century?

# THE PETERBOROUGH DITCH MURDERER JOANNA DENNEHY

There are virtually no female serial killers, or so the old cliche goes. Needless to say, it is completely untrue, although the vast majority of serial killers do tend to be male. Yet, while they may be greatly outnumbered by their male counterparts, there is still no shortage of cold-blooded, calculating females to be found in the annals of serial murder.

The British criminal justice system considers Joanna Dennehy to be such a danger to the public that she has been given a rare "whole life sentence"—meaning that she will spend the rest of her life in prison, without the possibility of parole. Such sentences are reserved for those offenders who are the very worst of the worst. Dennehy is only the third female in British history to have received one. (The other two recipients, Rosemary West and Myra Hindley, were covered in the first book in this series, *Serial Killers: The Minds, Methods, and Mayhem of History's Most Notorious Murderers,* Visible Ink Press, 2021).

Just what is it that made this apparently ordinary young woman such a menace to her fellow human beings?

Joanna Dennehy was born in August 1982, in St. Albans, Great Britain. Her parents worked blue-collar jobs: Dennehy's father was a security guard, and her mother was in the food product industry. Based on what little is known about her childhood, it was like that of millions of other British children and does not appear to have been marred by abuse or other familial issues. Indeed, Dennehy's sister served honorably in the British Army, including service in Afghanistan, before forging a successful career on her return to civilian life. Both she and Joanna had been raised in the same environment and parented in the same way.

"Our parents were hard working," recalled sister Maria Dennehy in a 2014 interview with the BBC. "We were very spoilt as children, always on holiday. My parents gave her [Joanna] a good education. She was very academic, and used to read books, and liked to learn a lot of stuff."

Joanna did indeed do well in school—a solid, if unspectacular, student. All cannot have been sweetness and light, however, because the young Joanna became a regular runaway. This began at around the age of 13. When she began to use drugs, her disappearances became more frequent, until at the age of 16, she finally stopped returning home at all. Joanna also became more difficult to handle, her behavior going beyond that of the usual rebellious streak shown by most teenagers.

Now estranged from her parents and sister, she moved in with an older man and had two children with him. It wasn't long before there was domestic violence, but not in the way one would suspect. Dennehy was the one doing the beating, smashing the father of her children in the face over and over again. In 2009, after suffering one beating too many, he threw her out of the house and changed the locks. Sensing danger from his physically and emotionally abusive former partner, the man took his children and left town. Joanna Dennehy was never allowed to see them again.

Dennehy was bisexual and never lacked for partners. Whenever she was in a relationship, monogamy seemed like an alien concept for her.

Although lacking a moral compass as most of us would think of it, Joanna Dennehy did live by a sort of moral code of her own devising. The victims she selected were all adult males. No women or children came to harm at her hands. It is difficult to obtain firearms in the United Kingdom; Dennehy's preferred murder weapon was a three-inch, curve-bladed knife. All her victims were stabbed in the heart.

Some serial killers murder over the space of years, or even decades. The 30-year-old Joanna Dennehy's killing spree took place over a single ten-day period in the spring of 2013. It is likely that she would have continued killing men if she had not gotten caught and taken off the streets of Peterborough, where the crimes took place.

Dennehy had a reputation for toughness and belligerence. People in her neighborhood referred to her as "the man woman" due to her surly and combative demeanor, plus her hair-trigger temper. She was also nicknamed "Star," referring to the small black star that was tattooed on her face, just beneath one eye.

Yet there was another side to her. Those who knew Joanna Dennehy also said that she could be friendly and a charmer. She had a weird kind of charisma and a nontraditional attractiveness that drew people to her. Depending on her mood, they could be embraced with open arms or grabbed by the throat and told to "fuck off."

Lukasz Slaboszewski was a 31-year-old immigrant from Poland. After coming to the United Kingdom in 2005, he had suffered with an addiction to opioids, primarily heroin. Slaboszewski had been working to turn his life around, however, receiving help for his drug abuse problem with a course of methadone treatment. He was also holding down a steady job, earning a living as a warehouse worker.

A Cambridgeshire city 76 miles north of London, Peterborough takes its name from a medieval abbey dedicated to St. Peter, who is also celebrated by the city's more modern Peterborough Cathedral, consecrated in 1238.

The precise date of his death is unknown. Slaboszewski disappeared sometime after March 19, 2013. He had made references to having an English girlfriend, which with hindsight, seems to refer to Joanna Dennehy. It is likely that she made sexual advances toward Slaboszewski in an attempt to lull him into a false sense of security. When his guard was down, she fatally stabbed him in the chest, then put his dead body in a trash bin. It is not known how long she kept it there before disposing of it on farmland.

John Chapman, 56, was a military veteran, having served in the Royal Navy during the Falklands War against Argentina in 1982. Chapman struggled with alcoholism but was doing his best to make his way in the world. On March 29, Dennehy stabbed him to death inside his own home. In both murders, the fatal wound was delivered to the heart, although Chapman also sustained penetrating trauma to the neck.

The serial killer did not have to look far for her first two victims. Both Slaboszewski and Chapman lived in the same set of low-income bedsits as she did. ("Bedsit" is a British term for a single-room rental property, usually a combination of bedroom/living room/food preparation area.) She would have encountered them both as they entered and left their respective bedsits, doubtless sizing each one up as a potential victim.

The bedsits were corun by 48-year-old Kevin Lee, who became Dennehy's third victim on the same day that she killed Chapman. The two knew each other. Not only was he Dennehy's landlord, but he had also entered into a sexual relationship with her. She used that to lure him to his death, sending him a message promising to set up a sexual encounter. It was an ambush. When Lee arrived, Dennehy stabbed him in the heart, then phoned an accomplice named Gary Richards and bellowed the Britney Spears song "Oops! I Did It Again" at him.

As much as she hated men, Dennehy had two male accomplices: Leslie Layton, 36, and Gary "Stretch" Richards, 47. The two helped her dispose of her victims' bodies. When police analysts looked at Layton's phone, they found a photograph of John Chapman's body.

Dennehy appeared to have an emotional involvement with Richards. The pair were caught on CCTV camera holding hands, and Stretch would write her love letters. She would later write that she loved him too but added that it was a strictly platonic affair.

> Dennehy dumped the bodies of all three of her murder victims in ditches, hence earning her crimes the name "the Peterborough Ditch Murders."

Dennehy dumped the bodies of all three of her murder victims in ditches, hence earning her crimes the name "the Peterborough Ditch Murders." After killing three men, she had developed a taste for murder and the notoriety that it would bring her. Now, she wanted more.

Hereford is a historic town on the border between England and Wales. It is almost 150 miles away from Peterborough. Richards drove Dennehy to Hereford in search of more prospective murder victims. Robin Bereza and John Rogers were out taking a walk, minding their own business, when she pounced on them and attacked each man with a knife. Other than the fact that they were male, the choice of victims was entirely random. Each was simply in the wrong place at the wrong time.

The 64-year-old Bereza described the attack when he testified in court. "I got worried then, frightened," he recalled, asking Dennehy as she came toward him, "What are you doing?"

"I'm hurting you," was her answer, stabbing him twice in the upper torso. She left him bleeding on the ground, with injuries serious enough for him to be life-flighted to a major trauma center. He was fortunate to survive.

Richards and Dennehy drove off, looking for their next victim. It had to be a male, Dennehy insisted, and the man must be walking a dog. Women and children were not eligible targets. They eventually caught sight of 56-year-old John Rogers.

Dennehy stabbed Rogers more than 40 times, in the chest, back, and abdomen. Afterward, he told prosecutors that she had been completely emotionless throughout the attack, showing no signs of anger, joy, or any type of feeling whatsoever. Even when her victim fell to the ground, Dennehy kept stabbing him. Then she took his dog and fled the scene. Fortunately, she soon got bored of the pet, and it was recovered shortly afterward and returned to its owner.

Rogers required major surgery but survived the attack. He died of unrelated causes in 2014.

It would later come to light that Dennehy had, to some degree, tried to model herself on the American bank robbers-murderers Bonnie and Clyde, who went out in a blaze of gunfire at the end of a lengthy crime spree. They died in a shoot-out with law enforcement, the car they were sitting in being riddled with bullets. Not so Joanna Dennehy, however—she surrendered without resistance to an armed police squad when they located her. No shots were fired.

Perhaps surprisingly, Dennehy made no effort to defend herself in court. She pleaded guilty to having murdered Lukasz Slaboszewski, John Chapman, and Kevin Lee. She also pled guilty to two further counts of attempted murder, based upon her attacks on the two dog walkers.

The defense team for her accomplices, Layton and Richards, maintained that Dennehy had manipulated both men and, because she had committed all three of the murders herself, should bear the lion's share of the culpability

Leslie Layton was sentenced to 14 years' imprisonment for the crime of help-

Bonnie and Clyde's names have been synonymous with *crime spree* since the 1930s, after a two-year interstate escapade that included bank robbery, assault, kidnapping, and murder, including that of nine police officers.

ing Joanna Dennehy remove, transport, and dispose of the bodies of her victims. The fact that he had obstructed a homicide investigation was also considered by the judge. Gary Richards was given a life sentence, with the possibility of parole after 19 years.

Psychological evaluation of Joanna Dennehy revealed that she had strong sadomasochistic tendencies. This condition involves getting sexual gratification from inflicting pain on others, preferably while also debasing them. She liked to hurt her sexual partners, and sometimes, she liked them to hurt her back.

She also enjoyed humiliating and emasculating her victims, even after their deaths, which is why she took the time and trouble to change Kevin Lee's dead body into a dress. After dropping the body off, she deliberately bared the dead man's buttocks, pulling the dress up. It wasn't enough for her to have killed him. She had to humiliate him as well.

Her clinical diagnosis also categorized her as a psychopath, which was clearly borne out by the three murders and two attempted murders she committed in 2013. Joanna Dennehy liked stabbing men and the rush that came along with it.

Joanna Dennehy (right) stands trial at the Old Bailey, with Gary (Stretch) Dennehy (2nd left), Leslie Layton (5th left), and Robert Moore (center, a friend of Dennehy's who was not involved in the murders but provided Dennehy with a false alibi) in the dock.

Ego-driven and with little to nothing in the way of impulse control, Dennehy pled guilty with a certain sense of pride because she wanted to be perceived as a dominant force in ending the lives of three men. She killed not out of lust, but for the attention and notoriety committing high-profile murders would bring.

Far from trying to duck responsibility for her crimes, Dennehy got off on the idea of being seen to be some kind of badass. No doubt this helped her standing in prison, where alpha personality types tend to dominate the pecking order.

Yet Dennehy changed her story in 2014, claiming that she was not actually responsible for the murder of John Chapman. She insisted that Layton had been the true killer, and she said his motive was an attempt to impress her. Whether this is actually the truth is anybody's guess, and one is forced to wonder how many more times Dennehy's story is going to change as she languishes behind bars.

Dennehy is undeniably a fantasist and a pathologic liar. At their first meeting, she told landlord Kevin Lee and his business partner, Paul Creed, that she had already committed murder—of her own father. He had raped her, she claimed, and gotten her pregnant. The baby had died, and she had killed her dad. That had earned her 13 years in prison, she added. In reality, Joanna Dennehy's father was alive and well, and there is no proof to back up her claims that he abused her in such a way. There was indeed a multitude of scars on her body, many localized on her abdomen, but she had inflicted them upon herself. They were not signs of torture or abuse. She found pain to be a turn-on, particularly during the physical act of sex, when she would sometimes take a knife to her own skin, cutting herself with long strokes of the blade.

It is debatable whether somebody of Joanna Dennehy's ilk can feel an emotion such as love, but after she was sent to prison, she began a relationship with another female inmate, named Hayley Palmer. Palmer was serving a 16-year sentence for robbery and was released in the spring of 2021. Now that she has obtained her freedom—which Joanna Dennehy will never have—Palmer nonetheless claims that she is planning to marry Dennehy as soon as possible. As Dennehy is permitted no visitors, how such a marriage might happen is anybody's guess.

In 2018, the news media reported that Dennehy and Palmer had tried to kill themselves as the fulfillment of a suicide pact. Britain's *The Sun* newspaper stated that Dennehy's throat was cut, and Palmer had her wrists slashed. Prison guards found them both together in a cell, drenched in blood.

Like a leopard who can't change its spots, Dennehy continues to make trouble behind bars and is considered Britain's most dangerous female inmate.

Once her injuries had healed, Dennehy was moved to another prison. The facility, Her Majesty's Prison Low Durham, housed another infamous female serial killer: the aforementioned Rosemary West, of the infamous Cromwell Street "House of Horrors." Shortly after her transfer, Dennehy's craving for the spotlight once again reared its head. She is alleged to have made threats to murder West as soon as she got the chance. Whether this was a legitimate threat or simply more grandstanding on Dennehy's part will never be known; as soon as the rumor made its way to prison authorities, they promptly transferred West to another prison.

Joanna Dennehy has always been far from a model prisoner, to put it mildly; indeed, there are some who believe that she is the most dangerous female inmate in the entire British penal system. In 2016, she hatched a plot to escape from prison. Access throughout the facility was secured by biometric touch pad readers, requiring the fingerprint of a prison officer to open them. Dennehy's cold-blooded plan was to murder an officer, hack off her fingers with a knife, and use the amputated fingers to make her escape. Unfortunately for Dennehy, her sheer effrontery was matched only by her stupidity. She wrote the plan down and kept notes in her cell—which were duly found by prison officers during a search. She was promptly sent to solitary confinement, where she would have no contact with the two accomplices she had also enlisted in the escape plot.

At the time of writing, Dennehy is still behind bars and is likely to remain there for the rest of her life. Denied the spotlight she so desperately craves, the convicted serial killer spends part of her time writing letters to men on the outside. The letters contain details of her crimes, sexual tidbits, and other information used to titillate and attempt to manipulate them. Joanna Dennehy has proven once again that a leopard never truly does change its spots.

# CHILD KILLER – OR FALSELY ACCUSED MOTHER? KATHLEEN FOLBIGG

It's fair to say that most serial killers do not target family members. There are, of course, exceptions, such as American murderer Edmund Kemper, whose very first victims were his grandparents. Killing close to home is a great way to get caught. Whenever a person goes missing, invariably the first people to fall under suspicion are the most immediate family members—spouses, siblings, and sometimes parents.

Australian mother Kathleen Megan Folbigg was the mother of four children: Laura, Sarah, Patrick, and Caleb. Over a ten-year period, every single one of them died—all before reaching the age of two.

On February 20, 1989, Caleb Folbigg died in his crib. He was just 19 days old. Kathleen found him at around three o'clock in the morning, her hysterical screaming waking her husband up from a sound sleep. "My baby!" Kathleen shrieked. "There's something wrong with my baby!"

This was every parent's worst nightmare: sudden infant death syndrome (SIDS), or cot death—or so it appeared.

Almost two years later, on February 13, 1991, Caleb's brother, Patrick, died. He was eight months old and had been diagnosed with epilepsy. It was believed that he may have suffered a seizure, which caused his death.

Two and a half years later, in the summer of 1993, 10-month-old Sarah Folbigg died under similar circumstances. Her father stated afterward that Kathleen had seemed particularly irritable, if not angry, with their daughter.

In 1999, her sister, Laura, died at the age of 18 months. Like her brothers and sister before her, she had stopped breathing. An autopsy was performed. The only abnormality noted was a case of very mild myocarditis, inflammation of the heart tissue. This alone was unlikely to have caused her to die; although myocarditis can be fatal, it typically requires a much more serious case than was seen with Laura Folbigg.

Although none of the deaths were considered suspicious by themselves, when taken in totality—four deaths, nearly identical in nature, taking place in the same household—it is easy to see why the police suspected that a killer was at work. Sickeningly, the evidence pointed toward the dead children's mother as the prime suspect. She had been the one to discover all four of them after their deaths.

The case went to trial in 2003. The prosecution's argument was that each death had been due to the cessation of breathing, something on which both sides could agree. The question at the heart of the matter was, Exactly what had caused each child to stop breathing?

> The question at the heart of the matter was, exactly what had caused each child to stop breathing?

Kathleen Folbigg was charged with having smothered all four of her children until they were dead. Her entire legal defense was predicated on one simple concept: she had not killed any of her children, let alone all of them. The deaths were simply one big, terrible coincidence. They had all had a recent illness or medical condition, such as a respiratory infection or epileptic seizure, which had contributed to each tragic outcome.

Unsurprisingly, the experts testifying on behalf of the prosecution disagreed. Quoted in an April 2001 story in the *Sydney Morning Herald*, a forensic pathologist laid out the math, which concluded that the likelihood of all four children having died of natural causes was greater than a trillion to one. In the extremely unlikely event that there was no foul play and these were legitimate deaths, then the death of the Folbigg children represented one of the biggest statistical anomalies on record.

To make matters even more complicated for Kathleen Folbigg, murder ran in her family. In 1969, when Folbigg was 18 months old, her father had killed her mother by stabbing her repeatedly. Young Kathleen recalled nothing of the event but spent years in foster care and children's homes. She left care and struck out on her own as soon as she possibly could, taking whichever low-paying jobs a teenager could get.

An entry in the adult Kathleen's diary stated, "Obviously, I am my father's daughter." On the face of it, this seems completely damning, but context is everything. She could have felt herself to be her father's daughter in many ways. They could have shared a temper, a sense of humor, a dislike for a certain food, or, as the prosecution would have pointed out, the capacity to commit murder.

Some of her diary entries were extremely damning and undoubtedly contributed to her conviction. If they are considered in a certain light, a series of statements can be interpreted to be admissions of guilt. For example: "I think I am more patient with Laura. I take the time to figure what is wrong now instead of just snapping my cog [losing my temper].... Wouldn't of handled another like Sarah. She's saved her life by being different."

An empty crib is a quiet crib.

Another entry referred to her husband: "He has a morbid fear about Laura.... Well, I know there's nothing wrong with her. Nothing out of ordinary any way. Because it was me not them.... With Sarah all I wanted was her to shut up. And one day she did."

Kathleen Folbigg made a number of ominous comments about her second daughter. "She's a fairly good-natured baby—Thank goodness, it has saved her from the fate of her siblings. I think she was warned."

Folbigg had mental health issues and was prone to mood swings. Her children frustrated her every bit as much as they brought her happiness. In fact, by her own admission, there were times at which she actively hated them. The real question was, did they make her angry enough to kill them? Were her journals the confessions of a cold-blooded killer, or simply the scribblings of a mother struggling to cope with depression and a significant amount of stress?

This was by no means a clear-cut case. For one thing, none of the deceased children bore obvious marks or wounds that would have suggested a pattern of physical abuse, although Sarah Folbigg's lungs did show signs of minor bleeding, which pointed to the possibility that she had been asphyxiated. There were no broken bones, and no other unexplained burns or bruises anywhere on their bodies.

It is a tragic fact of life that young children can, and too often do, die in their cribs for no apparent reason. Frequently, the parents have done absolutely nothing wrong. When this occurs in the first year of life, the coroner may classify it as SIDS. This is sometimes a diagnosis of exclusion, when no other apparent cause for death can be determined, but there are also specific findings that point to the condition as the cause of death in a young child.

Scientists still do not know the exact causes of SIDS, although studies have identified a number of risk factors that render an infant vulnerable to the syndrome. Certain genetic disorders can predispose a child to dying of SIDS. Laura and Sarah Folbigg did indeed have the specific genetic mutation that would have increased their chances of suddenly dying in their sleep. The mutation in question can cause cardiac dysrhythmias in an otherwise healthy heart, which are frequently fatal.

Unfortunately for Kathleen Folbigg, the only way to determine whether this particular gene is part of a child's genetic makeup would be to perform gene sequencing. This was eventually done, but crucially, it did not take place until after she had been tried and sentenced.

SIDS babies tend to be found prone, in the face-down position. All four of the Folbigg babies were lying on their backs when they were discovered. This was seen as a mark against the possibility of natural death and in favor of probable smothering.

At the conclusion of her trial in 2003, Kathleen Folbigg was found guilty, primarily because the prosecution made a compelling case that the possibility of her *not* having murdered her own children was so great, it was effectively zero.

> SIDS babies tend to be found prone, in the face-down position. All four of the Folbigg babies were lying on their backs when they were discovered.

After being convicted of murdering three of her children (Laura, Patrick, and Sarah) and one count of manslaughter for the fourth, Caleb, Folbigg was sentenced to 40 years' imprisonment. The first 30 years were to be served with no possibility for parole whatsoever, and until 2019, it looked very much as though she would serve out the entire term.

No matter how ironclad the prosecution's case seemed to be, some cracks have appeared in it over the two decades since the guilty verdict was rendered. Science has advanced, and some of those advancements have cast doubt on the guilty verdict handed down to Kathleen Folbigg.

Could it be possible that, rather than being a serial murderess, Kathleen Folbigg is actually the victim of a massive miscarriage of justice? At the time of writing, a group of scientific experts has re-examined the evidence and concluded that there is, in fact, reasonable doubt as to whether she killed her children. One of the fundamental axioms of any fair legal system is that when reasonable doubt exists, the defendant should be acquitted.

Could the Folbigg babies have all suffered a genetic predisposition for conditions that can lead to SIDS?

The truth concerning Kathleen Folbigg's guilt or innocence remains opaque. It is simply not possible to determine with any degree of accuracy whether she killed some, all, or none of her children. At the time of her conviction, she was dubbed "Australia's worst female serial killer." She has spent 19 years behind bars for crimes she may not actually have committed—indeed, for something that a number of leading medical experts say was no crime at all, but rather, a tragic set of circumstances beyond anybody's control.

She is the one person in this book who probably deserves to be given her freedom back. Now, almost 20 years after her conviction, opinion on the matter is still divided. Folbigg has her supporters, many of whom have extremely strong scientific backgrounds and are experts in their field. On the other hand, there are others who remain convinced that the four deaths were simply too improbable to be ascribed to coincidence. After an appeal for the evidence to be reassessed was denied, Folbigg's defenders have set up a petition, hoping to amass enough signatures to gain her case some traction within the Australian legal system. Their ultimate goal is to get her a pardon.

Is she truly a serial killer, or is she a falsely accused victim? Only Kathleen Folbigg knows the absolute truth. Many of the individuals who appear in this book went to prison insisting that they were innocent. Time may ultimately prove that Folbigg, who steadfastly maintains her innocence, is actually telling the truth.

# THE MONSTER OF THE ANDES
## PEDRO LOPEZ

In the context of the serial killer phenomena, one word appears over and over again: monster. This term appears repeatedly throughout the literature and media coverage of serial murder, and it is easy to see why. These are men and women who perform the most gut-wrenching of acts, often without batting an eye. The things they do are, indeed, monstrous.

Some believe that because of its frequent usage, the impact of the word "monster" has become diluted. While that may or may not be true, it is undeniable that some of the murderers who have been given that appellation truly do deserve it. One such individual is Colombia-born Pedro López, the so-called Monster of the Andes.

How did this seemingly ordinary working man earn the dubious description? By murdering children—possibly hundreds of them. The true scope and extent of his horrific crimes only became apparent after his arrest in 1980.

What little is known of Pedro López's childhood comes from his own verbal testimony, which automatically makes it suspect. Great credit must be given to journalist Ron Laytner, who interviewed López extensively about his life and the murders he committed and published the results in numerous newspaper articles.

Born in October 1948 to a prostitute in Colombia, he was abandoned on the streets as a young boy, for which he never forgave his mother. A number of other serial killers who experienced a similarly traumatic childhood went on to project this anger and hatred they felt for their own mother on other female victims, usually adult women. This was not the case when it came to López, who exclusively targeted little girls. After abducting them, he sexually molested them before strangling them to death. To keep these heinous acts from being discovered, he buried each victim in a shallow grave before moving on to the next.

It has been claimed that the reason López's mother disowned him and threw him out of her home was because she caught him sexually molesting his sister. Having lost his family, López then lived as a street urchin in Bogotá, Colombia's capital city. He resorted to theft and begging to survive. Unsurprisingly, it wasn't long before his life of petty crime landed him in jail, at the age of 18. Colombian prisons had (and still have) a well-deserved reputation as some of the toughest in the world. To survive serving time in one, an inmate had to be tougher. López proved that he was as tough as they come when a small gang of fellow inmates attacked him one day, administering a fearsome beating as part of a brutal gang rape.

Rather than go off half-cocked, López instead chose to bide his time and plot revenge. Over the space of several days, he carefully crafted a shiv with a razor-sharp blade. Doubtless thinking that their unprovoked assault on the young man was now forgotten, his attackers were taken by surprise when their victim struck back.

Knowing that he had no chance of defeating them all at once, López contrived to lure each of his assailants to his prison cell one by one. Smarter men would probably have wondered why the lights were

out, but the first three inmates went along anyway. Once inside the cell, they found López waiting for them with his home-made weapon. Showing not the slightest compunction whatsoever, he stabbed each of them to death. The fourth managed to escape with his life.

At the age of 18, Pedro López had just committed his first three murders (that we know of). His reputation as a man not to be messed with was cemented, at the cost of two more years added to his prison sentence. Those murders would be the start of a killing spree that spanned multiple decades and countries.

Nestled high on a plateau among the Andes Mountains, Colombia's capital city of Bogotá is a place of both extreme wealth and extreme poverty. During López's youth, it was known as one of the most violent cities in the world.

It is not known exactly when López first turned his attention toward young girls, but we do know that he began killing slowly and infrequently at first, finally ramping up to a point where he was murdering on average two of them every week. The vast majority of his murders took place between 1977 and 1980.

During the late 1970s, Pedro López was an itinerant migrant worker living in Peru. It is believed that during this period of his life, he began to rape and murder in earnest. Some police estimates said that he was responsible for at least 100 killings in Peru, if not more. Many of them took place in rural and mountainous areas, and it was in one such place that he was caught and almost killed.

López was interrupted in the middle of an attempted child abduction. This part of the country was not governed by the law of cities and nations; tribal law held sway and was renowned for being both brutal and decisive, which is how Pedro López found himself naked and undergoing the most painful torture the tribespeople could devise. After the passage of a period of time deemed sufficient by the tribe, his fate was to be thrown into a shallow grave, just like those in which he interred the bodies of his victims, and buried alive. That would have involved a slow and unpleasant death, and had things actually panned out that way, the lives of hundreds of young girls would have been saved.

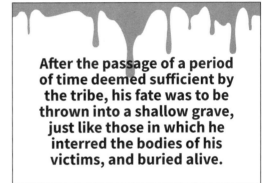

**After the passage of a period of time deemed sufficient by the tribe, his fate was to be thrown into a shallow grave, just like those in which he interred the bodies of his victims, and buried alive.**

Instead, López was saved at the eleventh hour by a well-meaning missionary from the United States. Unwilling to see a man put to death in such a manner, no matter what he had been caught doing, the missionary instead volunteered to take responsibility for López and drive him to the closest police station. She was taking a risk with her own personal safety by transporting a man with López's violent background, but the tribespeople made sure he was tied up securely before placing him in the back of the missionary's vehicle. Unbeknownst to her, she had saved a life at the future cost of hundreds of others.

Tribal justice and so-called civilized justice were two very different things. The Peruvian authorities had no suspicion that they held a serial killer in their jail cell. The most they could do, given the circumstances, was to deport López back to his native Colombia.

From here, his next stop was Ecuador. His near-miss with the Peruvian tribespeople did not make him any more cautious; in fact, if anything, it only increased his desire to rape and kill. He spent the bulk of his time roaming around the country, finding vulnerable little girls who he could charm into coming along with him. Unlike some abductors, López didn't violently snatch his victims. Instead, he preferred to charm them, taking advantage of the children's sweet and innocent nature.

His MO was to wander the streets, markets, and public places— seemingly at random, but actually on the lookout for a specific type of young girl. Once one caught his eye, López began to follow her. He stayed well back, making sure he wasn't spotted. This was even more important when the girl was accompanied by a parent or an older sibling. He would hang back, observe, see where they went and what they did. Sometimes, this stalking process went on for several days. López was constantly alert for a window of opportunity, however brief it might be, to catch his target on her own. Then he would move in, offering the child a present, usually some small, shiny keepsake that was calculated to turn a young girl's head.

Just like that, he was able to entice the child away. Having gained her confidence to some degree (or at least, won her over with a gift), he would lead the girl off, far away from the place of abduction. He had already dug a grave for his latest victim before setting out. By the time her parent or custodian noticed that she was missing, it was too late.

In April 1980, while he was living in Ambato, Ecuador, his past finally caught up with López. The region had been hit with torrential rains, followed by heavy flooding. Fast-flowing river water washed away large swathes of mud from a riverbank. Once the waters had subsided, citizens were horrified to discover the decomposing remains of four little girls, lying in muddy holes in the ground.

There was an immediate public outcry. This went far beyond kidnapping, a crime to which the police often turned a blind eye. It was obvious to everybody that the children had been murdered, and the perpetrator had to be found immediately. Ambato went on a state of high alert, with both its police and citizenry watching out for the monster who would have done such a thing.

Did Pedro López hear about the discovery of his victims' bodies? It is almost inconceivable that he would not have. Common sense would have dictated that he lie low for a while or relocate to another city in the region. Instead, displaying not the slightest hint of self-preservation, he was back on the prowl again the following day, stalking an 11-year-old girl in broad daylight.

Fortunately, the girl's mother saw him staring at her daughter. She confronted him in the middle of a public square, and a large group of fellow citizens grabbed López, physically restraining him and wrestling his would-be victim away. In hindsight, he was lucky not to have been beaten to death by the crowd before police officers arrived to arrest him. Few things are guaranteed to enrage people more than a child-killer.

Ambato, Ecuador, is a regional capital high in the central Andean valley, surrounded by volcanoes, a center for the area's trade and industry.

Once he was in their custody, López tried to play it cool. He had been caught in the act of trying to abduct a young girl, it was true, but there was no real evidence linking him to the murder of the four whose bodies had just been unearthed by the river. Knowing this, the police planted one of their own alongside López in his cell. This mole's only task was to gain López's confidence and get him to talk.

It took weeks, but finally, Pedro López did begin to talk. He simply couldn't help himself, and once the flood gates opened, he ended up confessing to hundreds of rape-murders. The arresting officers listened to his self-professed catalog of horrors in shocked disbelief. Then, to prove his word, they accompanied him to some of the body burial sites, where they dug up the remains of more than 50 young girls. None was older than 12, with the youngest being just eight years of age.

The murderer did not even put up the pretense of being sorry for having taken the lives of so many innocent children. Although he claimed responsibility for each rape and killing, there was no contrition in Pedro López's voice when he talked about them. In fact, quite the contrary—he seemed to be almost proud of what he had done. Before long, even though he was held in police custody, he had become public enemy number one, the most reviled and hated man in all of Ecuador.

The more little bodies of murdered children were recovered from shallow graves, the more anger toward López grew, and understandably so. It was necessary for him to be kept in an isolated jail cell for his own protection. Had he been released into the general population, he wouldn't have survived a day. Word got out that a bounty had been placed on his head by the families of those he had killed. The truth is that practically every convict in Ecuador would have happily killed Pedro López for free.

One of the most remarkable aspects of the Pedro López case is the sentence that he received. Despite the vast number of lives that he snuffed out, the maximum penalty that he could be given under Ecuadorian law was 16 years' imprisonment. If he kept his nose clean while behind bars, there was even the possibility of getting a couple of years knocked off his sentence for good behavior—which is exactly what happened.

After completing 14 years of his 16-year sentence, López walked out of prison a free man in 1994—except, not quite. He may have discharged his debt to the Ecuadorian people, but now it was Colombia's turn to have a crack at him. Fortunately for him, rather than end up doing hard time in a penitentiary, López was instead committed to a mental institution, where he served just three more years under relatively easy conditions. In 1998, when offered bail, he accepted the terms laid out by the state—and promptly vanished, never to be seen again.

**In 1998, when offered bail, he accepted the terms laid out by the state—and promptly vanished, never to be seen again.**

Why did Pedro López commit the awful atrocities that he did? In addition to a hatred of his mother, he claimed that when he was a child living on the streets of Bogotá, he was repeatedly raped by an adult male. This was the source of much of his anger, causing him to want to do the same thing to innocent children himself.

The twisted amusement López took from his victims did not end with their death. He made a habit of keeping several dead bodies close together, sometimes putting them in the same grave. He liked to talk to them and have them talk to one another. On occasion, he would stage the corpses, sitting them up facing one another in a ghoulish tableau.

An accurate count of the victims of Pedro López will never be known. Although he was forthcoming about the number of murders he committed during his years as an active serial killer, López disposed of the bodies of his victims in a number of different ways. He was always on the lookout for major construction projects in progress, particularly those that involved building new roads or maintaining older ones. Once the construction workers had put down tools for the day and gone home, he would sneak onto the site after dark and bury bodies there. López did this in the hopes that the burial site would be built over when construction continued, thereby hiding the evidence of his crime forever.

Other victims' remains were lost thanks to the weather and the environment, their unmarked graves washed away by flooding or mudslides. Some were dug up by critters, their bones gnawed on and scattered far and wide.

The murders spanned the territory of three different nations: Ecuador, Peru, and Colombia. None of the law enforcement agencies involved shared data at the time, and there was no easy way for anybody to recognize that a serial killer was at work within and between their borders.

It has been estimated by some that the total number of murders could range anywhere between 300 and 400—if not more. Sadly, children disappear all the time, including in South America. Kidnapping was rife throughout the region, and police forces were both underfunded and overstretched. They had neither the time nor the resources to go looking for girls who had, it was just assumed, been kidnapped and sent far away to work a menial job. The possibility of a serial predator stalking the streets never came up on their radar.

Skeptics rightly point out that a serial killer is the very definition of an unreliable witness. Many grossly inflate the number of victims they have killed, usually from a desire to climb what they perceive as "rankings." Some believe that the more lives a serial killer has taken, the better they have performed. It is an attempt to stroke an already enlarged ego. There is no cast-iron guarantee that Pedro López killed 300 or more children, but there is also no guarantee that he didn't.

Wherever roads or structures were being built or repaired, López found a convenient long-term hiding place for his victims' bodies, making it difficult to confirm all of his confessions.

All of which brings us to the most disturbing aspect of the entire case. López dropped off the radar following his disappearance from the mental institution and has never been seen since. At least one child murder has taken place since that time which might be attributable to him—possibly more. This begs the questions: what happened to him, and where is he now?

At the time of writing, assuming López is still alive, he would be in his mid-seventies. He is still wanted by law enforcement, being rightly perceived as a threat to the children of Colombia and its neighbors. For years, he may well have been hiding within plain sight, living in relative anonymity while the search for him slowly cools and fades.

It is possible that he is dead, most likely of natural causes. He could also be ill, or infirm, and therefore incapable of murdering again.

If the study of serial killers teaches us one thing, it is this: once they begin killing, these monsters tend to keep on killing. If Pedro López is still alive and possesses a modicum of strength and intellect, then the children of South America are still not safe.

# BRITAIN'S HANNIBAL THE CANNIBAL ROBERT MAUDSLEY

**F**ew things illustrate the mass fascination with serial killers more than the character of Dexter Morgan. Featuring in a series of popular novels by author Jeff Lindsay and brought to life in a smash-hit TV show of the same name by actor Michael C. Hall, Dexter is a fictional police blood-splatter analyst with a dark secret—he is also a serial killer. What separates the character of Dexter from his real-world counterparts, the thing that allows us as an audience to root for him to some degree, is that he only kills other serial killers.

It's an interesting concept for a story, but does the concept of the so-called noble serial killer have any basis in reality? The short answer is this: not really. However, there is at least one serial killer who—some have claimed—murdered not for the fun of it but because he was targeting those that society considers to be the lowest of the low.

His name is Robert John Maudsley, and the constructed narrative that now surrounds him is both complicated and fascinating. It is also murky and inconsistent, as the primary historian—Maudsley himself—has told different variations on the story over the years. The news media have also played a role in distorting Maudsley's image, portraying him as a vengeful vigilante-type loner who killed for a greater good. In this case, at least, it turns out that the truth really is stranger than fiction—and far less clear-cut.

It is fair to say that Maudsley's childhood was far from an idyllic one. He was born in Liverpool in 1953 into a working-class, deeply broken British family. It was a toxic environment; in fact, social workers had judged the Maudsleys' home life to be of such high neglect that all four of Maudsley children were taken into the care of the state.

The children were placed in an orphanage, the day-to-day operation of which was overseen by nuns. It was a place of rules and regulations, even for a young boy of Maudsley's age, but the orphanage was a veritable heaven compared to the fractured household that he, his two brothers, and sister had been rescued from. Unfortunately, after a few years had passed, the Department of Social Services reversed course and decided that things had improved to the point where the Maudsley children could return home again.

It was a dreadful mistake.

For one thing, their parents had continued having children. The four Maudsley kids now had eight new siblings. The environment they went back to was one in which physical, mental, and emotional abuse was the norm. Although corporal punishment was commonplace during the 1950s and 1960s, the beatings meted out to Robert and his brothers and sisters would be considered child abuse today. Such violence was administered for the most minor of infractions, and sometimes for no apparent reason at all.

In an eerie foreshadowing of what his future would hold, the young Robert was kept locked up in a room all by himself. According to him, the only time the door opened was to admit his father, who was coming in to give him another beating. This occurred several times each day and involved more than just fists (which would have been bad enough)—Maudsley's father used household objects as weapons with which to batter his son.

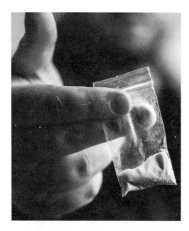

In London and addicted to drugs, Maudsley turned to sex work to fund his habits.

Just what had caused Robert to be the focus of his parents' abuse remains unknown. Things soon became bad enough that Social Services intervened once again, pulling him back out of his parents' custody and placing him into foster care. Asking where their brother had gone to, Maudsley's siblings were told off-handedly that he was dead. Children being children, they believed their parents' lie.

By the time he reached the age of 16, Robert was out on the streets. He began to engage in petty theft, breaking and entering into private residences, and then selling whatever he could steal. The local police caught him and quickly put a stop to that.

Like many who find themselves homeless, Maudsley gravitated to the United Kingdom's capital city of London, where he soon found that life on the streets was every bit as brutal and unforgiving as his abusive home environment had been. He claimed to have been sexually assaulted during this period of his life, which would have contributed to the rage he felt consuming him.

As a youth with no money and little in the way of job prospects, Maudsley had few options when it came to making a living. Even fewer of those options were legal or deemed socially acceptable. In the end, it came down to prostitution, selling his body in exchange for cash. He had been sucked into the world of drugs and soon became addicted. This could easily have marked the beginning of a downward spiral that ended with his death, as has happened to so many unfortunate souls who came to London in search of a brighter future.

Instead, fate took a different turn on March 14, 1974. Maudsley went home with a customer named John Farrell, who was willing to pay him for sex. Construction worker Farrell was 30, 10 years older than the rent boy he had picked up. The two men already knew each other, and this was probably not their first sexual liaison. Both men had to be quiet when they returned to Farrell's flat, because the landlord was watching television in a room nearby.

The commonly accepted version of the story maintains that at some point during their encounter, Farrell produced pictures of several young children and told Maudsley that he had sexually molested them. Quite what his motivation for doing this might have been is never made clear—it makes little sense that he would have admitted to a crime that would, if Maudsley had reported it to the police, have seen him sentenced to a lengthy spell in prison. What was in it for Farrell, other than risk?

At this point, Maudsley is supposed to have flown into a rage at the sight of the abused boys and leapt upon Farrell, venting his rage on the pedophile in front of him—but did he really? Not according to the statement that he made to the police following his arrest. Maudsley told officers that he had gone out that day with the express desire to hurt somebody and had even carried a knife with him as a means of doing so.

Maudsley's statement mentions nothing about pictures of children. Instead, it claims that he and Farrell got into bed together and engaged in consensual sexual activity, while a voice in Maudsley's head told him to kill the other man. Maudsley attempted to "masturbate the feeling away." Not surprisingly, this was unsuccessful. The two men eventually drifted off to sleep, but the homicidal urge was still there when Maudsley woke up. Before going to sleep, he had stashed the knife underneath the bed. He recalled being unable to get the weapon out of his mind.

Farrell and Maudsley spent a lazy morning together. The former could have had no inkling that the latter was seriously thinking about taking his life, but Maudsley was growing increasingly fixated upon the idea. Farrell did indeed pull out some pictures of other lovers he had brought home to his flat, but there is no proof that they were children; most likely, they were also rent boys, as Maudsley was. The age of consent for homosexual men in the United Kingdom was 21 then, which means it is likely that some of Farrell's partners were legally underage. (The current age of consent is now 16.) However, the oft-stated claim that Maudsley killed Farrell because he was a pedophile was not accurate.

It may be that something about the photographs intensified Maudsley's anger, however, because this was the moment when he grabbed the knife from under the bed and lunged at Farrell.

"All of a sudden, the feeling came on," he stated later. Robert Maudsley launched a frenzied knife attack on John Farrell, stabbing him repeatedly in the chest, back, and flank. Farrell tried to escape, but his attacker kept on swinging the blade. His victim never made it as far as the door. Maudsley recalled later: "I could have robbed the house, but all I wanted to do was kill someone."

This is an important statement because it challenges the widespread myth that he targeted Farrell on account of his alleged pedophilia. If

Maudsley claimed that Farrell's photo collection sparked his rage.

Maudsley's statement is true, then the specific identity of his victim was unimportant. He simply wanted to kill, period. There may also have been a financial aspect to the killing, because Maudsley stole money from Farrell prior to leaving his flat.

A number of accounts of this murder add that he then strangled Farrell to death with a garrote. Still others claim that he struck him in the head with a blunt instrument, though Maudsley himself noted that he thought Farrell's skull had struck the door as he fell.

Once his victim was dead, he told the dead body of his victim that he was sorry, then went to the bathroom and washed off as much of the blood as he could manage. He was able to scrub most of it off his skin, but his clothes were saturated. Maudsley called the police and reported what he had done, then went to his own flat and changed clothes. Once there, he felt the urge to kill rising again, and, uncertain if he would be able to suppress it, left and called the police again. He was picked up by a patrol car shortly afterward and taken into custody.

Detectives questioned Robert Maudsley at length. He made no effort to deny the murder or his responsibility for it. An evaluation of his mental health resulted in his being judged mentally incompetent to stand trial for the crime. Instead, he became an inmate of Broadmoor, Britain's infamous maximum security psychiatric facility. Broadmoor has housed some of the U.K.'s most notorious violent criminals, such as Peter Sutcliffe, the so-called Yorkshire Ripper.

**An evaluation of his mental health resulted in his being judged mentally incompetent to stand trial for the crime.**

Maudsley's time at Broadmoor came to a bloody and violent end in 1976. The big event of the day was a patients' soccer match, giving the residents a chance to blow off some steam and get some exercise. Maudsley, who was 28 at the time, enlisted the help of a fellow patient, 28-year-old David Cheeseman, to kidnap a convicted pedophile named David Francis. All three men had been participants in the soccer game. When it was over, Maudsley and Cheeseman pounced on the unsuspecting Francis, delivering a swift beating before dragging him away into a room used by the patients to change into their sports kit.

A little before 11 o'clock in the morning, the two aggressors barricaded themselves inside the room, and so began a ten-hour siege during which they would continually torture Francis. They used lengths of wire ripped from the back of a record player to bind their captive's hands and feet, then battered him repeatedly while horrified staff members tried to convince them to stop by yelling through the door. Their pleas were to no avail. Maudsley and Cheeseman kicked and punched the helpless Francis over and over again, in effect using him as a human punching bag.

By nine o'clock that same evening, it was over. David Francis had been beaten to the verge of death, and then fatally garroted by Maudsley. His two murderers proudly held their victim's dead body up to the window, showing it off to the Broadmoor staff who were assembled out-

In the wrong hands, everything is a potential weapon.

side. His skull had been smashed open, and brain matter was exposed. There would later be claims that a spoon was sticking out. This would eventually lead to Maudsley gaining a reputation for cannibalism— the common belief, according to one of the guards, being that he had scooped out and eaten part of Francis's brain. I could find no evidence to support the claim.

Shortly afterward, Maudsley and Cheeseman unblocked the door and gave themselves up. There was no point denying their guilt. The pair claimed that they had kidnapped and tortured Francis because they had found out about him sexually molesting another patient and wanted to exact vengeance upon him for that crime. The claim is an odd one, because in an earlier incident of hostage-taking at Broadmoor, Maudsley had buddied up with Francis to kidnap a different patient. He had no scruples about Francis's past behavior then, when it suited his purpose.

The court ruled Maudsley guilty of manslaughter. Rather than return him to Broadmoor, where his presence had been something of a minor disaster, he was instead sent to Her Majesty's Prison Wakefield. This was a Category A correctional facility that was home to some of the most dangerous criminals in the U.K. Some staff at HMP Wakefield had given it the less-than-affectionate nickname of "the Monster House." Harold Shipman, the so-called "Doctor Death," was just one of those incarcerated there.

It was no psychiatric hospital: the emphasis at Wakefield was on containing the inmates and protecting society from them, rather than on trying to cure the potentially incurable. As such, it was a good fit for Robert Maudsley, who, even though he was behind bars, was inevitably going to kill again.

That happened just a few months after he arrived. Salney Darwood, 46, was incarcerated on a life sentence, having been convicted of manslaughter. On July 29, 1978, Darwood ran afoul of Maudsley when he went to the latter's cell. Apropos of nothing, Maudsley attacked him with a crudely fashioned knife. After stabbing his victim, he then used an improvised garrote to strangle him to death. Darwood's body was stuffed underneath Maudsley's bed. The killer then cleaned himself up in the sink, as best he could, and set about finding somebody else to kill.

There was something about Maudsley's crazed affect that day that rang alarm bells for other prisoners. He tried to get numerous others to accompany him back to his cell. Nobody wanted to take him up on his offer, so he changed tack and went after 56-year-old Bill Roberts, using the same blade he used to stab Salney Darwood. After repeatedly stabbing Roberts, Maudsley smashed his head forcefully against the wall until he was dead. For the legal authorities, this was the last straw. For the safety of everyone concerned, they determined, he would be kept in strict isolation for the remainder of his sentence—and that sentence would extend to the end of his natural life.

> Maudsley was given the nickname of "Hannibal the Cannibal" by the British press, who sought to cash in with the fictional character created in the novels of Thomas Harris....

Maudsley was given the nickname of "Hannibal the Cannibal" by the British press, who sought to cash in with the fictional character created in the novels of Thomas Harris and portrayed to chilling effect in the smash-hit Hollywood movie *The Silence of the Lambs* by Sir Anthony Hopkins. Harris's Hannibal Lecter is an academic with an off-the-charts I.Q., an extremely smart man who appreciates the finer things in life. He is also devoid of anything approaching a conscience and is willing to kill whenever he feels like it. The parallels with Robert Maudsley are obvious, if a little stretched.

Lecter is a man of culture, a devotee of the arts, who understands and appreciates gourmet food, fine wines, sophisticated literature, opera, and poetry. Maudsley is reputed to share many of the same interests. He is exceptionally intelligent and about as far from the stereotypical movie murderer as it is possible to get. Yet none of this detracts from the fact that he is responsible for killing four people in cold blood.

One of the iconic scenes in Jonathan Demme's movie adaptation of *The Silence of the Lambs* involves a face-off between Jodie Foster's FBI profiler, Clarice Starling, and Lecter, in the latter's prison cell. The cell itself is made of transparent Perspex and is buried deep underground, an acknowledgment of just how dangerous the prison authorities consider Lecter to be. In real life, the cell in which Maudsley spent not just years but decades in isolation isn't all that different from the one featured in the movie. It was built especially for him in 1983, predating the movie by eight years. Its sole occupant was kept in solitary confinement for all but one hour each day, when a squad of prison officers accompanied him for his daily allotment of exercise.

As previously mentioned, a key part of the so-called "Hannibal the Cannibal" mystique surrounding him stems from the claims made in the British press that Maudsley had eaten part of the brain of one of his victims. I have been unable to find any concrete evidence to back this up other than the eyewitness report that David Francis was found with a spoon inserted into his completely shattered skull, and in all likelihood, this was nothing more than a tall story.

As this book goes to press, 69-year-old Robert Maudsley has spent more than 45 years in either a psychiatric care facility or in prison— much of it in complete isolation, in the basement of HMP Wakefield.

A campaign has been ongoing in the United Kingdom to improve conditions for Maudsley in jail. Several different petitions, which can be found on change.org, currently have hundreds of signatories and use the rationale that Maudsley's actions were in fact laudable, even somewhat akin to a public service. He should therefore be given access to a wide variety of books and other reading material.

One signatory comments that: "If his crimes where [sic] only taking out paedo's and rapists he should receive a knighthood." Another agrees, saying, "I think he a hero for killing dirty pedos."

Rumored to have used a spoon to eat the brains of his Broadmoor victim, Maudsley would eventually be compared to, and give the nickname of, Hannibal.

This ignores the fact that not all Maudsley's victims were pedophiles or rapists, despite some very popular claims to the contrary. Many people take the view that he should be given somewhat better conditions in prison but never released, considering that there is no guarantee he would not kill again if given the chance.

During the Christmas season of 2021, Maudsley, then 68, petitioned to be allowed to be put into the general population. This is somewhat understandable, considering that he has spent more than 40 years in solitary confinement, with little in the way of human contact. His petition was denied, as was the appeal he subsequently lodged in response.

Unless something changes significantly, Robert Maudsley will most likely die alone in his cell, which he, his family, and his supporters contend is completely unfair. The authorities, on the other hand, have taken the position that even though decades have passed since he committed his last violent crime, it would still be too risky to allow him to interact with other prisoners. That risk would extend not just to any potential victims but also to Maudsley himself; there would be no shortage of "up and comers" in the prison system who would like nothing more than to make a name for themselves by maiming or killing a high-profile murderer such as he.

Much debate has taken place concerning Robert Maudsley's motive for murder. When asked about the reasons behind his killings, Maudsley laid the blame at the door of his parents. He claimed that his mother and father had been so abusive to him during his childhood that he had nurtured a blistering rage for them that grew stronger with each passing year. When he was killing his victims, Maudsley went on to explain, he was exorcizing that rage, which he felt more appropriately should have been vented on them—but no longer could be.

He maintained that if he had murdered his parents when the opportunity presented itself, he would never have killed another victim. Whether this is true is impossible to determine. It is fair to say, however, that the vicious and sustained abuse Maudsley suffered as a boy must have had some lasting and significant impact on his life. One does not simply brush off that kind of trauma and walk away without any ill effects.

As a teenager, he made multiple visits to mental health institutions. Talking frankly with the psychiatrists, he admitted to hearing voices speaking to him from inside his own head. Those insistent voices were instructing him to

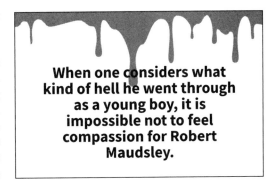

When one considers what kind of hell he went through as a young boy, it is impossible not to feel compassion for Robert Maudsley.

do one thing: murder his mother and father. He was so emotionally disturbed that on more than one occasion, he tried to take his own life.

When one considers what kind of hell he went through as a young boy, it is impossible not to feel compassion for Robert Maudsley. Such consideration also raises the question: if he had been born into a loving, ordinary family, as every child deserves to be, would he still have gone on to commit four acts of lethal savagery in later life? Or would he have gone on to be an ordinary member of society (if, indeed, there truly is such a thing) and lead a happy, albeit unremarkable life of peaceful domesticity? We can never know for sure, of course, but the latter path seems most likely.

When the age-old debate of nature versus nurture is raised, I suspect that the serial killer Robert Maudsley ultimately became would never have existed if his ruthless parents had not beat it into him during his formative years. He claims to be undergoing a long-term nervous breakdown, brought on by the isolated conditions under which he serves his sentence, and that thoughts of suicide are never far away. He asked to be given a cyanide capsule to end his own life. The request was denied.

That, by itself, is a tragedy. Yet, to be clear, sympathy for him should only go so far. There is a real danger in turning a convicted murder into a folk hero, even one with such a sad and lamentable background. He is not some kind of lovable rogue. At the end of the day, the bottom line is that Robert Maudsley ended the lives of four men in cold blood. There is no guarantee that, if he were to be released, either into the general prison population or onto the streets of Great Britain, he would not do the same thing again. It is for this reason that the British Home Secretary will almost certainly never take the risk of giving him his freedom. He remains the United Kingdom's longest-serving prisoner.

# BODIES IN BARRELS
# THE SNOWTOWN MURDERS

It's fair to say that the little hamlet of Snowtown is in the middle of nowhere. Little more than a collection of stores and a few homes, this small town in South Australia would never have found a place in the history books if it wasn't for a series of brutal killings that took place in the 1990s. Although most of the murders took place elsewhere, for reasons that will soon become apparent, they came to be known collectively as the Snowtown Murders.

On August 31, 1992, 20-year-old Clinton Trezise became the first victim of the Snowtown killers when he was beaten to death by John Justin Bunting. Bunting had invited Trezise to his home in Salisbury North, a suburb of Adelaide, the capital of South Australia. Suspecting nothing, he had accepted the invitation. Bunting attacked Trezise out of the blue, claiming later to be motivated by his belief that his victim was a pedophile. He may have been influenced by rumors circulating that Trezise had a boyfriend with that particular perversion.

The assault on Clinton Trezise was savage. Bunting used a heavy object to smash the young man's skull in. Trezise raised an arm to try and fend off the attack, to no avail. His attacker battered the arm down, breaking bones in the process, before moving in to finish his helpless victim off.

Clinton Trezise was a flamboyant man who liked dressing in brightly colored pants. Unabashedly gay and totally out about it, it's easy to see why he caused Bunting to blow a fuse. Bunting was a petty and hateful man, consumed by prejudice and spite. In addition to feeling a vitriolic hatred of pedophiles, he was also a militant homophobe. He claimed to have been attacked and molested by an older male (a friend's brother) when he was eight years old. If true—and with a manipulative

An unremarkable suburb of Adelaide, Australia, Salisbury is about 80 miles (130 kilometers) from the murder campaign's eponymous city, Snowtown.

narcissist like Bunting, it is impossible to be sure—then this would go some way to explaining his deep-seated malevolence.

Bunting referred to gay men and potential pedophiles by the rather distasteful moniker of "dirties," gleefully boasting to his cohort that they were going to "off some more of them dirties" when they were about to commit future murders. In his warped mind, he was incapable of separating the concept that just because a man happened to be homosexual, that did not necessarily mean that he was a pedophile. (To state the obvious, the *vast* majority of gay men are not.) Bunting simply could not differentiate the two things—either could not or did not want to. To the deeply bigoted, logic and reason are often strangers.

The killing of Clinton Trezise was Bunting's first known murder. He had not yet fully assembled the gang of accomplices that would help him with future murders, but its foundations were starting to form, thanks to a pair of unlikely acquaintances. Bunting enlisted the help of two men to dispose of his victim's body. Robert Joe Wagner and Barry Lane were, it is fair to say, an unusual couple. Wagner was 20 years old, and Lane was in his mid-30s. Disturbingly, Lane was a convicted pedophile, and had set his sights on Wagner when he was just 13. He liked to dress as a woman and refer to himself as Vanessa.

This relationship amounts to one of the strangest aspects of the entire case. Between them, the two men represented everything John Justin Bunting despised most in the world. Both were gay, and one was a convicted child molester. The fact that they became friends with the pathologically bigoted Bunting was highly unusual, and the course of their association would be far from smooth.

The three men bundled up Clinton Trezise's dead body and, under cover of darkness, drove out into the sparsely populated countryside. It wasn't long before they found a suitable spot for burial. After he finished burying the body in a shallow grave, Bunting went about his life as if nothing out of the ordinary had happened. This is the phase in which a fledgling serial killer is at their most hesitant. They have just committed the first murder, disposed of the evidence as best they could, and spent a period of time waiting for the other shoe to drop. Will they be caught?

Time passes. After a while, a knock at the door no longer makes their heart race. The police haven't sniffed them out, they realize. They have killed and gotten away with it. Their mind turns to murder again. For Bunting, this period lasted for almost three and a half years. His second murder took place in December 1995. The victim was a 26-year-old man with special needs, by the name of Ray Davies. Bunting was married but was also sleeping with Suzanne Allen, who, in turn, had once been engaged to Davies but had broken it off after learning that he had sexually molested two of her young relatives.

The web of relationships grows increasingly tangled and convoluted at this point, so let's pause for a moment to establish some more of the key players in the Snowtown Murders.

John Bunting had moved in with a single mother named Elizabeth Harvey. Unbeknownst to Harvey, her sons had been sexually molested by an older man named Jeffrey Payne. One of those sons was a teenager, 14-year-old James Vlassakis. Feeling powerless to stop the abuse because Payne had told him he would murder the boy's mother if he told on him, James saw no option but to simply grit his teeth and endure it. It has also been said that James's half-brother, Troy, molested him as well.

Yet there was another option, and it arrived in the form of John Bunting. No sooner had he taken up residence with James's mother, than he made his animosity toward pedophiles abundantly

> **The fact that they became friends with the pathologically bigoted Bunting was highly unusual, and the course of their association would be far from smooth.**

clear. For someone who had been repeatedly abused by the object of his hatred, falling into line with Bunting's way of thinking would have been an easy sell. The more time the two of them spent together, the more James began to see Bunting as a kind of father figure, somebody to look up to—and eventually, to emulate.

Before long, Bunting and James developed a close bond. Displaying a level of trust that the teenager wasn't used to receiving, the older man told him that he had killed the missing Clinton Trezise and buried his body out on some farmland. It was a smart move on Bunting's part. Not only did it buy him some serious credibility with his starry-eyed protege, but it also made him an accomplice of sorts. By knowing about the murder and not going to the police, James was implicated too.

In addition to seeing his mother's new lover as a role model, James was also a little scared of him. So was everybody else in the house. It soon became obvious that Bunting was more than a little unstable, ranting and raging whenever the mood took him. On the other hand, he provided a strange kind of security of a type that Elizabeth Harvey and her boys had never known before.

To amuse himself and pass the time, Bunting liked to terrorize his suspected "dirties" by making anonymous threats over the phone. Sometimes he went further, damaging their homes and property, spraying obscenities on the walls, and smashing things. He enlisted James to help him, which the youth did without complaint. Less palatable to him were the times when Bunting tried to involve him in torturing and killing dogs. This was most likely an attempt by Bunting to "toughen up" James, to make him get over some of his natural squeamishness. As he saw it, it wasn't a great leap from killing an animal to killing a human being, and Bunting wanted him to get hands-on in future murders.

> To amuse himself and pass the time, Bunting liked to terrorize his suspected "dirties" by making anonymous threats over the phone.

Bunting was attempting to mold James in his own image, instilling the same outrage that he himself felt. Over time, he gradually succeeded. The resentment that the teenager felt at his own abuse was something that would fuel his participation in future murders. The older man was already plotting. One wall in the house, which he liked to call his "wall of spiders," was covered with note paper on which was scrawled the names of local men whom Bunting suspected of being "dirties." These suspicions were usually founded on little more than rumors and Bunting's gut instinct, though on occasion he turned out to be correct, as was the case with Ray Davies.

James Vlassakis was not involved in Bunting's second murder, but Robert Wagner and Elizabeth Harvey were. The two men accosted Davies, handcuffed him, and drove him to a secluded location where they would not be interrupted. Davies endured several hours of being savagely beaten. They took a sick delight in battering his genitals with a metal pole, causing them to swell grotesquely from internal bleeding.

At the end of it, Davies was still alive, but badly hurt. Rather than finish him off, they took the risk of stuffing him back into the car and taking him to Harvey's home. If Elizabeth Harvey found it strange that her lover and his companion had brought a half-dead man into her house, she soon got over it. Bunting explained to her that he was a pedophile and held the restrained man down while Harvey stabbed him in the leg with a knife—or so Bunting would later claim to her son James.

Another beating followed. Davies could not fight back. He was handcuffed and completely at the mercy of his captors. Finally, the two men tired of doling out the physical punishment. Robert Wagner took the jumper cables from the car and used them to strangle Ray Davies to death.

Like a detective's bulletin board festooned with evidence in a complex case, Bunting's wall turned into the sinister mind map of a man hellbent on creating his own cases.

Bunting had put some forethought into the murder. He had already dug a hole in the ground behind his home. He and Wagner threw their victim's body into it and covered it with soil. Davies had lived in a caravan in Suzanne Allen's backyard, and his disappearance might be noticed. To forestall any awkward questions, Bunting concocted a story about having scared him out of town with threats. Allen seemed to believe the tale and did not lose any sleep over the fact that Davies was gone and wouldn't be coming back. She might have seen things differently if she had known that she was also destined to become one of Bunting's future victims, less than a year afterward.

In addition to selling off the caravan he had lived in, Bunting also profited from the death of Ray Davies by fraudulently claiming his benefit payments. As nobody had officially reported him missing, this went undetected by the authorities and turned into quite a lucrative revenue stream for his murderer. Bunting must have realized that he could gain money, in addition to sadistic pleasure, by killing.

Eleven months later, he set his sights upon murdering Suzanne Allen. He had stopped having sex with her, which Allen wasn't very pleased about. She made every effort to get back together, but Bunting was having none of it. She bored him and had fast turned from being a pleasing diversion into an inconvenient annoyance. Her murder showed Bunting's claim that he was only killing dirties, sick men whom he believed the world was better off without, to be a lie. Suzanne Allen died because John Bunting wanted her out of his life and wanted a share of her money for himself. By November 1996, with the help of Robert Wagner, he made it happen.

Suzanne Allen died because John Bunting wanted her out of his life and wanted a share of her money for himself.

At his criminal trial, Bunting would deny having killed Allen, claiming that she died of a heart attack at home and that he had happened upon her body unexpectedly. Leaving aside his extensive record of lying to get his own way, the fact that he sold most of her furniture, personal effects, and made regular withdrawals from her checking account demonstrates what a fortuitous event Suzanne Allen's demise was for John Bunting. He had no qualms whatsoever about killing another human being when there was something in it for him, whether that something happened to be financial gain or personal pleasure.

No matter what really happened in the death of Suzanne Allen, the consequences cannot be denied. Bunting and Wagner decided to get rid of the body—why would they have felt the need if they had had no hand in her death?—and to make the process easier, they elected to dismember her body in the bathroom of her home. After chopping her corpse up into multiple pieces, the two men sealed them up in plastic bags. They disposed of the evidence of their crime in the same shallow grave that contained Ray Davies's body. Allen's body was placed on top of his.

Unlike Davies, however, Suzanne Allen still had a family to miss her. The police were informed of her disappearance and began to make inquiries. Seeing that money was being regularly taken out of her bank account, they reasoned that she was probably still alive but had chosen to drop off the grid, for some reason best known only to herself. There was no real suspicion of foul play, especially after officers contacted a man reputed to be the closest thing she had to a boyfriend. That man was, of course, John Bunting, and his lies were convincing enough to throw the police off the scent. Suzanne Allen was alive and well, he claimed, but simply wanted to keep to herself. As far as law enforcement was now concerned, there was nothing left for them to do.

Ten months passed with no further deaths. Then, in September 1997, Bunting began to feel the old, familiar itch to commit murder again. He had spent his time building up his cult of personality. In addition to brainwashing James Vlassakis into sharing his bigotry and hatred, Bunting had somehow managed to get Robert Wagner to think along the same lines. The formerly gay Wagner now mouthed the same homophobic hate speech as he did, and he even went so far as to eschew sexual relationships with men in favor of the company of a woman.

Their next victim, a teenaged, male-to-female transexual named Michael (Michelle) Gardiner, was an acquaintance of Wagner's girlfriend, who was a single mother and sometimes accepted the 19-year-old's offer to babysit. The fact that Gardiner was also gay and often dressed as a woman likely didn't endear him to Wagner or John Bunting. The two of them abducted Gardiner and drove him far from his home. Judging him to be just another dirty person, Bunting and Wagner resolved to execute him. First, however, they forced him to call a girlfriend to tell her that everything was all right. The phone call was long distance, which struck the friend as odd, as she recalled during a police interview. She told police that Gardiner's voice sounded unusually stressed for no reason she could fathom, but she never saw Gardiner again.

Although the specifics of Gardiner's murder are unclear, Wagner and Bunting strangled him to death and and then stuffed the body into an industrial-type drum or barrel. It would be more than three years before police officers finally discovered the barrel and opened it. The length of rope used to murder Gardiner was still knotted around his neck.

Just a few weeks after the death of Gardiner, Bunting and Wagner decided to scratch another "dirty" off the wall of potential targets. They chose someone that Robert Wagner knew intimately: his former molester and then later, his lover, Barry Lane. Quite why Bunting had given Wagner a free pass concerning his homosexual lifestyle, when he was not willing to extend one to Lane, is unknown; however, Wagner turned on his former lover with an anger and a ferocity that Bunting gleefully egged on.

Word had reached Bunting that Lane had been telling people about his involvement with the disposal of Clinton Trezise's body. Whether it was true or not, Bunting's paranoid nature meant that he now saw Lane and his tendency to gossip as a definite threat. Killing him would not only increase his personal security but would also remove another pedophile from the face of the Earth. For John Bunting, it was a win-win situation.

Much like Wagner, Barry Lane had switched his attention from males to fe-

Michael Gardiner's remains were stuffed into the first of what would be many victim-storage barrels.

males. This was a temporary state of affairs, however, and by the time Wagner and Bunting took him captive, he was involved with 18-year-old Thomas Trevilyan. Doubtless, Bunting was repulsed at seeing a 42-year-old man involved with a man less than half his age, and for Wagner, now in his twenties, this must have conjured up memories of his own teenage years with Lane.

The abduction and murder took place on October 17, 1997. Once again, when it came to cashing in on the crime he was about to commit, Bunting had planned ahead. He forced the terrified man to phone his mother and subject her to a torrent of verbal abuse, with the intention of making her think that Lane was disowning her and the rest of the family, that he wanted nothing more to do with them and was leaving the area for good. In a way, he was.

After hanging up the phone, the two men started to torture Lane. Based on statements given later by James Vlassakis, they managed to get Thomas Trevilyan to participate. Their implement of choice was a pair of pliers, which they applied to different parts of Lane's body. Taping his mouth shut over a makeshift gag muffled but could not eliminate his screams. The torture session ended when Barry Lane's tormentors strangled him. His body was wrapped up in a carpet and then went into a barrel for storage. Bunting had made sure to secure access to his bank account before killing him.

In a detour from what would become the killers' MO, Trevilyan's death was staged as a hanging suicide.

In less than a month, Trevilyan was also dead. The method of death was not consistent with the murders John Bunting had been responsible for up to that point. His lifeless body was found hanging from a tree branch in what looked at first like a suicide. Much like Barry Lane, however, Thomas Trevilyan had begun to tell people about his role in committing murder. He may not have been a "dirty," in Bunting's eyes, but his loose lips meant that he could not be allowed to live.

Trevilyan did have a history of serious mental health issues. On the day before his death, he chased a child and puppy with a kitchen knife, threatening to cut the puppy's throat. (Fortunately, a passerby intervened, and nobody was harmed.) A witness saw the disturbed young man in the company of Bunting and Wagner later that same evening. The three of them were driving to an undisclosed location. James Vlassakis would later state on the record that the two men had been responsible for hanging Trevilyan from the tree and then staging the scene to make it look like a suicide.

This was the most subtle of the murders so far. Bunting restrained himself from brazenly continuing to take money from the dead man's bank account, not wanting to tip off the authorities that there was a sinister dimension to this apparent suicide. As far as anybody knew, an emotionally disturbed young man had tragically taken his own life. It looked as if his killers were going to get off scot-free.

Perhaps not wanting to push their luck too far, Bunting and Wagner took a few months off from killing. They did nothing more until April 1998. Gavin Porter, 29, was a friend of James Vlassakis, and at the time of his death, was living with Bunting and Elizabeth Harvey at their home. He did not fit the profile of Bunting and Wagner's usual choice of victim. He wasn't gay and did not have a reputation for interfering with underage males. It may simply have been a case of Bunting growing antsy to kill again and finding his next target conveniently close to home.

If James Vlassakis's testimony is to be believed, Bunting and Wagner waited for him to go out to the movies for the night, then murdered Porter while he was gone. James returned to the house and was met by the gleeful pair of killers, who showed him the body of Gavin Porter, who appeared to have been fatally strangled. And that wasn't all. Removing the lid from a storage barrel, Bunting told James to look inside. The tangled mess of limbs and tissue crammed into the barrel was, Bunting explained, all that was left of Barry Lane and Michael Gardiner.

Porter's body would soon end up in a storage barrel of its own. Bunting kept the barrels in his shed. This was another opportunity for James Vlassakis to go to the police and turn Bunting and Wagner in. Rather than do that, however, he chose to keep assisting them with their murderous spree. Gavin Porter had disappeared from his home, and James began telling people that he had simply moved on, hoping that his vague reassurances would avert suspicion. As with other victims, the conspirators continued to collect the dead man's benefits payments. John Bunting had gotten the PIN number to his debit card, and the authorities were none the wiser.

Four months afterward came the murder of 21-year-old Troy Youde. This was the half-brother who had sexually abused James Vlassakis years before. This made him just another "dirty" in Bunting's eyes, and killing him with James present would bind his young protege to him even more closely than he already was. In addition to James Vlassakis and Robert Wagner, Bunting enlisted a fourth accomplice for the killing: Mark Ray Haydon. Between them, they had plenty of assembled muscle to take down an unsuspecting young man.

The four aggressors waited until Youde was fast asleep in bed, picked up some blunt weapons, and stealthily crept up to the door of his bedroom. Then they struck. The assault was as savage as it was unprovoked. All four men beat Youde remorselessly. After punching, kicking, and battering their victim, he was made to repeat a series of very deliberate phrases into a tape recorder. These messages were to be used later in an attempt to convince people that Troy Youde was still alive.

Bunting forced Youde to his knees and made him apologize to James Vlassakis for having molested him as a youth. He was made to address the grandiose Bunting as "Lord God" and the other men "master" or "sir." Acquiescing did not save him from further torture with the now-common set of pliers. Finally, Bunting fashioned a rudimentary tourniquet from a piece of rope and the handle to a car jack and wrapped it around Youde's throat. Twisting the handle caused the rope to constrict, cutting off the blood flow to and from his brain, putting pressure on the windpipe and reducing the flow of air. Soon, the unfortunate young man was dead. His body was placed into a fresh barrel. Because of his height, it was necessary for them to saw off one of his feet to get the lid back on.

> This was the half-brother who had sexually abused James Vlassakis years before. This made him just another "dirty" in Bunting's eyes....

By the time police officers opened the lid on the barrel containing his dismembered remains in 1999, there was no body of Troy Youde to be discovered. The body parts had deteriorated and decomposed significantly between the time of his death in August 1998 and their discovery the following year.

No sooner was Troy Youde dead than Bunting and his cronies began siphoning funds out of his account, and the gang moved on to its next victim: 18-year-old Frederick Brooks. Brooks was the son of Bunting's latest romantic dalliance, but that didn't stop the older man from taking a dislike to him right away. Bunting declared that the young man was a pedophile and belonged on his spider wall of dirties, though he had no proof with which to back up this spurious claim. More likely, Bunting simply didn't like the look of the young man, or Bunting didn't like that Brooks didn't seem to be impressed by Bunting's big man act.

It was now September 1998, and Fred Brooks confessed to having molested underage girls. This "confession" was extracted by means of torture, and it was tape recorded by Bunting in between beatings. He was rendered helpless by having his wrists handcuffed behind his back. A sparkler was inserted into his penis and lit. Brooks was in so much pain that he would have said literally anything to make it stop. Not only did he repeat back word for word everything his abductors wanted him to say, but he also gave up his banking details so they could continue to profit from his death.

Once they had what they wanted, Bunting and his accomplices gagged their victim and taped his mouth shut, burned him repeatedly with lit cigarettes, and then fatally strangled him. In a brazen move, James Vlassakis impersonated the dead Fred Brooks and met with a social worker. The objective was to continue the flow of cash benefits, which was successful—for a time. The social worker hadn't the faintest idea that the real Frederick Brooks was dead and decomposing in a 40-gallon barrel.

The murders were now happening monthly. The next to die was 29-year-old Gary O'Dwyer, whose home was close to Bunting's and who was perceived as being vulnerable because he lived alone. Bunting had a greedy eye on O'Dwyer's finances and used the same lazy and tired excuse about him supposedly being a pedophile as the reason to kill him. Using James Vlassakis as an intermediary, Bunting set up a small social meet-up with O'Dwyer, who failed to smell a rat. It may have been that he was simply desperate for company.

The murder took place inside O'Dwyer's own home. Bunting had brought a case of beer along with him. After a few drinks had been passed around, he launched a surprised attack on O'Dwyer. Once he was subdued, the torture began. One of Bunting's favorite implements was an autotransformer, a device used to apply varying amounts of electricity to his victim. Attaching a pair of crocodile clips to sensitive parts of the body, such as the nipples or testicles, Bunting sadistically applied shocks of increasing voltage, relishing the sight of his victim screaming and squirming in agony.

After Bunting grew bored of the torture, he strangled Gary O'Dwyer and placed his body into another barrel. His possessions, in-

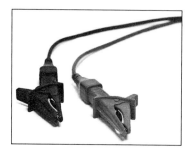

Also known as alligator clips, crocodile clips have spring-loaded jaws with metal teeth that can be attached to specific points to create a circuit, allowing electric current to flow between them.

cluding furniture and electrical appliances, were either sold or given away to Bunting's friends.

November 21 would see the final Snowtown murder of 1998: that of 37-year-old Elizabeth Haydon, the wife of Bunting's accomplice, Mark Haydon. Fred Brooks was her nephew. The reasons for Bunting choosing her as a target are unclear. She didn't fit the usual profile of people Bunting hated, most of whom were men. He had taken a dislike to Elizabeth Haydon and referred to her contemptuously as a whore.

Killing the family member of one of his cronies brought with it an increased level of risk that Bunting's nefarious activities might be exposed, but he didn't seem to care. Having gotten away with murder too many times already, Bunting was beginning to fancy himself as being untouchable. He and Wagner waited until Mark Haydon was otherwise engaged before making their move. It may also have been the case that Haydon knew about the murder in advance and tacitly endorsed it happening, removing himself from the scene before it took place, and pretending to be surprised afterward. This was certainly something that the police and prosecutors came to suspect.

The exact circumstances of Elizabeth Haydon's murder will never be known. Much of what we know about the Snowtown killings comes from James Vlassakis, who provided insider information when he agreed to testify against Bunting and those accomplices of his who were more actively involved in the murders. James was not present for Elizabeth's death, but it is reasonable to assume that she was tortured in the same manner as Bunting's other victims before her body was stuffed into another barrel for storage.

It soon dawned on the killers that they were fast running out of room in which to store the increasing number of barrels they were racking up. They were also beginning to stink. They attempted to solve this problem by renting out a building in Snowtown that used to be the town's bank but had been standing empty and unused for quite some time. Once they got the keys, they transported the barrels there and rolled them down to the vault. It is likely that Bunting only ever saw this as a temporary solution. He had filled each of the six barrels with acid, presumably in the hopes that the bodies would liquefy more quickly and would soon be unrecognizable as having once been human beings.

The final killing occurred on May 9, 1999. The chosen victim was 24-year-old David Johnson, the stepbrother of James Vlassakis. Bunting used James to get Johnson to Snowtown on the flimsy pretext of buying a second-hand computer and pounced on him when he stepped inside the bank. Johnson was not gay, but Bunting insisted that he was and used that as an excuse to kill him. Johnson had heard about some of the murders from James, and it was about to cost him his life.

David Johnson was quickly overpowered and placed in handcuffs. In between beatings, he was made to read "proof of life" sentences into Bunting's tape recorder. He also gave up the PIN for his debit card, the proceeds of which would add to Bunting's revenue stream. Johnson attempted to fight back, but he was no match for Bunting and Wagner, who subdued and then fatally strangled him. Like the others, his body was put into a barrel, but not before his murderers had cut off strips of flesh, which they subsequently cooked and ate.

Nobody's luck holds out forever, and several missing persons cases had been opened with respect to the victims of the Snowtown Murders. The police grew suspicious when they found that some of the missing people were continuing to claim their financial benefits despite seeming to have dropped off the face of the Earth. Inquiries were made, and one name popped up again and again in connection with the subject of each investigation: John Justin Bunting.

Detectives obtained a warrant for a wire tap, which gave them direct access to the calls being made to and from Bunting's phone. What they heard in some of the ensuing conversations only served to make them more suspicious that they were dealing with a murderer. What they were not aware of at this point was just how many people Bunting was responsible for killing. They put a tail on Bunting and Wagner, tracking their every move.

On May 20, 1999, based on a tip-off about some barrels being stored there that "smelled really disgusting," the police raided the former bank building in Snowtown. What they found inside made even seasoned officers gag. The vault stank so badly, officers had to don breathing masks to cope. This had not been a problem for John Bunting, who had no sense of smell.

Only the final murder, that of David Johnson, had been committed in the bank itself. Like so many serial killers before him, John

When missing persons cases began to seem like potential murder and fraud, detectives homed in on Bunting. Tapping his phone, they learned enough to step up surveillance.

Bunting had gotten sloppy. He had failed to clean up after himself. Strewn across the concrete floor was an array of implements that the gang had used to torture Johnson before his death. The transformer used to electrocute his victims was still there, along with an assortment of knives. Duct tape was used to seal the victim's mouth, and rope was the means of strangulation. A pair of pliers had been applied to various sensitive areas, including the victim's toes. Lying on the floor was a set of handcuffs. There were even personal effects belonging to David Johnson, including his wallet. No effort whatsoever had been made to hide any of them. It was almost as if Bunting had no fear of being caught.

The skeletal remnants of early murder victim Clinton Trezise had been discovered in 1994 by farmers working the field. He was put into the ground naked, so there was no clothing to give a clue as to who he was. The remains themselves were so badly decomposed that identification would have been extremely difficult. Trezise was not officially declared missing until October of the following year, and despite his disappearance being featured on national television on more than one occasion, no connection would be made between his absence and the dug-up remains until 1999, when police searched the bank and made a grisly discovery in the vault: the remnants of eight human beings, in six storage barrels, each in various states of decomposition due to the ravages of time and the acid in which they were immersed.

The Snowtown murderers had finally been rumbled.

The Snowtown murder trial ran for just short of a year and remains one of the most complex and exhaustive ever to take place in Australia. The notion that a gang of serial killers, who liked to torture their victims and live on the profits afterward, horrified and fascinated the public in equal measure. They quite rightly wondered just how John Bunting and his gang had gotten away with it for so long.

The judge and jury were given every horrific detail of the pain inflicted by Bunting and his gang upon their victims. Most of this came from the prosecution's star witness, James Vlassakis, who cooperated fully with the investigation and provided information that could have been obtained from no other source. Prosecutors played some of the tapes Bunting had recorded, and the hushed courtroom heard the dead victims reading statements that he had scripted for them in advance. They also heard the torture sessions in all their brutality.

Arrogant to the last, Bunting yelled out in court: "I decided to take action, and I took action. Thank you."

At the trial's conclusion, the jury found John Justin Bunting guilty on eleven counts of murder. He was 36 years old when he began his life sentence. He will never be released from prison.

At the age of 31, Robert Wagner was convicted on ten counts of murder. He had admitted to three of them and was convicted of seven more to which he did not plead guilty. Like his partner in crime, John Bunting, he will spend the rest of his life in prison.

> **Snowtown itself has been scarred by its dark past. The ... name evokes images of torture and murder that many of its residents would just as soon forget.**

Mark Haydon was convicted not of murder but on multiple counts of assisting Bunting in disposing of his victims' bodies. He was sentenced to 25 years' imprisonment. Several attempts to obtain early parole were quashed, much to the relief of the next of kin of his victims. He is currently on track to be released from prison in 2024.

In exchange for his cooperation, James Vlassakis was sentenced to 26 years behind bars. He had pled guilty to four counts of murder. Like Mark Haydon, he will probably be released in the next few years. What happens to both of them once they regain their freedom remains to be seen.

Snowtown itself has been scarred by its dark past. The small town was thrust unexpectedly into the spotlight in 1999, and although the media furor has long since died down, the town's name evokes images of torture and murder that many of its residents would just as soon forget. On the other hand, Snowtown has seen an increase in tourism in the two decades since the murders, as curious sightseers stand outside the bank and wonder about the horrors it used to contain. This was amplified in 2011 with the release of a fictionalized version of events in the movie *Snowtown*.

The bank building that lies at the heart of it all currently sits unused, and although there have been discussions regarding turning it into a crime museum, none of them have come to fruition at the time of writing. A home is attached to the bank and has seen several different owners take up residence. To their credit, they have resisted any urge to cash in on the grisly reputation of the property. Many in town think that the bank should have been demolished, in the hopes of expunging Snowtown's undeservedly black reputation. Sadly, that ship has long since sailed.

For John Justin Bunting, torture, murder, and dismemberment all seemed to come naturally. As a young man, he had spent some time working in a crematorium. This gave him exposure to dead bodies, inuring him to the sense of revulsion that many people feel in the presence of a corpse. He also had a spell working in butchery, slaughtering animals and cutting them apart. He loved to talk about just how much pleasure the killing gave him. When taken together, both jobs served as a kind of training for the murders he would go on to commit.

He also took delight in torturing, killing, and skinning animals, primarily dogs and cats, which he trapped for the purpose. Politically speaking, Bunting was drawn to right-wing ideologies. He had shown an interest in white supremacy and Nazism.

Why did he kill? Some have said that it was all about the money. Over the course of the murders, Bunting and his accomplices defrauded their victims of tens of thousands of dollars. There are far easier ways to commit fraud than murder, however, and most of them are far less risky. The simple truth is that John Bunting killed because he liked it. The act of murdering those who he hated—those he believed, rightly or wrongly, to be either gay or a pedophile—stroked his ego.

A background in butchering carries certain advantages in a serial killer's career.

Despite his tough-guy persona, John Bunting was a physically short and emotionally fragile man, one with a desperate need to be the center of attention and call the shots. He took pleasure in perverting others, particularly those such as James Vlassakis, who were easily in-fluenced, to his own ends. He fancied himself a vigilante, cleaning up the streets of scum, wiping out those he felt had no right to live. He saw himself as doing a public service, rather than committing the cold-blooded murder of innocent human beings.

Bunting explained his rationale thusly: his victims were all deviants in one way or another, afflicted with an incurable disease, such as pedo-philia or homosexuality. By killing them, he was administering the only cure possible for said disease. Whether Bunting genuinely believed this or not is open to debate, but he failed to explain exactly how the sadistic tortures he inflicted upon each victim helped effect such a "cure." Bunt-ing's explanation holds no water when examined closely. The bottom line is that every single murder he carried out was for personal gain, be it financial or emotional in nature. Once detectives tallied up the numbers, they estimated that Bunting had profited from his victims to the tune of $95,000—if not more.

Sometimes, he killed to protect himself. Both John Bunting and Robert Wagner had big mouths. They boasted about people they had killed to others. Sometimes, a short while after these outbursts of brag-gadocio, they would think better of it and decide that the person they had blabbed to now knew too much, was no longer to be considered trustworthy, and had to be eliminated.

For the people of Snowtown, unfairly linked forever with what is arguably Australia's worst chain of homicides, there is likely to be no forgiveness for those who put their hometown on the map for the very worst of reasons. It can only be hoped that someday, vivid memories of bodies kept in barrels will fade from the collective consciousness, and Snowtown will go back to being just another small town—albeit one with a very dark history.

# Further Reading

Sources for this book included numerous police and legal reports, articles, news media in various forms, and documentaries. For those wishing to read further into the cases spotlighted here, what follows is a list of recommended books by authors who have written about them in greater detail—or who have otherwise expanded upon the contents of this book.

Appleby, Timothy. *A New Kind of Monster: The Secret Life and Chilling Crimes of Colonel Russell Williams.* Toronto: Vintage Canada, 2012.

Benns, Matthew. *When the Bough Breaks: The True Story of Child Killer Kathleen Folbigg.* Milsons Point, NSW: Bantam, 2003.

Callahan, Maureen. *American Predator: The Hunt for the Most Meticulous Serial Killer of the 21st Century.* New York: Penguin Books, 2020.

Cameron, Stevie. *On the Farm: Robert William Pickton and the Tragic Story of the Vancouver's Missing Women.* Toronto: Knopf Canada, 2010.

Douglas, John E., and Mark Olshaker. *The Killer across the Table: Unlocking the Secrets of Serial Killers and Predators with the FBI's Original Mindhunter.* New York: Dey St., 2020.

Elkind, Peter. *The Death Shift.* New York: Penguin Books, 1989.

Estep, Richard. *American Hotel Story: History, Hauntings, and Heartbreak in L.A.'s Infamous Hotel Cecil,* 2021.

Estep, Richard. *Serial Killers: The Minds, Methods, and Mayhem of History's Notorious Murderers.* Visible Ink Press, 2021.

Fournier, Gregory A. *Terror in Ypsilanti: John Norman Collins Unmasked.* Tucson, AZ: Wheatmark, 2016.

Gibb, David A. *Camouflaged Killer: The Shocking Double Life of Colonel Russell Williams.* New York: Berkley Books, 2012.

Hunter, J. T. *Devil in The Darkness: The True Story of Serial Killer Israel Keyes.* RJ Parker Publishing Inc., 2016.

Jackman, Tom, and Troy Cole. *Rites of Burial.* New York: Pinnacle, 1992.

King, Stephen. *Misery.* London: Hodder, 2019.

Leake, John. *Entering Hades: The Double Life of a Serial Killer.* New York: Berkley Books, 2009.

Ling, Justin. *Missing from the Village: The Story of Serial Killer Bruce McArthur, the Search for Justice, ... and the System That Failed Toronto's Queer Communi.* Toronto: McClelland & Stewart, 2022.

Marshall, Debi. *Killing for Pleasure*. North Sydney, NSW: Random House Australia, 2011.

McNamara, Michelle. *I'll Be Gone in the Dark: One Woman's Obsessive Search for the Golden State Killer*. New York: Harper Perennial, 2019.

Rule, Ann. *Green River, Running Red: The Real Story of the Green River Killer—America's Deadliest Serial Murderer*. New York: Gallery Books, 2019.

Sackman, Bruce. *Behind the Murder Curtain: Special Agent Bruce Sackman Hunts Doctors and Nurses Who Kill Our ... Veterans*. Post Hill Press, 2020.

Schaefer, G. J., and Sondra London. *Killer Fiction*. Feral House, 2011.

Stewart, James B. *Blind Eye*. New York: Simon & Schuster, 1999.

Sutton, Colin. *Manhunt—How I Brought Serial Killer Levi Bellfield to Justice*. La Vergne, TN: John Blake Publishing, 2019.

Williams, Stephen. *Invisible Darkness: The Horrifying Case of Paul Bernardo and Karla Homolka*. Toronto, ON: S.D.S. Communications Corporation, 2014.

# Index

Note: ill. indicates photos and illustrations.